Bolognese Longsword

for the Modern Practitioner

Arik Mendelevitz

Fool of
Swords

Contents

FOREWORD 8

CHAPTER 1
The Purpose of This Book 10

CHAPTER 2
Don't Know Much About History 12

CHAPTER 3
The Principles of Bolognese Fencing......16
Structure...16
Measure 16
Tempo 16
Gioco 17

CHAPTER 4
How Do I Hold This Damn Thing? 18
Parts of the Sword 18

CHAPTER 5
Cuts...29
Cutting Diagram.....................................33
Full Cuts vs Half Cuts 38
Three Sizes of Cuts 38
Falsi 40
The Three Advantages 42
How To Stop a Cut. 46
How To Get Around a Cut. 49
Cutting Patterns 51

CHAPTER 6
Thrusts..54
Inside vs Outside Lines...........................54
Stringere..54
Hunt The Debole......................................58
How To Collapse a Hard Thrust 64
Thrusting Patterns...................................69
How to Prep a Cut or a Thrust 69

CHAPTER 7
Guards...70
Choose Your Guard, Any Guard...........97
Throw Any Blow 99
Four Corners Drill...................................99

CHAPTER 8
Blade Actions......................................106
Three Turns of the Sword.....................106
Proportion..108
Counter-finds...115
The Three Choice Problem 118
Half-Swording 120
Covered vs Uncovered Attacks............121

CHAPTER 9
The Shitty Parry Drill........................124

CHAPTER 10
Footwork...132
Defensive vs Offensive Measure..........132
Footwork Actions...................................134
The Three Turns of the Feet..................141
Concordant vs Discordant Actions.....143
The Glove Game......................................146

CHAPTER 11

Provocations 148

CHAPTER 12

Tempo, The Best-O? 150
The Five Tempi 150
Counting Tempi 157
Three Micro-Tempi 159
Acting In/Out of Tempo 161

CHAPTER 13

Gioco 162

CHAPTER 14

Feints 164
Feint-Direct 165
Feint by Disengagement 166
Attack to Hit 168
Attack to Miss 169
How to Teach Feints 171

CHAPTER 15

Grappling 178
Outside and Inside Yields 182

CHAPTER 16

Drills 184
Blocked vs Variable Drilling 184
Cooperative vs
Noncooperative Drills 185
Complexity vs Intensity 186
Building an On Ramp 187

CHAPTER 17

Fencer Alignment Chart 192
Aggressor vs Counterpuncher 193
Hard vs Soft 194
Area of Excellence 196
The Funnel 196
Denial 197

CHAPTER 18

Strategy 198
Hand Hits 198
Attack Where They Will Be 199
High vs Low Guards 199
Getting Over Roadblocks 201
Fighting From Principle ....
208

CHAPTER 19

Tournaments 212

CHAPTER 20

Equipment 216

Passing The Knowledge On 222
Appendix I: 101 Curriculum 224
Appendix II: Rank Examinations 234
Glossary 243
Works Cited 246
Further Reading 248
Acknowledgements 249
About the Author 250

For my parents and
all the years they
sat there so that a
young boy could
learn to swordfight.

"Our best chances
of success come
when we are fully
committed to
everything that
we are doing in
that moment."

Luke Wilson, Professional Juggler

Foreword

One of the greatest accomplishments a martial artist can attain is seeing people you've helped along their own journeys match and even surpass your own accomplishments. When Arik asked me to write a forward for his Bolognese longsword manual, I realized that I had made it as a practitioner of historic swordplay.

I was well into my own career as a competitive fencer and a student of La Verdadera Destreza as described in the writings of Luis Pacheco de Navarez and interpreted in Mary and Puck Curtis' *From the Page to the Practice* when a 14-year-old Arik first walked into our local SCA fighter practice with his parents.

Teenage Arik was a very different person from the focused scholar that he is today. He was brash and full of himself and he was so focused on winning fights that he sometimes lost sight of values important to the wider HEMA community like honor on the field.

It has been a true privilege to be there as Arik grew from that teenager to the man and the scholar he has become. It's been an honor to have been able to help him in some small way as he has worked tirelessly to fine-tune his skills with the rapier, sidesword, and grappling.

Arik has been an elite fighter for several years now. When the SCA recognized Arik as a Master of Defense, I told him that in addition to the qualities of skill at arms, scholarship and teaching, and leadership, he brought something truly unique to the community. Starting with the pandemic and continuing through today, Arik has found a true generosity of spirit that has impelled him to share his ever-growing body of knowledge with the broader HEMA community within and outside the SCA.

While the world shut down due to COVID, Arik continued to train. He created a virtual training program that he offered to practitioners from all over the country. As restrictions lifted, he started traveling to run workshops on Nicoletto Giganti's system for rapier combat even as he began to compete in HEMA events as well as SCA tournaments with great success.

Ever one to find something new to work on, Arik started working through the Anonymous Bolognese, a treatise on Italian sidesword and longsword combat.

Not satisfied with merely being an excellent rapierist, he dove into a book covering sidesword and longsword fencing.

I'm a specialist. Destreza is a great system for one-handed swords with a reasonably complex hilt like sideswords and rapiers. Later authors continued the tradition and adapted it to the use of the smallsword and saber. I've always been rapier-focused and have chosen to go deep and narrow. Not Arik. While he started with the rapier and it's always been his best game, he chose to learn and master a new system for different kinds of swords, which he has tested to great effect on the field.

This book represents the culmination of half a lifetime's study, competition, and work for Arik. It demonstrates his devotion to the art and the historical context that it was developed under as well as the generosity of spirit that creating such a work takes. I hope that you gain as much from reading it as he put into writing it.

Jim Lai
Master of Defense - Society for Creative Anachronism

1: The Purpose of This Book

I wrote this book for two audiences: teachers and students. For fencing teachers, maybe you've spent years teaching the Bolognese art and are looking for a new perspective or a guide to a different weapon. Maybe you've taught Italian rapier or German longsword and are trying to expand your repertoire to something new. Perhaps you are just now starting to take those first steps from just being a student of the art to being in a position to pass it along and are looking for a "how to" guide by someone a little further down the path. Regardless of which of these describe you best, just know that you have found your way to a tool that represents years and years of intense dedication that will hopefully provide you with some helpful guidance as you find your way.

Maybe, though, you're not interested in trying to keep the attention of two dozen college kids all at once as you rattle off obscure Italian terms, and are instead just looking to hit people better. Well, good news, this book is for you too. Even if teaching others is something that doesn't particularly hold your interest, my goal is for this book to serve as a guide to a deep, rich art passed down to us by some of the worst writers in fencing history. I'm not exaggerating—just try reading Marozzo without looking at the intro or having a background in all of this. The Bolognese art contains thousands of plays, but the authors were clearly writing for an audience far different from our own. While it is always a noble pursuit to look back to the original material in any study, it can be helpful to have someone you have more in common with break that all down in a way that you can more easily digest. Of course, the best way for most people is to learn from a knowledgeable instructor face to face. However, that isn't always possible due to things like geography and finances. You also don't have to worry about waking the book up right after you get out of the shower and need to double check that one random thing before your brain will let you go to bed.

Regardless of where you are coming from in picking up this text, I hope that it will serve you well. While reading it straight through will definitely make more sense than just skipping around, particularly if you aren't previously familiar with most of the vocabulary, I don't really expect people to blaze through it in just a few sittings. In my own study, I treat most of the fencing books on my shelves as reference material. They are resources I can rely on to help answer this or that question, as opposed to novels with a clear narrative that goes from A, to B, to C. I suspect this book will largely be used the same. That said, now that this book has gone from my hands to yours, it is no longer mine to dictate how you use it. Here's hoping it serves you well.

2: Don't Know Much About History?

If you're picking up this book, there's a decent chance you're at least somewhat familiar with what's going on. If not, don't fret, this chapter is written specifically for you.

In the past few decades there's been a resurgence of interest in medieval and renaissance European combat, particularly through things such as HEMA (historical European martial arts), the SCA (society for creative anachronism), WMA (western martial arts), and HMB (historical medieval battles). Throughout all of these, perhaps the single most prevalent weapon has been the sword in two hands, or as we often refer to it, the longsword. Now, the concept of wielding a bladed object in two hands is not unique to any one culture. We see this happening all across the world, ranging from the Maori powhenua, to the German zweihander, to the Aztec two-handed macuahuitl.

While a book covering two-handed swords across the world is something I'd be more than happy to personally throw money at, that's not the aim of this text. Instead, what I would like to introduce you to is the *spada a dui mani* (sword in two hands) of the Bolognese school of fencing. For context, Bologna, a city in Northern Italy, is the home to Europe's oldest university and served as a nexus for thought throughout the medieval and early modern eras. The Bolognese school of fencing is less a school in how we think about it in modern terms; it was more a collection of fencing instructors who worked in and around Bologna throughout the sixteenth-century who all used roughly the same terms and concepts to explain to their students how best to succeed with a sword.

The earliest documented instance of a paid fencing instructor in the city of Bologna was Filippo Dardi. We have documentation showing that he became licensed to teach fencing by the city starting in 1412, and in 1443 began to receive a regular stipend from the city government in order to subsidize the martial education of the city's youth. In 1434 he seems to have written a treatise on both geometry and fencing, the publishing of which led to him receiving a professorship, teaching math at the University of Bologna. Unfortunately, no one in our community has been able to find this treatise. So if you've got access to some historical archives and want an idea for a project, I might have something for you.

Without Dardi's book, the writings we have from the Bolognese system go from the
1513 poem *Viridario*, by Giovanni Filoteo Achillini, to the 1572 treatise *Dell'Arte
di Scrima Libri Tre* by Giovanni dall'Agocchie. The other works we have include
Antonio Manciolino's *Opera Nova* (1523), the Anonimo Bolognese (1500-1550?) and
Achille Marozzo's *Opera Nova* (1536).[1] These treatises encompass a wide array of
weapons, ranging from the single-handed sidesword all the way to the poleax and
partisan. The nice thing about what they wrote down is that it comprises a complete
system with techniques and concepts from any one weapon being shown to be
applicable to any other. While only two books out of the tradition show us specific
longsword techniques,[2] my goal here is to take the lessons from the tradition as a
whole and apply them to the tool at hand.

Something to take note of is that this form of combat is largely focused on
two people who are not wearing armor, are on foot, and are facing each other
with matched weapons. While there's no doubt these very same techniques were
employed on the battlefield or in the street, what we are shown seems to be much
more suited to the dueling list or the tournament field.[3] As such, my aim here is not
to teach you how best to perform some sort of street self-defense or how to cleave
through an army of oncoming peasants, but is instead to help provide the modern
reader with a way of understanding how best to employ this way of sword fighting
for our modern recreations and tournaments.

Additionally, while there are numerous weapons presented to us throughout
the tradition, the aim of this book will be to exclusively focus on how it applies to
fighting with a longsword. This is partly due to the popularity of longswords among
modern historical fencers, partly due to my own personal interests, and partly to
help focus the scope of the book.

[1] Some also include Angelo Viggiani's 1551 Lo Schermo in this list.
[2] Manciolino offers one page on general longsword advice but doesn't cover any
  specific techniques.
[3] We do see a few snippets of mismatched fights, but those are the exception and not the rule.

Who Were Each of Our Authors?

I will endeavor to not be a man of too many words.[4] I know of other people in the field who have spent months at a time digging deep into the biographies of each of these authors, figuring out how they connected to each other and what roles they played in the history of the great city of Bologna. While I'm sure an entire book could be written about the life and times of each of the authors from our tradition, my goal here is merely to provide a brief overview in order to give us a little bit of historical context. If none of that interests you, feel free to skip ahead a chapter or two where we get into how to most effectively swing a sword.

Giovanni Filoteo Achillini

Giovanni Filoteo Achillini, a courtier to the Bentivoglio family and a poet whose work is largely lost to time, is mostly known as the brother of the philosopher Alessandro Achillini. His poem *Viridario* is the first written description we have of the uniquely Bolognese method of fencing. While he wrote the poem in 1504, he did not publish it until 1514 in Padua, where he served as a professor of natural history after being forced to flee Bologna when Julius II conquered it from the Bentivoglios.[5] While it only describes fencing sword and buckler (a small shield) fighting, it still shows us multiple plays taking from a complete system built upon by other authors further down the line.

Antonio Manciolino

Manciolino published the first full-length book about what we would now call Bolognese fencing. We believe the text was originally published in 1523, but the earliest versions we have now are from the 1531 printing. The book primarily focuses on sword and buckler fighting, but also goes over as well as how to use two swords at once as well as how to use a variety of polearms. While the longsword is mentioned, it is unfortunately not given its own chapter. Manciolino is the first of the Bolognese authors to break down not only what each guard and blow was, but also gives us a wealth of fencing general strategy.

---

[4] Jherek Swanger, 204, with one of the world's greatest footnotes.
[5] https://theartofarms.substack.com/p/what-is-viridario-who-was-achillini

Achille Marozzo

Marozzo is by and far the most famous of the Bolognese authors. This is largely due to the fact that he, as the owner of a textile mill, had the largest budget of any of our authors, giving us the only clear pictures of what almost every guard with each and every weapon may have looked like. His book was initially published in 1536 and was also republished over thirty years later in 1568, showing us how relevant the system continued to be. His is one of the most expansive books we have, covering every weapon in the Bolognese system with multiple chapters dedicated to the practice of the longsword. We also know that he studied under the tutelage of master Antonio di Luca, of whom it was said, "as many warriors came out of his school as did out of the Trojan horse." [6]

Anonimo Bolognese (MSS Ravenna M-345/M-346)

Unlike our other sources, the Anonimo is two overlapping handwritten manuscripts as opposed to a singular printed work. As the name implies, we do not currently have any way of telling who the author was. While the manuscripts currently reside in a library in Ravenna, the similarities with the Bolognese authors are so striking that almost everyone considers it to be from the Bolognese tradition of fencing as opposed to being based in any of the other Italian lineages. Along with not knowing who the author is, we also do not have a date for when it was written. The best guess is somewhere between 1500 and 1550. Along with Marozzo's work, the Anonimo is one of the most comprehensive, with over four hundred plays for the sword in one hand and is the only other book in the tradition with a dedicated chapter to longsword fencing. It is the only book in the tradition that depicts any sort of armored combat, something much less common in sixteenth-century duels than it had been in earlier eras.

Giovanni dall'Agocchie

Giovanni dall'Agocchie, publishing in 1572, is the final master in our tradition. Having written almost three decades after any of the other authors, we see a few of his guards depart significantly from the other authors. While he unfortunately does not cover the longsword directly, he is perhaps the clearest writer out of the whole tradition and helps clearly explain several of the core tenets of the art in a way the other authors are not always able to do.

[6] Marozzo, "The Duel", 75.

3: The Principles of Bolognese Fencing

You can try to focus on this or that technique, but at the end of the day the fencer who bases their fight on solid principles is always going to win over the fencer who merely has a bag of tricks at their disposal. Now these are all topics we are going to explore later in this book, but I figured it would be good to lay them out now to provide you the beginnings of a framework that you can start to fit all the other pieces into as you go along.

The first of these is **structure**. Another way of thinking about this one would be to refer to it as "mechanics," which both covers the shapes in which you hold your sword out, but also encompasses how you hold your body as a whole. Ideally you should not only avoid providing your opponent with any weak angles that they could easily collapse right into your face, but also your whole musculoskeletal structure should support what you're doing. From your dominant hand through your shoulder, into your hip, and down into your back foot there should be an unbroken chain of structural support. Additionally, make sure that you're using the big muscles to do the majority of the work with the smaller muscle groups only coming in to help guide your action a small bit here or there. If you're relying on your rotator cuff to do the work of your lats and your delts, you're going to have to look up a good physical therapist fairly quickly.

Next is the pillar of *misura* (measure). If you aren't there when they're trying to hit you, but they're always where you can reach them whenever you choose to strike, the fight is yours. I know people who don't have a great grasp on blade-on-blade mechanics but have impeccable measure control. Between the two, I'd take having perfect measure over perfect mechanics any day.

After that comes *tempo*. Controlling space is great, but without control over time it's only going to do you so much. With the two together, you're now able to be in the right place at the right time. Knowing how to use mechanics to intercept your opponent's blow is an incredibly powerful tool. Too often though we get caught up in this or that blade mechanic without paying sufficient attention to when and where to use it. If you know how to be in that right place at the right time, it doesn't take all that much skill to just poke someone with your sword. Mechanics will help you get there more easily and will let you fight for far longer, but they alone aren't enough to keep you safe from your opponent's blade.

The final, and most distinctly Bolognese pillar we have is ***gioco*** (play). Out of the whole Italian tradition, this one is really just limited to Fiore and then the Bolognese authors. Specifically, there are the ideas of *gioco stretto* (constrained play) and *gioco largo* (unconstrained play) that dictate whether or not it is safe for you in any given tempo to take your point off-line. If you try and go big when you were supposed to go small, your sword isn't going to get there in time. Similarly, if you try and always go through, you'll find that there's times when it actually would have been the smarter tactical choice to take the seemingly long way around.

4: How Do I Hold This Damn Thing?

With two hands!

Okay, okay, enough with the jokes for now. Assuming you have a longsword trainer nearby (or an equivalent broomstick) I want you to go ahead and look at it. You'll note that there's likely a blade (unless you have a broomstick, in which case use your imagination). That blade is going to have two edges. Underneath those you should see the quillons (cross guard), a handle, and then a pommel at the end. Take your dominant hand and grab the handle below the quillons, pushing the heel of your palm into the handle such that your hand should be lined up the same way as the blade. [7]

If you're perfect, push your hand up against the quillons. If you're like me and every once in a while get hit by that new person even when you thought you really had that parry down, slide your dominant hand back ever so slightly. The other thing to remember here is that you want the bones of your forearm to line up with the handle and the blade.

[7] I do know some lefties who fight longsword with their right hand on top. Feel free to experiment with what feels best for you. That said, I am going to be using "dominant hand" throughout this book to describe the one closer to the hilt and "nondominant hand" to describe the one closer to the pommel.

If you grab the handle with it resting on the meat of your thumb, your hand and your sword are now making two intersecting lines and are going to be a whole lot less structurally sound when it's time to parry a cut from that one giant at your practice.

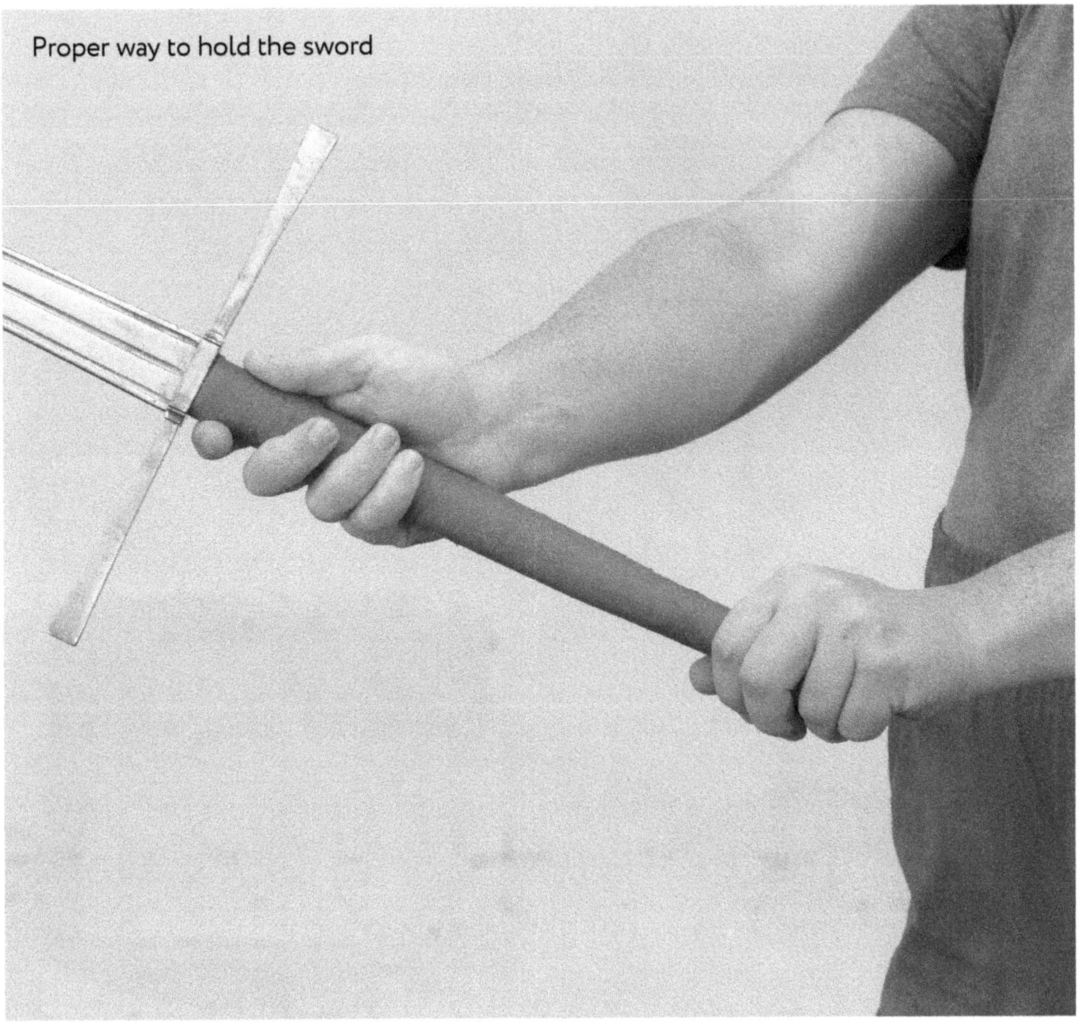

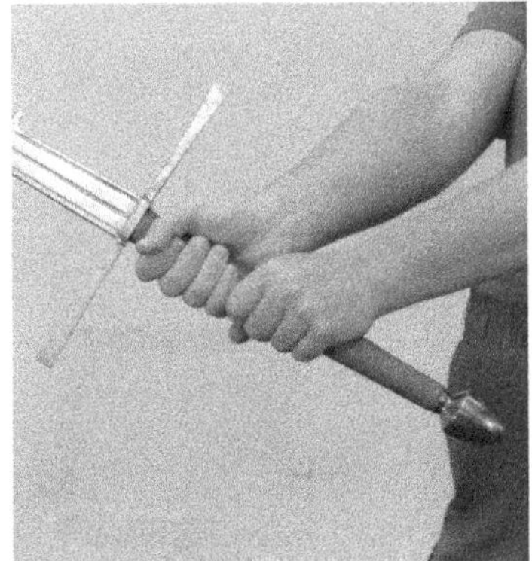

Proper way to hold the sword

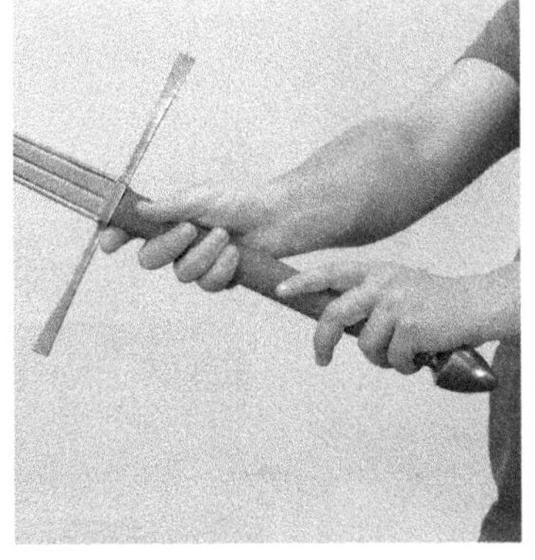

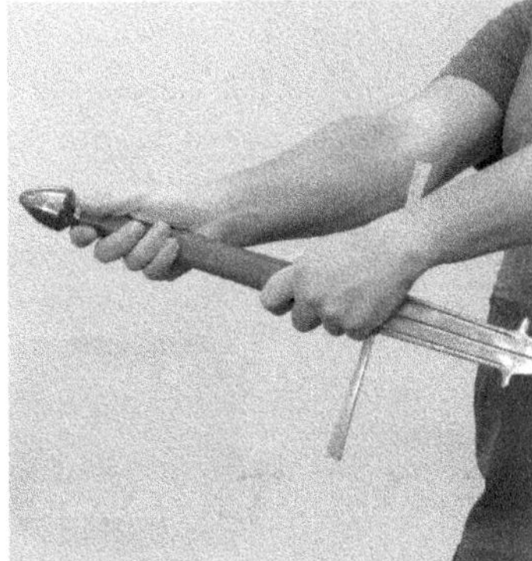

Improper ways to hold the sword

Now take your nondominant hand and make a loose circle with your thumb and index finger. Then, put that circle around your pommel. If your hands are touching, you're either gripping with them too close together or are going to need a longer handle for this system. If it's more comfortable to go an inch higher or lower, that also works. Everyone's hands are built differently.

The reason why we want our nondominant hand all the way back is simple: leverage. The further we scoot our hand back, the longer the lever we have. This not only means we can exert more force when our blade meets our opponent's, but also means that we can now move our sword faster, something that's especially important for when that very same opponent does something you weren't expecting them to do and you suddenly have to change plans on the fly. As such, our nondominant hand is going to be the one doing most of the work. For anyone coming into this with a background fencing with single-handed swords, this is an aspect that will take some time to get used to. An important thing to remember is that even if you can move your hands faster than your opponent can, there's no way you're going to out-speed them using just your dominant hand if they're using their back one.

Alright, I'm about to throw a little bit of bonus material your way. Now, if you're just starting out feel free to skip this part and only circle back to it once you've read the section on *gioco largo* and *gioco stretto* in chapter 14. If those terms are already familiar to you, keep reading.

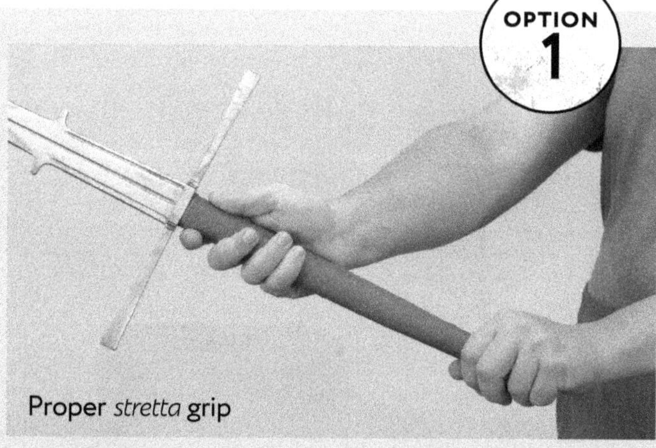

Proper *stretta* grip

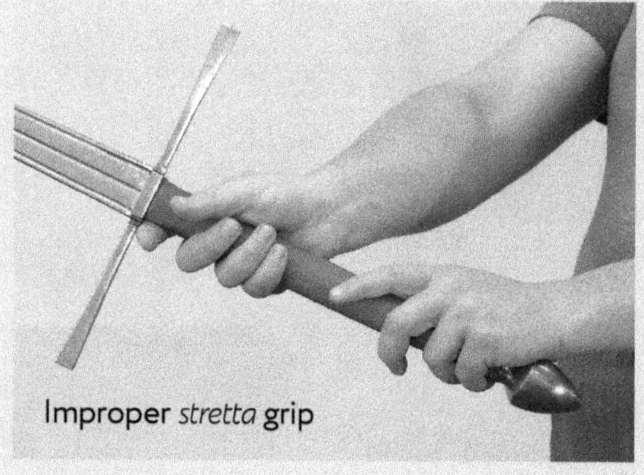

Improper *stretta* grip

There are two grips I tend to use depending on what mode of play I'm currently using. For what I like to call my *stretta* grip, I extend the index finger and thumb of my dominant hand, almost as if I'm pinching a key, to give me a bit more dexterity. This grip works great if you don't have to move too much, but it's not a position into which you should glue your hand.

Looking at the blade itself, we can divide it up a few different ways. To start with, you'll notice that your blade has two edges to it. The edge on the bottom, where your knuckles are pointing, is called the **true edge**. This is the edge you're going to want to do most everything with. If you think about using a hammer, your body is set up for you to really only use a hammer one way. You could try turning it around and attempt to pound nails in via a bicep curl, but you're not going to get very far. The other edge, the one closer to your thumbs, is what we call the **false edge**. This edge has its uses, but isn't the one you're going to use by default.

The other way we can divide the blade is lengthwise. The half of the blade that's closer to you is what we call the ***forte*** (strong). We'll talk about this more in detail in the chapters on cuts and thrusts, but this is the part of the blade that's going to provide you with way more leverage. So, if you're trying to bully your opponent's blade around, this is the part you're going to want to use. The other half of the blade, the part that's further away, is called the ***debole*** (weak). This is both the part you're going to hit other people with as well as the part of your opponent's blade you're going to want to attack through.

Option two is what I call my *larga* grip. Here I bring the index finger of my dominant hand back so that it's next to my middle finger, and then loosely touch the tip of it to my thumb.

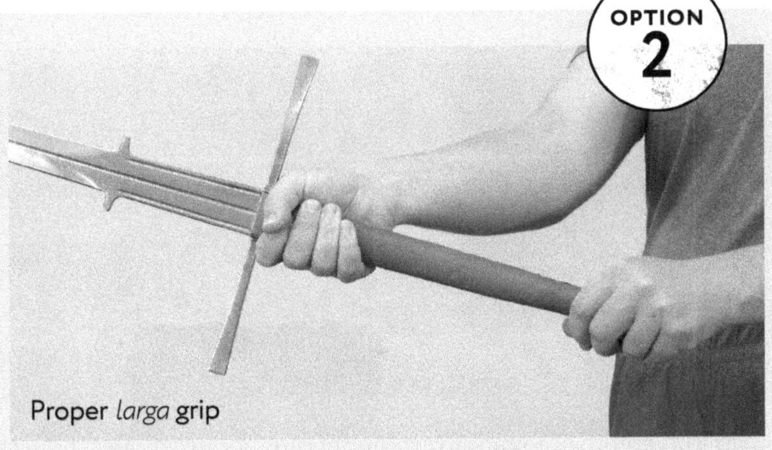

Proper *larga* grip

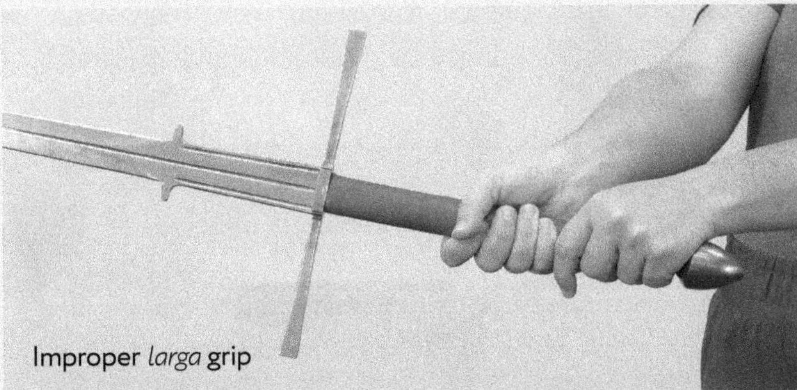

Improper *larga* grip

This makes it a lot easier to perform those larger sweeping actions we see in *larga* play, but sacrifices a bit of fine motor control in the process.

Okay, but what about the rest of your body? Glad you asked! In swordplay it's easy to get caught up in what the sword itself is doing. I'm going to let you in on a secret, though. If you have perfect footwork, you get to win every fight regardless of how good your blade mechanics are. If the rest of your body doesn't support what the sword is trying to do, that sword is going to have an awfully hard time getting where it wants to go.

To start off, I want you to go and pick up your sword again, just the way we discussed above. Now take your nondominant hand off the grip of the sword and use it to grab your blade, assuming you're not using a sharp. Now take the sword and pull it down behind your head.

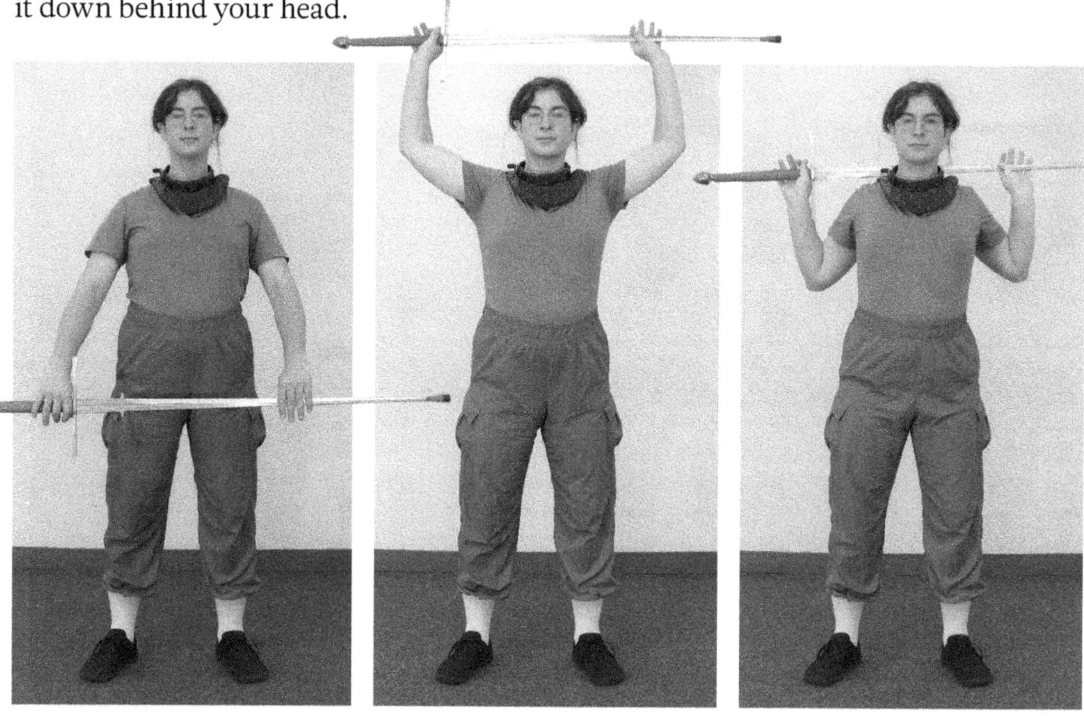

Did you feel those back muscles engage? Great! Now keep them engaged, let go of the blade, and hold the sword out in front of you. This teaches your body to do as much work as possible with the large muscle groups, instead of relying as much on the smaller ones to do all the work. Those big muscles between your shoulder blades, can do a whole lot more for you than the four tiny muscles in your rotator cuff. Not only will using those larger muscle groups mean you'll get tired less quickly, but it will also mean that you have a far lower chance of injury.

Next step, take your pelvis and tuck it under your ribs. Another way of thinking about this might be that you engage your glutes a bit in order to push the bottom part of your pelvis forward. Now, you don't want to keep your muscles overly tight while you're actually fighting, but you might have to add a bit of tension into the system to get everything you want in place to start.

Not tucking your pelvis in
Tucking your pelvis in
Tucking your pelvis in too far

Finally, I want you to start by standing with your feet shoulder-width apart. Next, take one of your feet and move it roughly 1.5x the length of your own foot forward. From there, bend both of your knees to the point that your back heel comes up off the floor. We're going to be exploring positions that involve both the right and left foot being in front, so try this exercise with both feet.

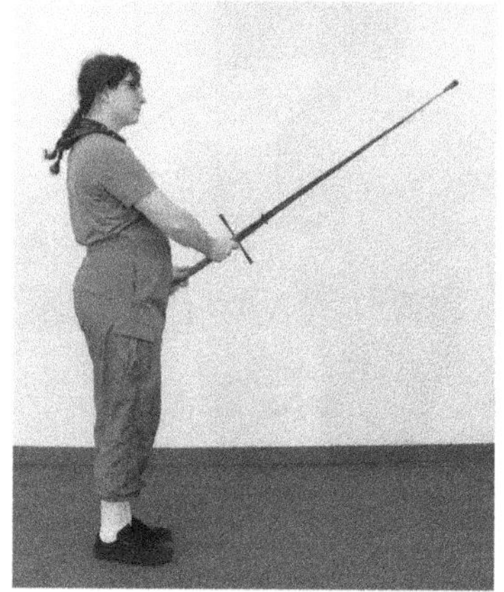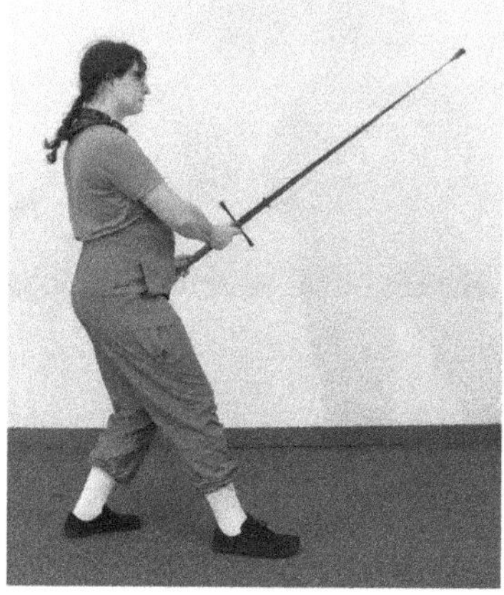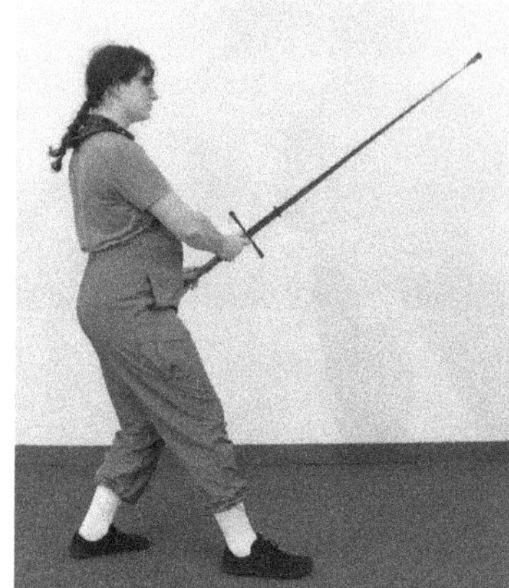

While you'll want your front foot pointed straight forward, you should keep your back foot should be somewhat turned out.[8] The exact degree to which it's turned out will depend a bit on what guard you happen to be forming at any given moment, so don't worry about it too much right now. Besides, we're all built differently, so different people are inherently going to stand differently. The one thing to be careful about is where your front foot is pointed. If you try and step forward with that front foot and it's no longer pointing the same way you're moving, you're going to start doing some real damage to your knee. I know someone who is no longer able to fence because they went for a big lunge, but with the front foot turned in at almost ninety degrees and their knee proceeded to try and leave their body. Fencing is some of the most fun you'll ever have and you'll likely have some amount of minor injuries as a result. That said, I highly doubt that you're ever going to need what you learn here to save your life. Having a bit of fun with your friends is great, but let's try not to have it be at the expense of your ability to walk.

While we're talking about knees, try pushing out slightly with your knees while you're in your stance. You don't need to go so far as to have your foot start to lift off the floor, but it's better to err on the side of pushing out than it is to have your knees start knocking together. A fun way to get a feeling for this is to get a friend, have them face you, put one of your knees against theirs, and then have both of you try and push out.

[8] Dall'Agocchie, "The Art of Defense". 12.

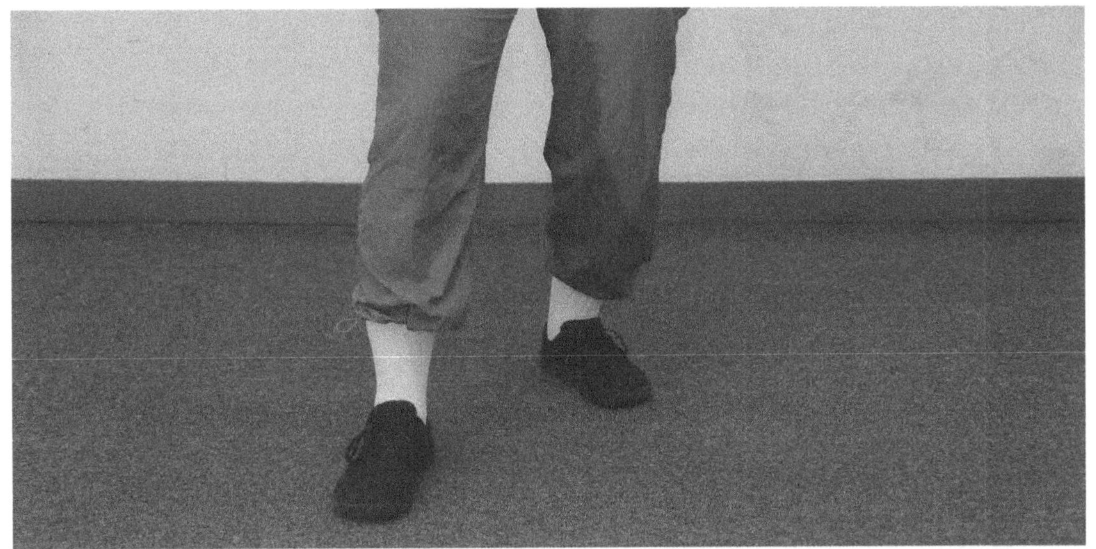

These exercises should help keep your knee in the right spot so you can keep fencing for decades to come.

Here's an exercise to help you see that you've got everything lined up right, so that you can win by using proper structure as opposed to trying to muscle your way through things. Have you and a partner stand in your respective stances facing each other. Now each of you extend the same hand (both right or both left) and lean forward. If you don't have everything lined up, particularly if your elbow is flaring out as opposed to pointing downward, you'll suddenly find yourself being pushed backward.

Properly aligning your structure

Improperly aligning your structure

5: Cuts

To start, remember that even though your training longsword shouldn't be sharp, it's representing something that is. For anyone who's not a vegetarian or a vegan reading this (sorry, Mom), I want you to try cutting through a thick piece of meat with a sharp knife. Now did you hit your food as hard as possible in order to split it cleanly in half? No, that would be silly. Now remember, the same thing applies to swords. They're large knives, not just pointy clubs. Hitting people harder would not have made your sword go through them any better. Using proper body mechanics and lining up the edge just right will help, but swinging for the fences is just going to convince people to stop playing with you. It's also just a really big, committed. movement that's going to leave you open to getting hit more. If you can no longer reasonably say "bonk" after you hit your opponent, you're hitting too hard.

With that said, let's take a look at what constitutes a good cut. One of the overarching themes here is going to be **sword, body, foot**.[9] This is also something we'll return to when we look at thrusts. Swords are sharp, and it doesn't take all that much force to get a sharp piece of steel to go through skin. I've had the chance to play with sharps a small bit and the point of a sword will go straight through a wool doublet and right into your vital organs with the force it takes just to tap someone on the shoulder. The thing you're going to want to focus on is getting the sword out quickly, not hitting as hard as you can. For anyone coming in with a background in striking arts, this is going to feel weird. A good roundhouse punch is going to come in with as much force as possible in order to give you the best chance of knocking your opponent out. If you do the same thing in any fencing tournament I happen to be running, I will not hesitate to inform you that you are done for the day. Also, even if you aren't hurting anyone, you leave yourself wide open by doing this and are going to win far fewer of your matches.

At any given moment, what is the fastest part of your body? It's definitely not your head or your chest, so those two are easy to rule out. Your foot can get you places pretty fast, but it can't spring forward at the speed of your hand, particularly when it's holding up your weight. As such, we want to get the fastest part of us out

[9] Anonimo Bolognese, 55.

first. Bonus points, if you're close enough to your opponent that moving your arms alone has hit them, you've finished! You hit them with your sword and there's no reason to keep moving into them, possibly with even more force.

Let's say that you started a little farther out. In that case extend the cut forward with your arms and then lean your upper body forward a bit. Not only will this increase your reach, but it will also mean you provide less target area to your opponent, because a good deal of your torso has now been effectively withdrawn. It also ensures that you're protecting yourself by first and foremost placing the sword in the way and only then moving your body in.

If that still hasn't done it, then it's time to step. We'll get into footwork a bit more

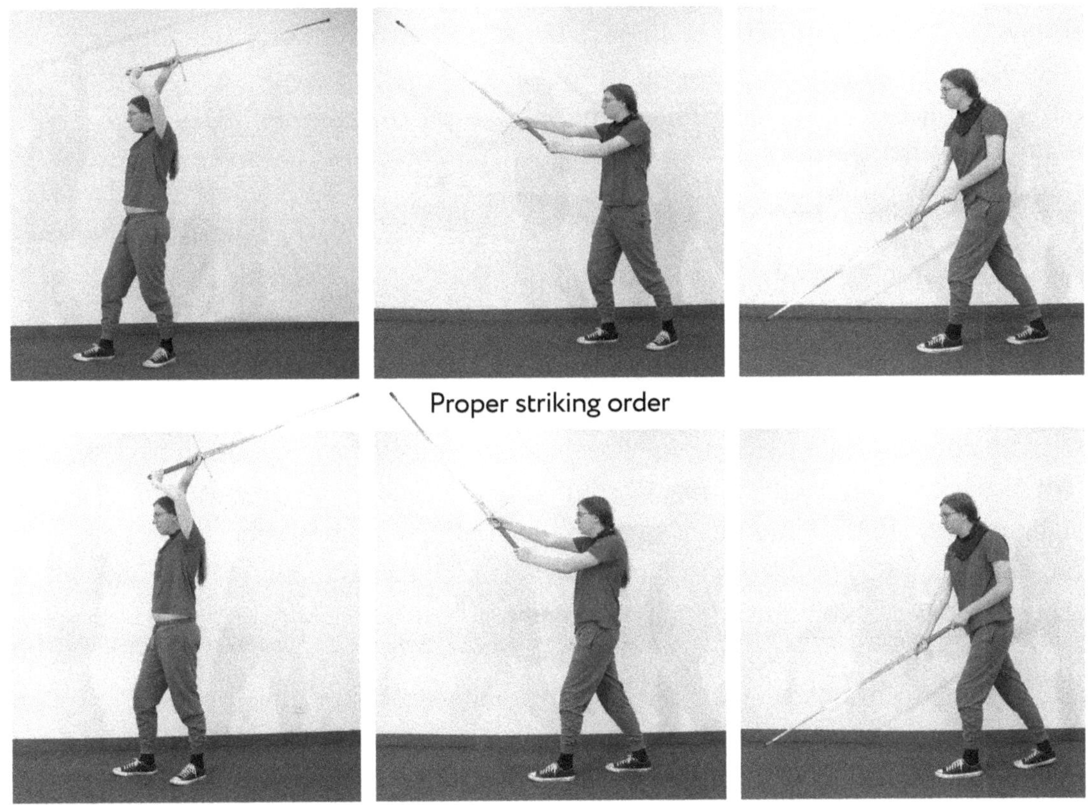

Proper striking order

Improper striking order

later but for the moment let's start by performing a simple passing step: start with one foot back and then bring it forward past your other foot. For right now, if you're gripping your sword with your right hand on top, let's have you start with the left foot in front and then have you pass your right foot forward. If you have your left hand on top, then start with your right foot in front and pass your left foot forward.

Now try doing this a few dozen times. Sword, then body, then foot. If you need to, feel free to start by doing these as distinct stages, stopping at each before you move to the next one. Once you've got that down, start to slowly smooth out the transition between them. Only once you can go from one to the other smoothly should you start to throw in any real speed. Remember, this learning process of crisp, then smooth, then fast is something you're going to keep using every time you want to try and incorporate a new fencing action into your game. It might feel tempting to skip ahead to doing things fast, but if you want to be able to do this safely and at a high level, you're going to have to start by taking it slow and isolating each piece.

On top of keeping your opponent safe and getting yourself in as fast as possible, the other thing that sword, body, foot will do for you is give you a more secure way of entering the fight. By moving the sword in first, we've led with the one thing that doesn't have nerve endings to block the path of our opponent's sword. If they do something unexpected at this stage, it's fairly easy to get our sword out of there. If, however, we've already stepped in by the time we realize something's gone awry, it's going to be a lot harder to keep ourselves from getting hit. Instead we want to clear the way before we go in.

The other piece to this is that your hands and your torso move across a spectrum, whereas your feet move as a binary. If you start moving your hand forward, it's pretty easy to stop and have it change course at any point along its path. Same thing goes for leaning your body forward and back. Your feet, however, don't get that choice. Once you've brought your foot into the air, it has to come down. If you start stepping forward, it's going to be real hard to have that foot go back without landing you on your face. You can make it go a little bit to the right or a little to the left while it's still in the air, but you can't safely pull it back the same way you can with your hand. From a tactical perspective, this means that stepping your foot toward your opponent is an inherently riskier move than moving your arms in or leaning forward.

Additionally, thanks to our friends in the modern Olympic fencing world, we know that moving sword, body, foot will actually get you there faster than moving them all at once.[10] It might feel like you're forcing your foot to wait for an eternity, but by moving your arm first it breaks your inertia, getting you to the target in an overall faster fashion. I don't know about you, but I'm happy to shave off any excess time from my motions in a fight that I can.

Once you've figured out how to go forward, now you've got to figure out how to go back. This part is easily overlooked, but it's often more important than attacking in proper order. If your plan didn't work, it's important to be able to bail. Especially with sharp swords, hitting your opponent isn't really the thing

---

[10] Chen, "Biomechanics of fencing sport", 2017.

that matters—not getting hit is. If they haven't hit you, you can always come back and try and hit them again later. If you hit them but can't get out cleanly, it doesn't matter that you "won", you're still not going back home.

Going backward, the order is going to be a bit different than from when we came in. Instead of going sword, body, foot, this time we're going to go body, foot, sword. The most important part here is to leave the sword out there the whole time you're coming in and the whole time you're coming out. If you threw a strike and stepped in, but your opponent is still standing, you're going to want to keep your sword out and between their sword and you for as long as possible. So, if you bring the sword back first on your way back out, you're handing your opponent a free shot. Remember, your goal is to make your opponent's life as difficult as possible and handing them your face on a silver platter isn't going to help you in that aim.

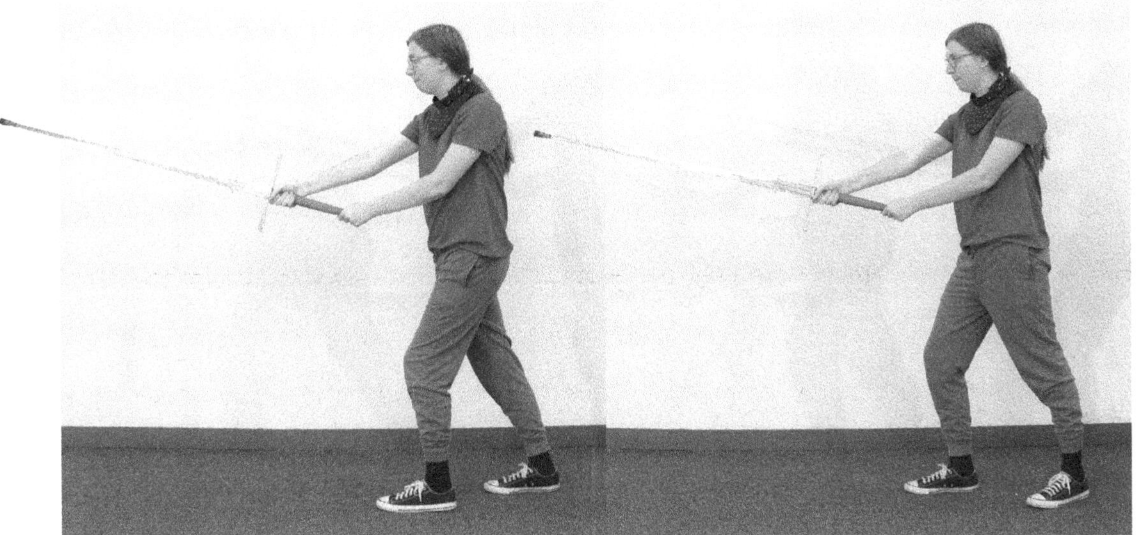

Proper recovery

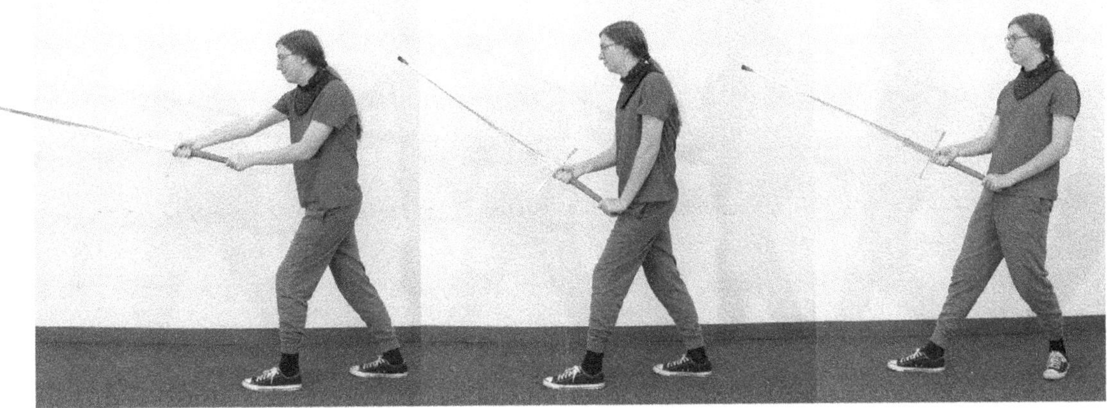

Improper recovery

Now you're going to want to pull your head back first for a few reasons. The first is that it is going to break your inertia, making the rest of the movement a whole lot easier. Next is that your face has a whole lot of important stuff in it and is generally one of the worst places to get hit with a sharp piece of steel. Finally, it gets the weight off your front foot, making its retreat a whole lot easier.

Once you've pulled your head back, now bring your front foot back. There are a few ways to do this, but for the moment just take what was your lead foot and pass it back so that it lands behind your other foot. We'll get into more detail about the different possibilities here once we get to the chapter on footwork.

Finally, now that you're out of range, bring your sword back to your starting guard. If you managed to step back but are still where your opponent can reach you, skip this step and keep your sword in front of you. Messing this up is a fairly common mistake, where people complete their cut and then forget about their hands, leaving them out there as a target. Leaving your hands out is a great way to tell your opponent that it's time to bop you right on the hands. Remember, if they can reach you, keep your sword in between their sword and you.

Getting hit in the hands in measure

Now we begin our climb up Mt. Vocab. Mt. Vocab can definitely seem intimidating, particularly for anyone like me who doesn't speak Italian. That said, in the end it's going to be a whole lot easier to describe something with just a couple precise terms that other folks will also be familiar with than it would be to try and list out a long English description for each and every movement and guard. With that said, let us begin our journey.

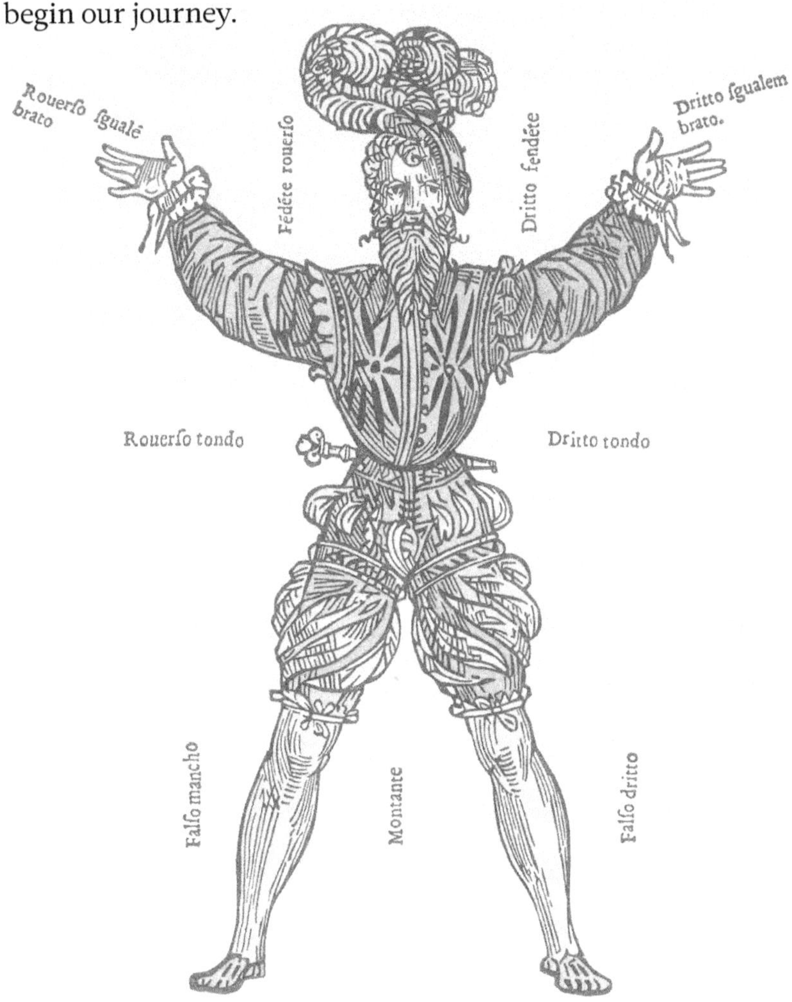

Marozzo's cutting diagram

The Bolognese masters give us names for several different cuts. The total number can seem a bit overwhelming at first, but the good news is that you really just have to learn them all for one side and then they're essentially the same for the other side. For all cuts originating from our dominant side, they are described with the term **mandritto**. The literal translation for this is "from the right", but if you're a lefty and you fight longsword with your left hand on top, for you a *mandritto* will be any cut originating from your left side. For all the cuts originating from your nondominant side, the term is **roverso**.

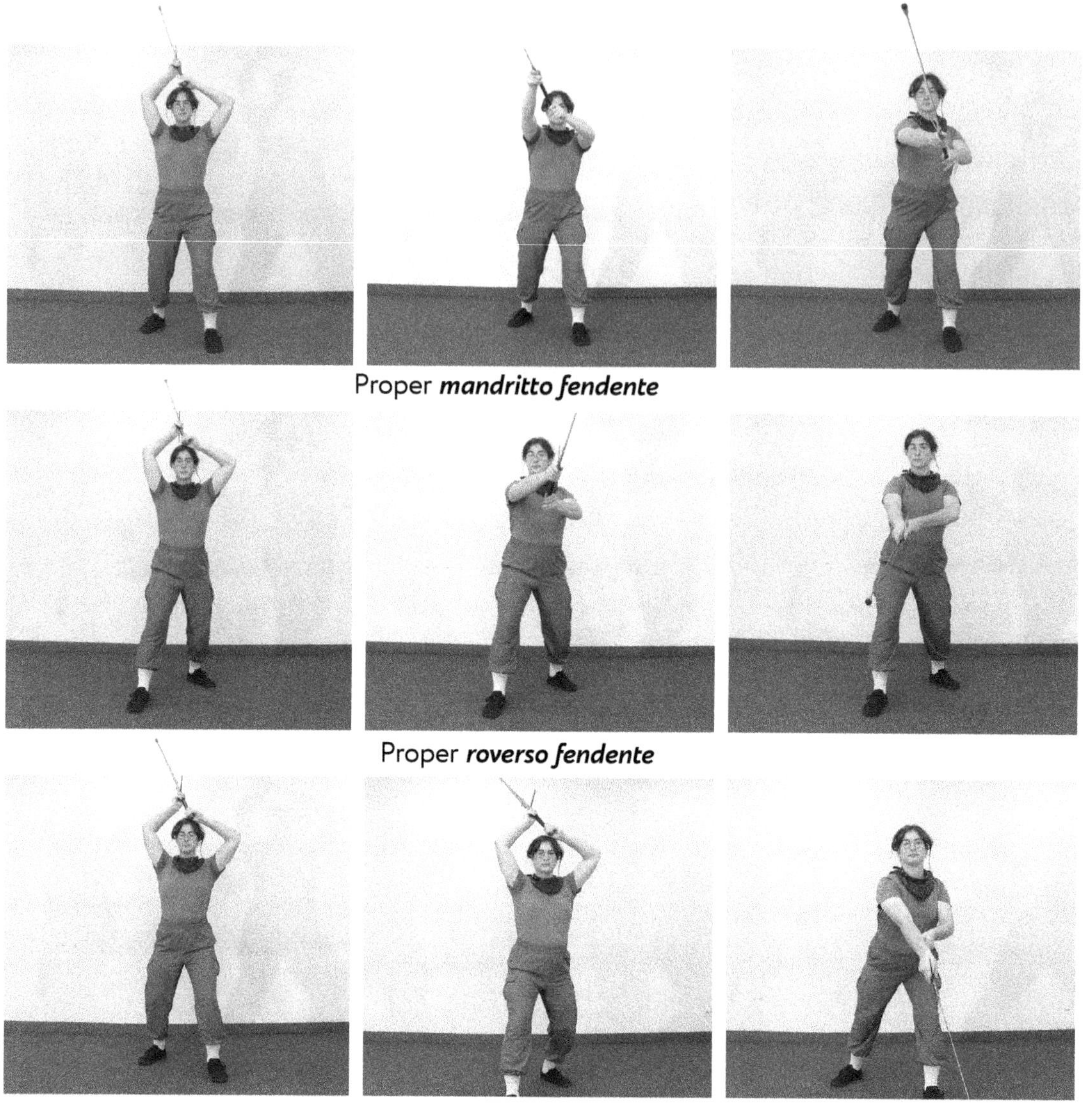

Proper *mandritto fendente*

Proper *roverso fendente*

Improper *mandritto fendente*

Starting from the top down, the first cut is the *mandritto **fendente***. This is a cut that goes from right to left, going not quite straight down. Dall'Agocchie describes this as cutting from the head on one side and going toward the foot on the other.[11] Remember that the cut is defined based on its trajectory, not its target. So, if I cut down at the same angle and hit you in the neck instead of going through your skull, it would still be considered a *fendente*. As you might have guessed, doing the same cut but from left to right would be a *roverso fendente*. Out of all the cuts we have, this one is the most structurally sound. If you're starting in a high guard, the *fendente* can be a really menacing move as we as humans don't like things coming down toward our heads.

[11] Dall'Agocchie, 8.

Next is the ***sgualimbratto***. This cut, which each author seems to spell differently, is the default cut in the Bolognese system and comes down at a forty-five-degree angle, going from shoulder to knee.[12] Sometimes in the manuals you'll see the authors just say to cut a *mandritto* or *roverso* without specifying the line. In almost every instance what they mean is a *sgualimbratto* thrown from one side or the other. While structurally a little less sound than the *fendente*, the *sgualimbratto* tends to be a lot better at getting around people's defenses.

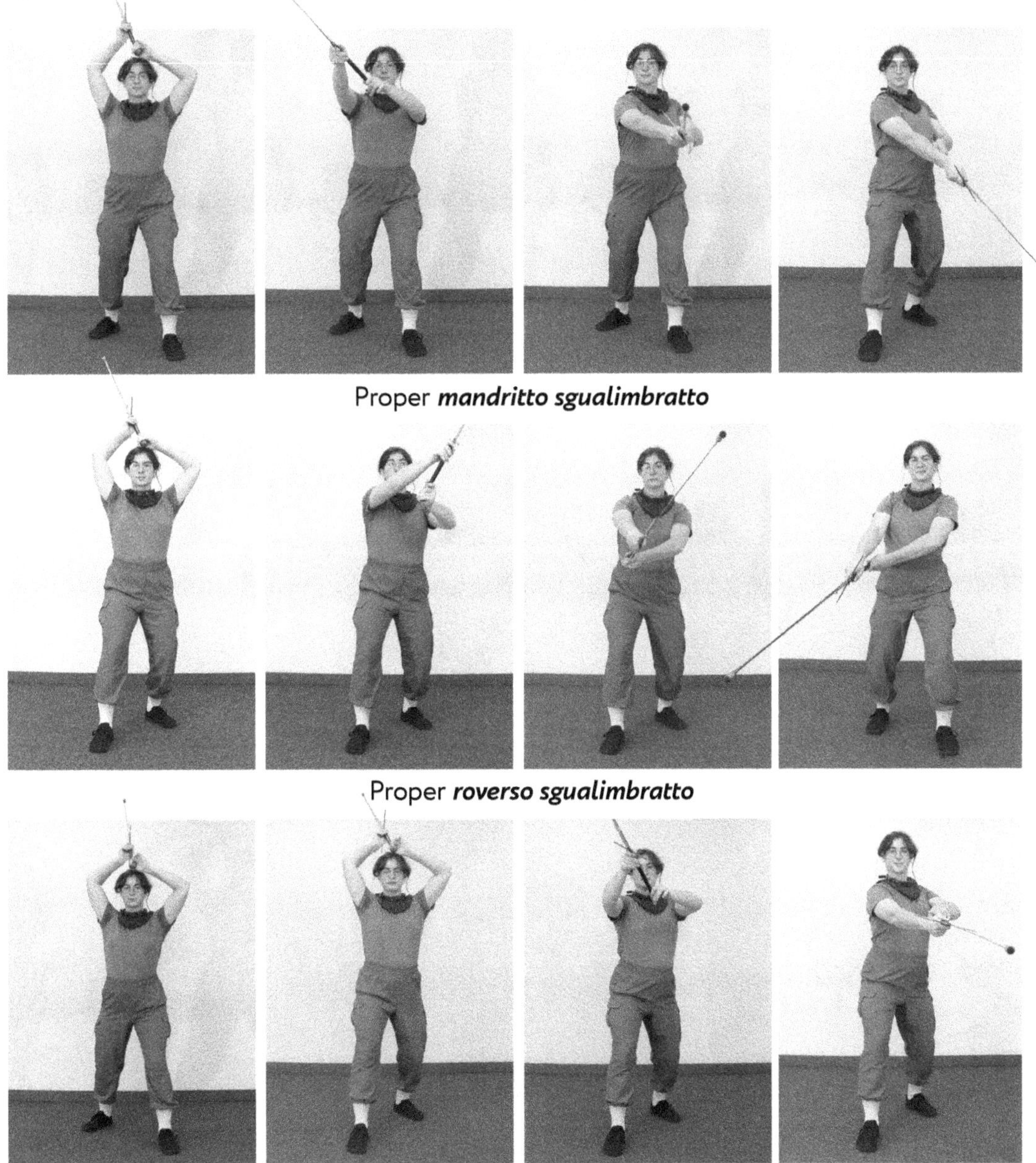

Proper *mandritto sgualimbratto*

Proper *roverso sgualimbratto*

Improper *sgualimbratto*

[12] Dall'Agocchie, 8.

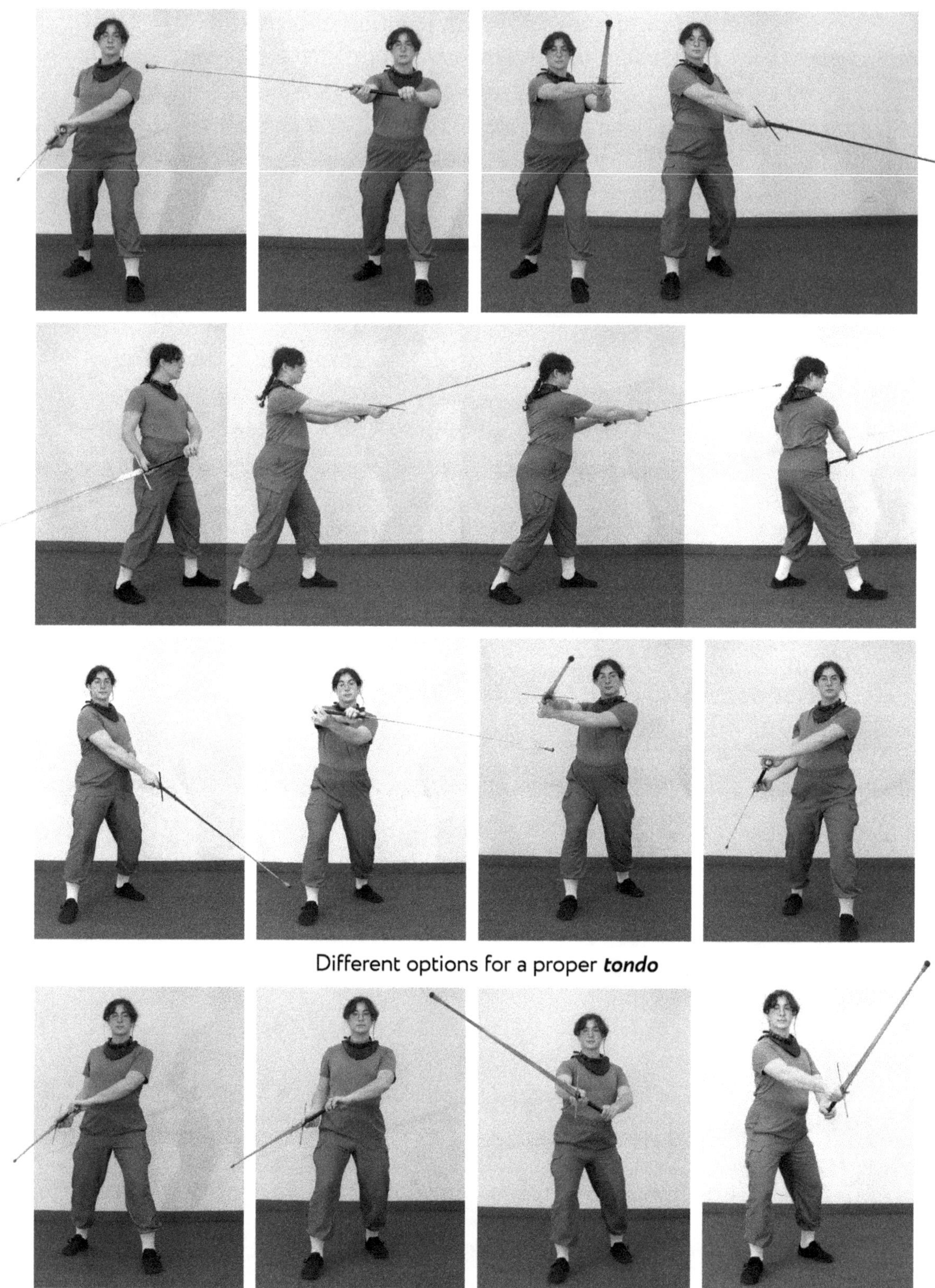

Different options for a proper *tondo*

Improper *tondo*

The next cut we have is the ***tondo***. While the word literally means "around", what it means in this context is a cut that goes horizontally across your opponent's body. Structurally speaking, this is the weakest of all the cuts. That said, it still has its place. It can be especially hard to block and also requires very little aiming. If I want to throw a *fendente* or a *sgualimbratto* to my opponent's leg, I have to really make sure that their leg is going to be within the trajectory of my cut. If instead I throw a *tondo*, as long as I'm close enough I know that it's going to connect with one leg or the other. The *tondo* can be a really versatile cut, as it can both strike our opponent "right below their beard" or take out a leg. If you happen to have anyone coming out of the German traditions at your local practice or tournament, they tend to use what's essentially a high *tondo*, especially once they get in close. So even if this isn't a cut you use a lot, it's good to know how to deal with it.

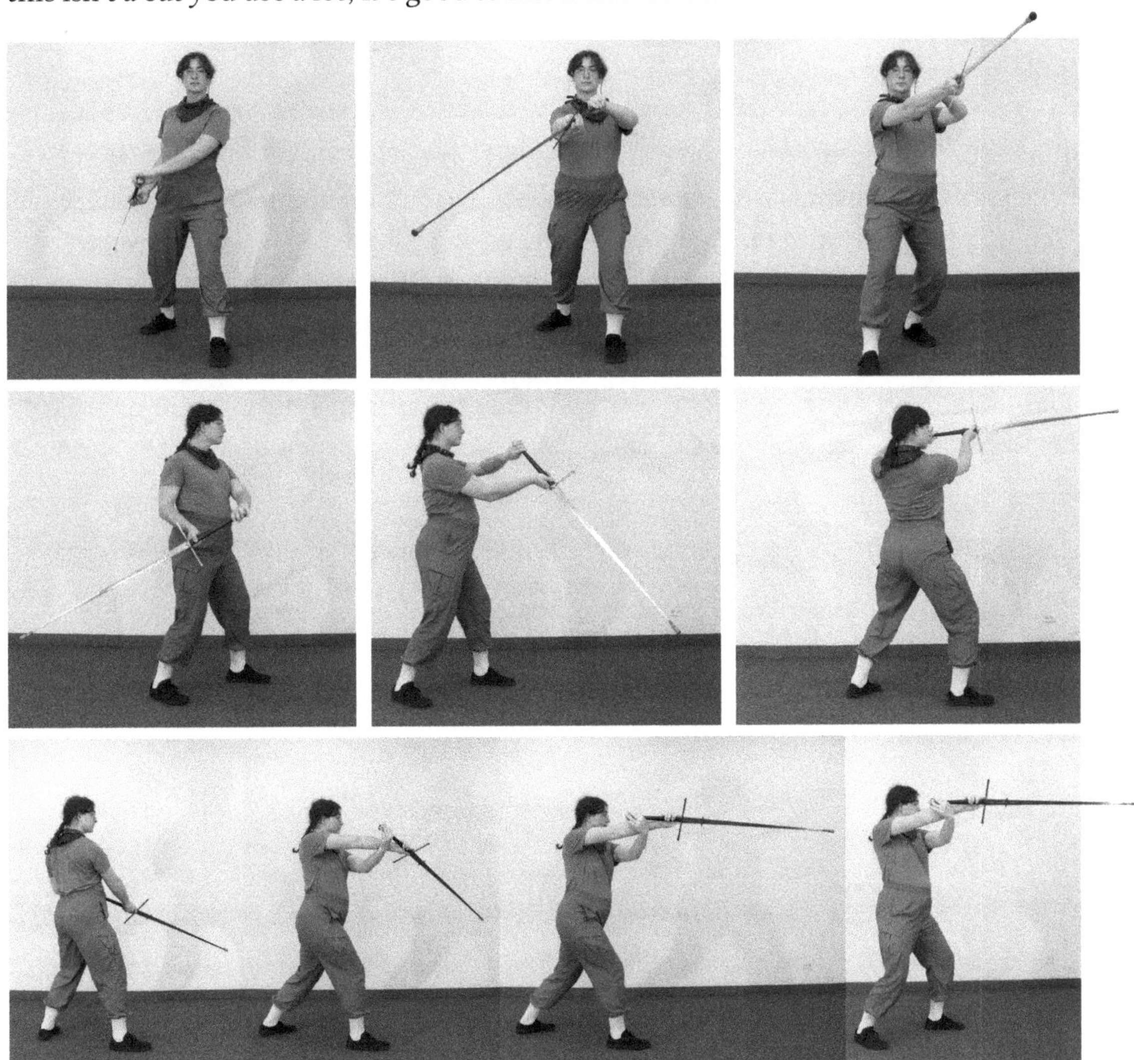

Different options for a proper ***ridoppio***

Following that, our next cut is the ***ridoppio***. This is just a diagonal rising cut that aims up toward your opponent's shoulder.[13] While you do have to go against gravity when using this cut, your bones are still pushing in the same direction as the cut with the ground to support you, so if you do it right it can meet a descending cut with a surprising amount of structure. This cut is really good for threatening your opponent's arms in a way they often won't expect.

The final cut here is called the ***montante***.[14] This one doesn't show up all that much, but it's just a rising cut that goes straight up the middle. Seeing as your mid-line is generally where all the best parts are, this cut can serve as a really threatening action that gets to the heart of our psyche. The Anonimo tells us this is done as a false edged cut, but we see it performed as a true edge cut in some of the other treatises.[15]

Full Cuts vs Half Cuts

Oftentimes the manuals will refer to an action as a *mezzo* (half) *mandritto/roverso*, differentiating that from a *tutta* (full) *mandritto/roverso*. This describes how the cut ends, but not necessarily how it begins. So, if your cut ends in presence (with your tip pointed at your opponent), say you cut into their hand but stop so that you end with your sword pointed at your opponent instead of passing all the way through, then that would be considered a half cut. Alternatively, if your cut cleaves all the way through or goes past your opponent, then it would be considered a full cut. As a note, it doesn't matter if your sword went through a full circle or not to get to its end target. The half/full cut designation is only concerned with where the cut ends.

Three Sizes of Cuts

There are three joints in the arms we can rotate around to generate force for a cut. With the fingers being stuck wrapped around our handle, our first option is what's called a **wrist cut**. Try holding your sword out and making a circle just using your wrists, without having to bend your elbows.

---

[13] Dall'Agocchie, 8.
[14] The large Spanish montante two handed sword is named after the cut it was often used to perform.
[15] Anonimo Bolognese, 61.

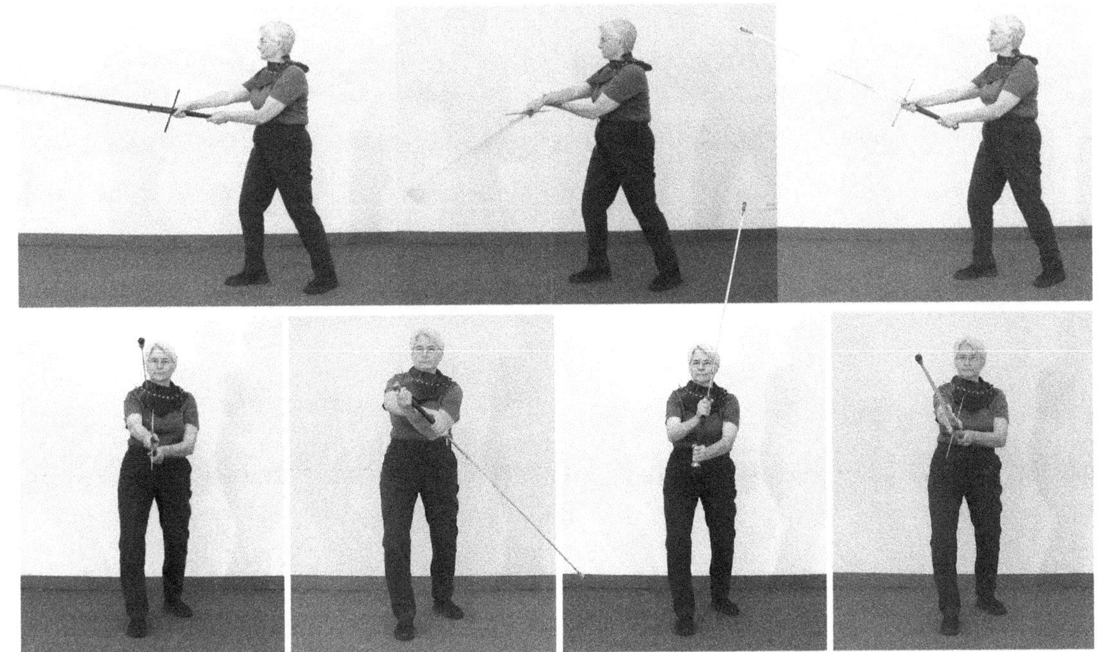

Wrist cut

The next option is what we call an **elbow cut**. Hold your arms out again. This time though, when you go to prep your cut use both your wrists and your elbows to pull the sword around, but don't use much of your shoulders in order to do it.

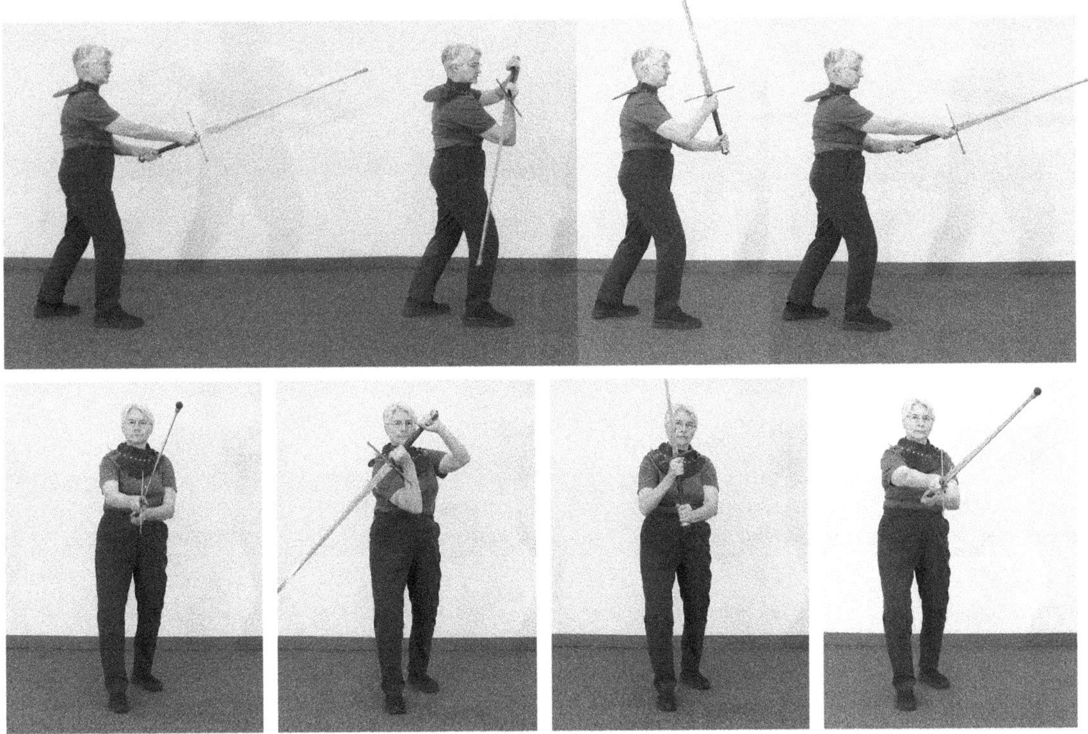

Elbow cut

Our final one is, you guessed it, a **shoulder cut**. For this, bring the sword all the way around using all three of the major joints in each of your arms.

Shoulder cut

Falsi

So far all of the cuts we've gone over have been with the true edge. True edge cuts are a great default and are generally going to be a lot more structurally sound. That said, sometimes going around is just easier than going through. Any of the five cuts (from either side) could be done instead as a *falso*, a cut with the false edge. Two of these are given their own names though.

The first of these is the *falso manco*. This is just a false edge *roverso ridoppio*, so it's a rising cut from your nondominant side. To perform this, all you have to do is push on the pommel as you extend your arms out a bit. This cut is great both as a way to attack your opponent's arms, and to deliver a beat to their sword, clearing the way for your next attack.

Falso manco

Next, we have the *falso dritto*. This is the same thing as the *falso manco*, just on the other side. To perform this one you're going to need to use your shoulders a bit more as your hands are now crossed. Otherwise, though, it has all the same uses as the *falso manco*, just from the other side.

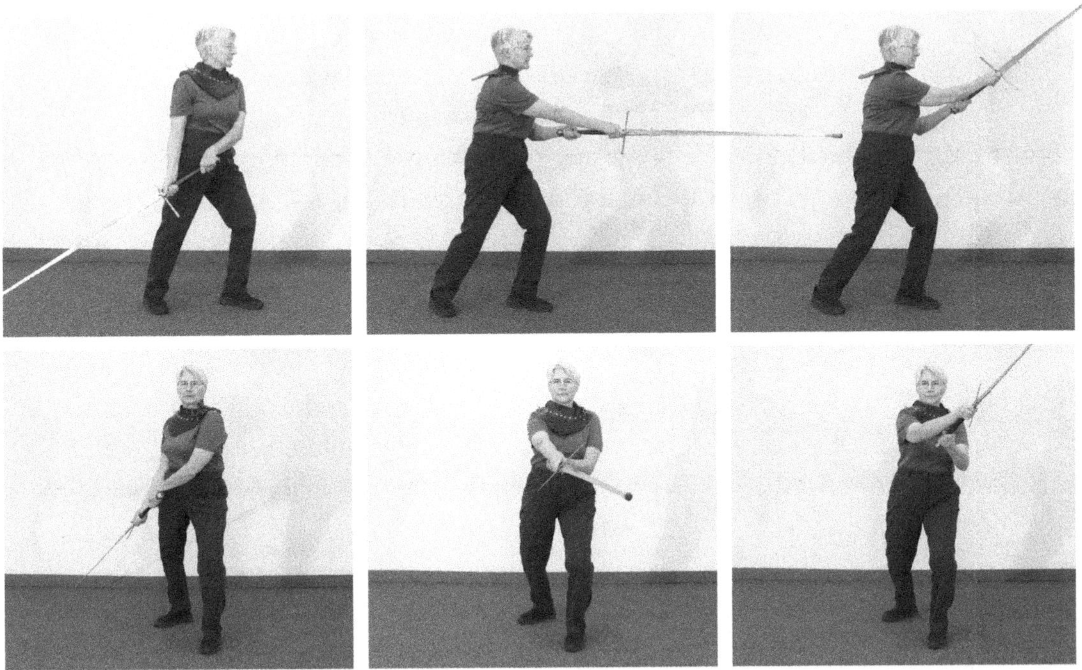

Falso dritto

Try this as an exercise: figure out how to do all the different cuts in a row. To start, just begin by performing them as true-edge cuts. This might look like a *mandritto fendente*, followed by a *roverso fendente*, then a *mandritto sgualimbratto*, a *roverso sgualimbratto*, a *mandritto tondo*, a *roverso tondo*, a *mandritto ridoppio*, a *roverso ridoppio*, and then finish it all off with a *montante*. Once you've done that a few times, try changing the order up, making sure you still do each cut at least once. After that, try doing them all as *falsi*. Next try switching up which ones you do with each edge and see what feels more natural to you and what needs more work.

The Three Advantages

Up until now, we've been focusing on how to throw a cut on your own, but what happens if your cut meets with someone else's cut? The good news is that we have an answer. When two blades meet during a cut, there are three things that define which one is going to be able to push through. The first advantage is that of the **true edge**, or just edge alignment more broadly.[16] You'll notice that your sword bends along one axis, but not the other. We want the one that doesn't bend to meet our opponent. The human hand is really good at swinging things one way, but not the other. Remember, if you're trying to put a nail in, you wouldn't try and hammer it palm down, or even worse, with the back of your hand.

If you think back to the beginning of the chapter, we also talked about how you slice through your food by pointing the knife the right way, not by hitting it harder. Next time you're eating dinner, try cutting through your food with your knife at a slightly off angle.[17] It doesn't really work. You might not have to actively think about it at this point, but your knife has to go in at a very particular angle without much room for error. Same thing goes for when you're trying to cut through someone's sword. Ideally it would be great if you could push your true edge through the flat of their blade, but if you have just a bit more of your edge in there and their sword connects just a bit closer to their flat, the difference is going to feel huge. Try this with a friend and a pair of training swords.

The next advantage is **leverage**.[18] When your two swords meet, the closer that intersection is to your hilt and the closer it is to their point, the stronger your position will be. Here's an exercise you can try at home. Hold your sword, or broomstick, out in front of you. Now have a friend press up against the true edge right below the quillons with one of their fingers. You'll notice it's pretty easy for

[16] Boorman, "Introduction to the Italian Rapier", 72.
[17] Please do not actually do this. We don't want you cutting your other hand by accident.
[18] Boorman, 80.

you to push right through them. Next, have them try but this time with their finger right under the tip. Now feel free to push down as hard as you can with both hands. You'll realize that despite pouring more strength in, the fact that you've handed your friend such a long lever to use gives them the clear advantage.

Leverage

Another way of thinking about this: your arms have muscles, your sword doesn't. Whenever your sword runs into someone else's, you want it to be closer to where you're generating force and farther away from where they're generating force.

The final advantage is that of **crossing**.[19] If I can get my sword on top of my opponent's sword and point my tip across theirs, not only do I have gravity on my side, but I've also now created a ramp to angle my opponent's sword away from my body and right into my hilt. In order to do this, you'll need to first get your cross over your partner's and then point your tip so that it aims just outside of their silhouette. Generally speaking, it's this advantage I see people forget about most. If you're wondering how someone just parried your powerful cut, it's probably because they just pointed across your sword.

[19] Boorman, 82.

Properly using crossing to intercept a cut

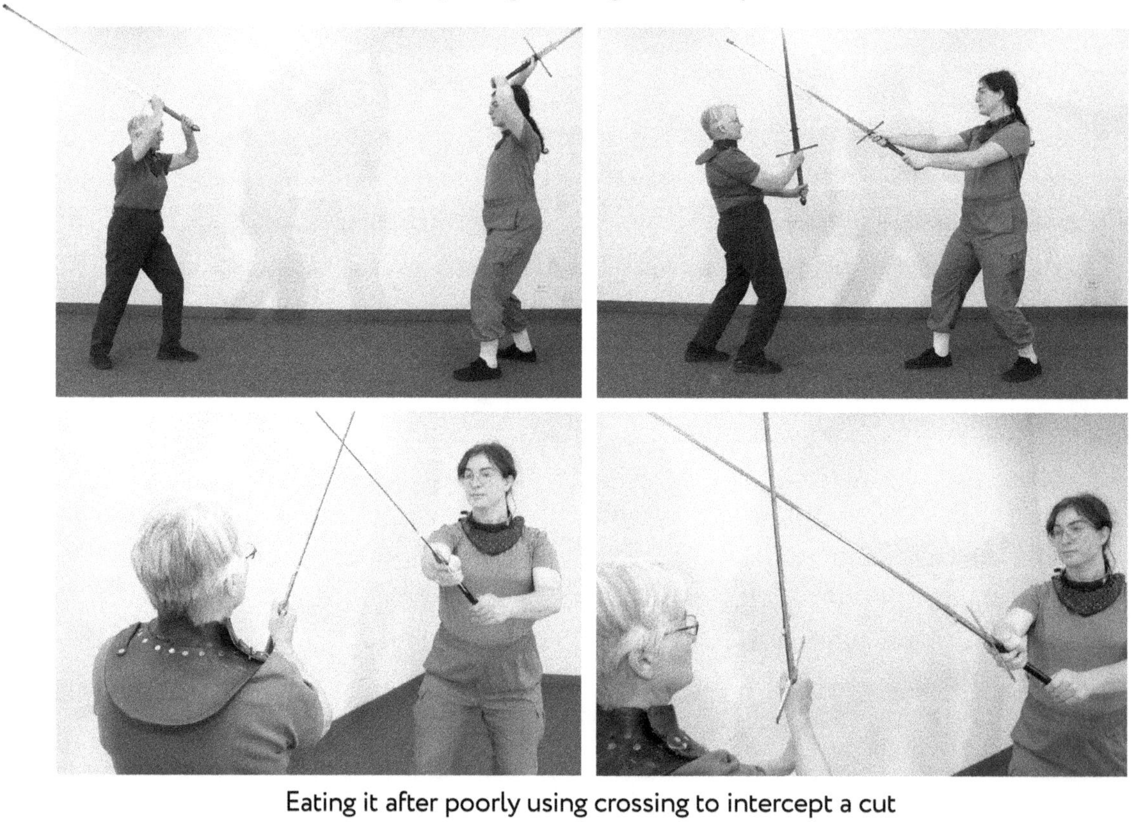

Eating it after poorly using crossing to intercept a cut

Similarly to how we lead sword, body, foot, here you want to make sure to move the point first and only then have the hilt follow. If you push the hilt out first, you're going to create a weak angle that your opponent will easily be able to point across and collapse into your face. You might feel like you need to shove the hilt out there because that's where your brain thinks your body ends, but now all of a sudden you have a several-foot-long finger that doesn't feel any pain at your disposal.

Crossing, where your sword points across theirs, can be accomplished in two different fashions. The first is to do it wholly with the sword, pointing all the way across your body. The other option is to use your feet and step in at an angle. Ideally,

Crossing just with bladework

Crossing just with footwork

Crossing with bladework and footwork together

you're going to end up using a little bit of both.

I generally recommend stepping to cross your opponent's line instead of swinging out as otherwise you make your follow up attack harder to get to while also trying to solve the problem with a weaker part of your blade.

How to Stop a Cut

If someone is throwing a cut straight at you, there are three main ways of using your sword to prevent getting bonked on the head. The first option is to execute a **parry**. Some instructors use this term to describe any and all defensive blade actions, but I tend to use it for a narrower scope. All this action requires is for you to take the tip of your sword and point it across the line of your opponent's cut, ending with your sword being in between their sword and you. This is really where that advantage of **crossing** comes in. As an exercise, grab a friend and have them slowly throw a cut into each of your four quadrants (upper-right, upper-left, lower-right, lower-left), and then stop each one with a parry. This might mean parrying a *mandritto fendente* aimed at your upper-left quadrant, a *roverso sgualimbratto* aimed at your upper-right quardrant, a *mandritto ridoppio* aimed at your lower-left quadrant, and a *roverso ridoppio* aimed at your lower-right quadrant. Try doing each one ten or twenty times and then after that have your partner start to change up the order on you.

One of the things you might notice, particularly if you and your partner are similarly matched in your understanding of mechanics or if your partner is significantly larger than you, is that it can be awfully hard to parry a strong cut by just standing there and moving your sword. Good news, there's another way. Instead of relying just on your arms to do all the work, use your feet. Try making an angled step where you come off to one side as opposed to straight forward/ back as you parry in order to better gain the advantage of crossing, so that your structure points in a straight line through their sword at a point where none of their body is standing behind it in order to provide backup.

The next option is a **collection** of your opponent's sword. Sometimes it's no longer worth it to try and solve the problem with subtle blade mechanics and instead it's time to dump all your stats into leverage and slam your quillons into your opponent's blade. For an example, have your drill partner slowly throw a *mandritto fendente* toward your head, with you wearing a fencing mask, and respond by forcefully shoving your hilt up into their blade with your quillons right above your eyebrows. Not only are **collections** a great way to tip the advantages in your favor, but they're also a great setup for pretty much any *presa* (grapple).

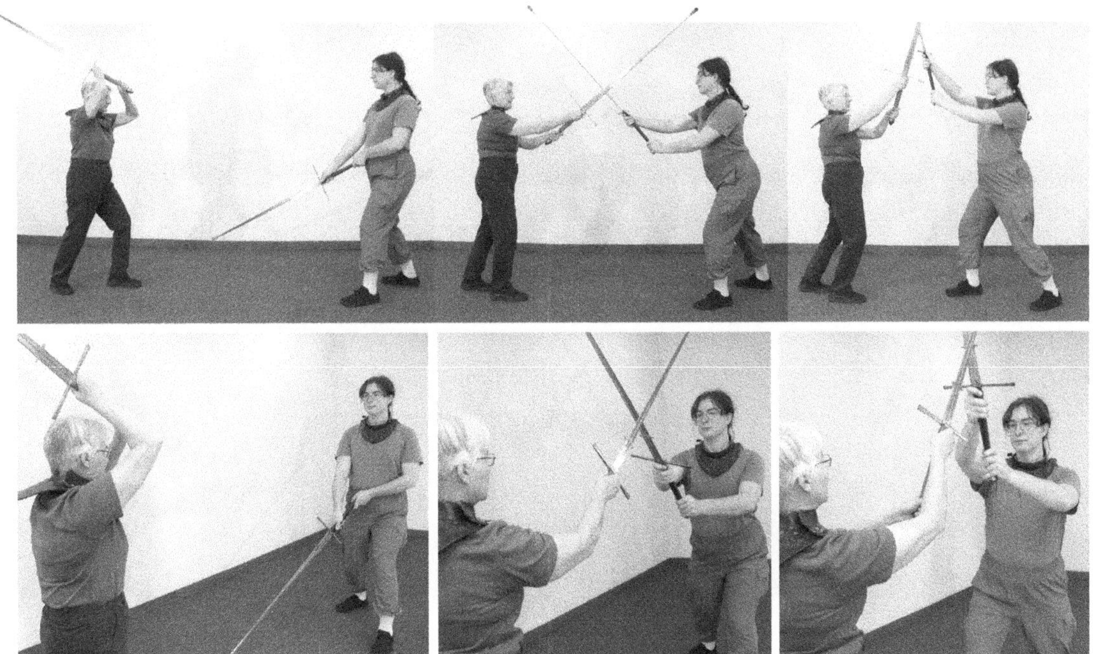

Collecting into *guardia di testa*

Option number three is what we call a **deflection**. This is just whacking their sword out of the way. If you stayed awake during your high school physics class, you might remember that force along one axis does nothing to affect force coming in along a different axis. If, for example, you let go of a helium-filled balloon it's going to go straight up. A sideways wind may push it to the left or the right, but unless that wind is also pushing down it won't affect the speed at which the balloon rises. So just because something is coming in straight toward you with more force than you'd like to try and stop, that doesn't mean that hitting it from the side won't derail it. To practice this, try having one partner throw a *mandritto sgualimratto* and then have the other person step out of the way as they throw a *falso manco* into their opponent's sword. Now try it with a *roverso sgualimbratto* against a *falso dritto*.

Deflecting a *mandritto sgualimbratto* with a *falso manco*

Sometimes, authors will instead refer to this as a **beat**. You can also use it against a thrust or a stationary guard. It's overall a great way to get you past the point of their sword so that you can start coming in closer and throw more threatening strikes.

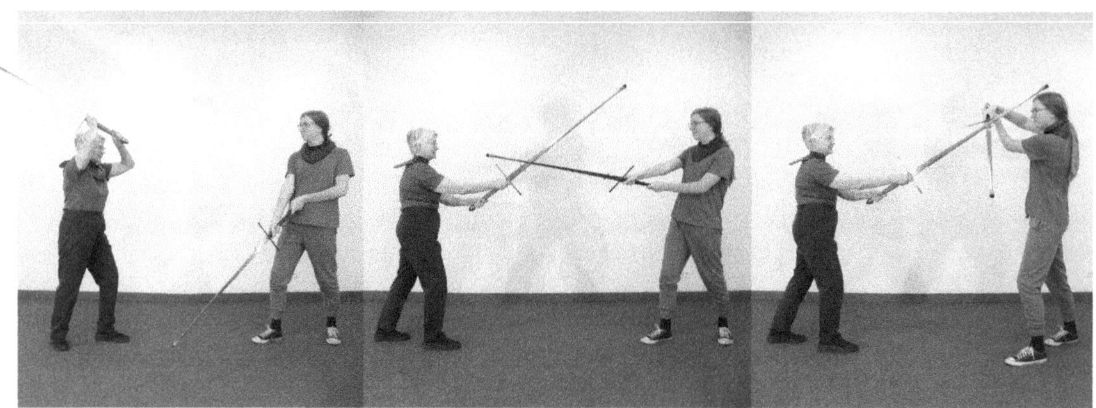

Poorly executed beat

Something to note here is that blade orientation matters a TON for these cuts in particular. If you don't quite strike with the edge of your sword when trying to hit their flat, this isn't going to work. You either have to get your false edge turned in all the way to hit their flat off to the side. Alternatively, you can wait just a hair longer and drop your false edge on top of theirs, pushing their blade further down and out of the way than they expected it to go. You can meet a descending action with a rising one here if you want; you just have to remember not to try and intercept it head on.

Another option for a deflection might be to strike their *mandritto sgualimbratto* with a *roverso sgualimbratto* of your own or for you to throw a *mandritto sgualimbratto* into their *roverso*. Note that your **deflection** doesn't necessarily have to be a rising cut, as in the earlier examples. However, it does need to be a *mandritto* against a *roverso* or vice versa. Theoretically you could step in at such an extreme angle that you could do a *mandritto* against a *mandritto* or a *roverso* against a *roverso*, but at that point you'd more than likely have a clear path to strike your opponent and wouldn't need to hit their sword out of the way to get there. Something to remember here is that all you need to do is deflect their blade far enough that it doesn't hit you. Any farther than that and you make it easy for your opponent to come around to the other side and strike you there. Fencing is a game far more about efficiency than it is about strength.

How to Get Around a Cut

Sometimes you can't go through, so you just gotta go around. But how do you do that? There are a few options we'll get more in depth with later on in this book, but let's look at one for the moment.

Let's say your opponent is throwing a *fendente* straight down into your head and you know you won't be able to take it straight on. Starting with a point-forward guard, one option would be to just cut over the top. You just push on your pommel and bring your blade over the top of theirs and on to the other side as you step out with your foot. Depending on how close you are, you can either come down on to their blade, locking it down, or you can skip straight to hitting them in the hands or the head.

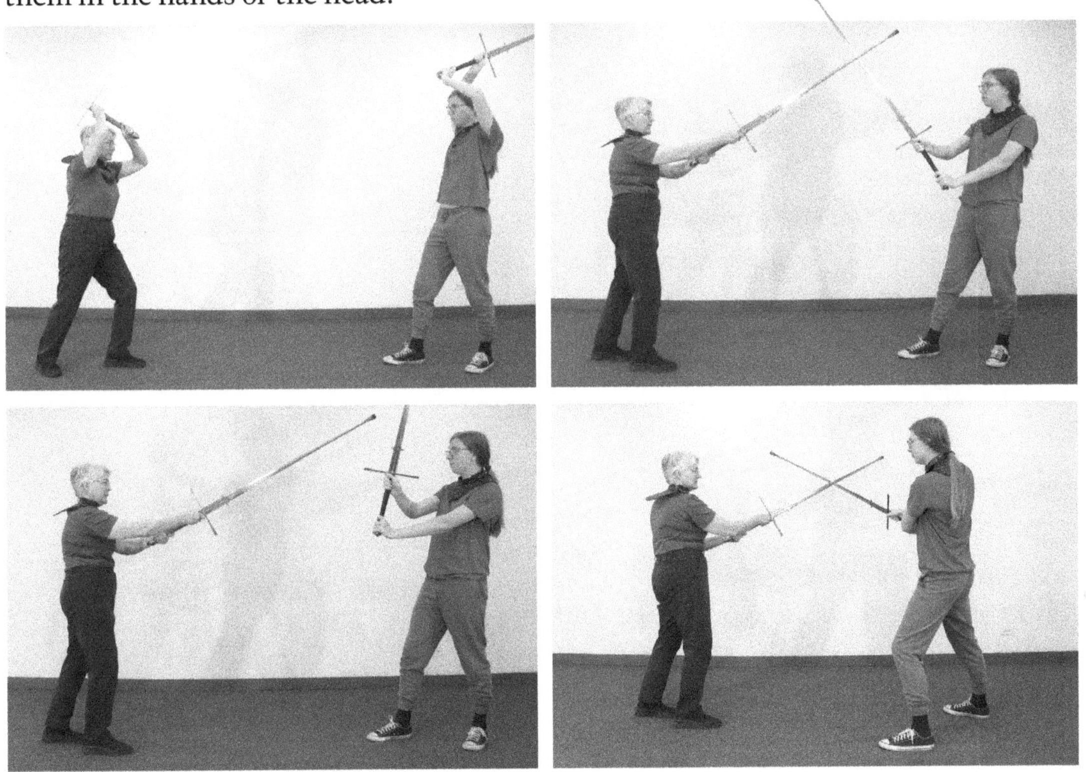

Sfalsare over the top of a *mandritto fendente*

Ribbon Cuts

Ribbon cuts are a pattern we see pop up over and over again. The phrase is a modern term stemming from the imagery of those little ribbons you see people pinning on their jackets. The name for them is modern, but we see them pop up all throughout the tradition. One example would be throwing a *falso manco* and then in one smooth motion coming around and delivering a *roverso sgualimbratto*. Alternatively, you could throw a *falso dritto* and then come up and around to strike with a *mandritto sgualimbratto*.

Ribbon cuts

Once you've tried these out, see what other cuts you can try and fit into the same overall pattern. Mostly they're just a convenient way of throwing an attack to one side and then the other without having to stop and reset in between. You also see them a lot as an initial attack to the blade, beating it away, followed up by a second attack to the hand or the body.

Spinto

A *spinto* is a cut that we push into our opponent. This doesn't mean laying our blade on them and sliding it forward. Instead, it's just pushing the edge of our blade directly into our chosen target (generally the head).

Sometimes this is done as it's the one opening available. Other times it's because we want to land a cut but don't want it to come with any significant force. This could be both not wanting to kill someone in a formal duel as well as just a way to be nice to your sparring partners.

Spinto

Cutting Patterns

There's more cutting patterns out there than I care to count and I highly encourage you to go out there and start creating your own. In the meantime, though, here are a few cutting patterns I've put together to help get you started moving around.

1. <u>Down from the left, up from the left, up from the right, down from the right.</u>
    - Do it with the true edge both ways.
    - Do it with the false edge both ways.
    - Start it with a true edge, then a false edge cut.
    - Start it with a false edge cut, then a true edge cut.

2. <u>Ribbon cuts</u>
    - Throw a *falso manco* to a *roverso sgualimbratto*. Then throw a *falso dritto* followed by a *mandritto sgualimbratto.*Do them all as wrist cuts.
    - Do them all as elbow cuts.
    - Do them all as shoulder cuts.
    - Do them all while alternating between wrist, elbow, and shoulder (doesn't have to be in that order).

3. Tondo Double Cuts
• Throw *mandritto tondo* with the false edge and then with the true edge.
• Throw a *roverso tondo* with the false edge and then with the true edge.
• Now do it all at head height.
• Do it all aiming at chest height.
• Do it all aiming at leg height.

4. Three of The Same
• Throw a full *mandritto sgualimbratto* aiming at head height.
• Throw a full *mandritto sgualimbratto* aiming at chest height.
• Throw a full *mandritto sgualimbratto* aiming at leg height.
• Do it again, but rearrange the order.
• Then throw a full *roverso sgualimbratto* aiming at head height.
• Then throw a full *roverso sgualimbratto* aiming at chest height.
• Then throw a full *roverso sgualimbratto* aiming at leg height.
• Now rearrange the order and do it again.

6: Thrusts

Something people often forget is that the longsword is a cut AND thrust weapon. Cuts are great and you should definitely use them, but make sure not to forget the weapon's reach is longest at its point. I cannot count the number of times I've seen a longsword fencer think of the fight as purely existing at cutting measure (distance), only to be surprised when their opponent pokes them with a lunge.

Before we get into how to properly deliver a thrust, first let's look at the concept of **line**. Broadly speaking, you have two major lines, the **inside line** and the **outside line**. Take your dominant hand and reach it forward as if you're going to shake someone's hand. The side where your palm is? Everything that happens on that side is on your inside line. Everything that occurs on the other side, whether it's your or your opponent doing it, is on your outside line. It's important to note here that if one fencer is right-handed and the other is left-handed, the swords can be said to be engaged on one person's inside line while at the same time being on the other person's outside line.

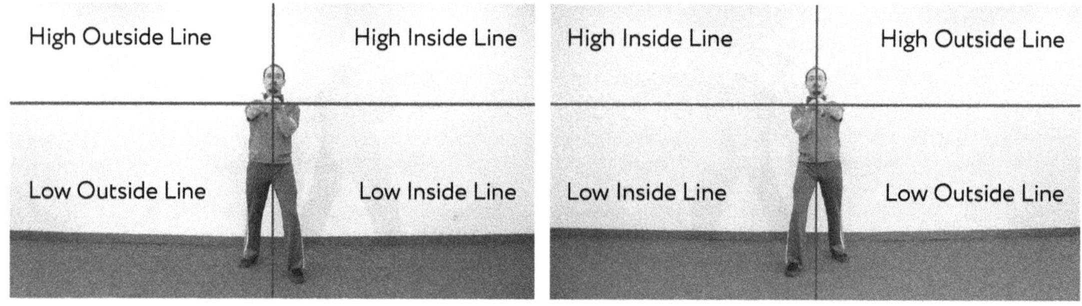

Right-handed

Left-handed

We also spend a lot of time talking about *stringere* or controlling the line. What this means is that you have control over the trajectory of where your opponent's sword either is moving or is likely to move. If my opponent wants to perform a thrust, then the line of their sword is not only the line segment extending from their pommel to their tip, but instead it keeps going as if their sword was infinitely long. If we're talking about a cut, then it's the entire trajectory along which the cut wants to travel. If I want to *stringere* their sword and control that line, I have to put the line of my sword in between the line of my opponent's sword and my body using good enough mechanics for them not to be able to just blow through.Now, what goes into a good thrust? The good news is that your aim matters a lot less here than it does with a cut. If you've ever had the chance to try cutting through tatami mats with a sharp sword, you'll have learned that if your edge is just slightly off, the cut is not going to do all that much. With thrusts though, you just need it to go forward. It takes a shockingly small amount of force for a pointy piece of steel to go through several layers of fabric and right into a person's vitals. This all means that there's a lot less focus on making sure it's a good strike when you're thrusting and you get to put more of your attention instead into how your sword interacts with your opponent's.

If your goal is to land a good touch against your partner with the point of your weapon, I suggest going through the following three steps: **Find, gain, strike**. For the **find**, this is you testing the waters to see what your opponent is going to do before you commit too much. If your partner starts with their sword pointed at you, extend your sword out a bit so that it crosses over your opponent's sword, ideally without touching it, and then step in to where you can hit them. Just like with the cuts in the last chapter, whenever we move in toward our opponent, we always want to go sword then foot. Even with the find, we always want to send the threatening piece of steel that doesn't feel any pain in first to see what's out there before we move our soft, squishy organs any closer toward danger. When you come in to find, try and do it within the first *palmo* (handwidth) of the blade, measuring from the tip going down. No need to step in too deep on this part. You're going to want the crossing point between your swords to be closer to your hilt/*forte* (strong) and closer to their tip/*debole* (weak).

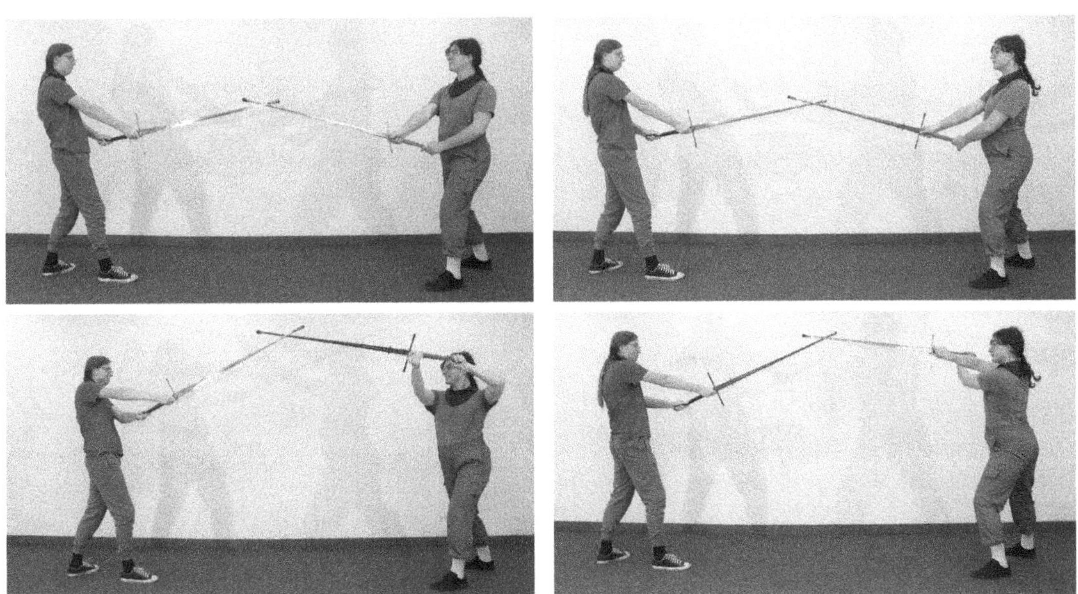

Finding in all four quadrants

Once you've done your find, assuming your opponent hasn't moved their blade, it's time to move on to the **gain**. If they have moved their sword, there's going to be a different answer that we'll get to in a bit, but never underestimate your opponent's ability to just freeze and not react. To perform the gain, just extend your point forward with your arms and lean in a bit with your upper body. Ideally this is done without any blade-on-blade contact, but as long as you have control it's fine if you make contact at this stage. Just note that by making contact at this point, you're giving your opponent more feedback to work with, and that touch neurons fire at about forty times the speed of sight neurons. Anyhow, by performing the gain, you're really locking in your opponent's sword, establishing a firmer control over it than we saw in the find, all before you make your final step.[20] This should end with their sword going from being withing that first *palmo* of your blade to taking it down to the *mezza spada* (middle of the sword) without having your tip go so deep that it gets caught in their quillons.

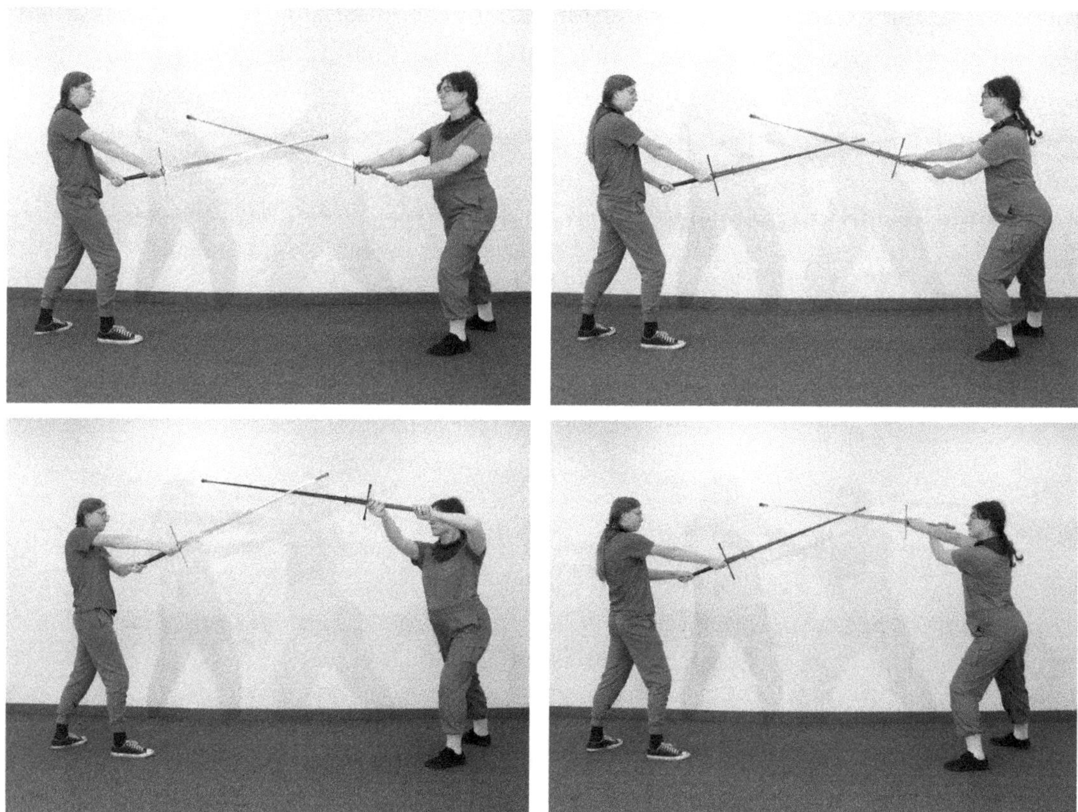

Gaining in all four quadrants

[20] As a note, differentiating the find from the gain is an idea that comes to us from much after the Bolognese era. Instead, they just use the term stringere to describe constraining their opponent's blade. I find, though, that splitting it into two distinct steps really helps modern students get the idea down better than just telling them to stringere their opponent's sword.

Finally, assuming your opponent still hasn't reacted, it's time to step forward and **strike**. If you've gotten this far without making blade contact, it's during this stage that you're likely going to want to touch blades as you want to be certain you have their sword locked in and they won't have much time to react at this point. You have a choice here of stepping forward either by extending the front foot forward, or by passing through with the back foot. Both are valid options and it really comes down more to personal preference as well as where your weight is at any given moment. If your plan is to advance the front foot forward, then my suggestion would be to make sure that the lean as a part of the **gain** doesn't shift weight toward that front foot as that'll make it a lot harder to lift it up. If, instead, your plan is to pass with your back foot, then go ahead and put all that weight onto the front foot so that it'll be faster for you to step forward with your back foot.

While all of this is a lot more straightforward with your opponent's blade in presence, the same idea can be applied in order to achieve a "virtual" *stringere* if their point isn't in presence. What's important here is that you're closing off their closest line of attack. Oftentimes this is accomplished just by pointing your tip right at their hands.

If there's a large difference in height between you and your opponent, or if they just have a tendency to fly back when you come in, you might have noticed that stepping forward once during the strike phase didn't get you there. That's perfectly normal. What matters here is not necessarily that you've hit your opponent, but that you've gained control of the line. As long as you are in a position where you only need to move your sword once to hit them and they need to move their sword twice (once to get around yours, another time to strike), the advantage is yours and you just need to keep going forward until you hit them. For your subsequent steps you can either gather the back foot forward and then advance your front foot again, or you can just do an infinite series of passing steps. Either way, the good news is that no one wins races running backward. So as long as you keep their sword locked down, you'll get there eventually. That said, be sure to pay attention as to whether or not your opponent has managed to slip their blade out. If you just keep running forward and forget about their sword, it's going to pop back up when you least appreciate it.

Be aware of where you're pointing when going from the gain to the strike. There are times when this will involve moving your point to cross so far over your opponent's sword during your gain that it points past their silhouette. That's fine, as long as you don't overdo it. As you move to strike, your sword will inherently begin to straighten out and come in line with your opponent. The key here is to make sure you aren't collapsing your blade in and creating a weak angle for your opponent to push through. Another thing that can help with this is when thrusting on the inside line to have your point cross their body and strike them in their armpit. If instead you're thrusting on the outside line, just aim for their sternum instead.

If your opponent doesn't have their sword pointed at you, you can also perform a virtual *stringere* against their blade.[21] This involves either pointing your tip directly at their hands or pointing the line of your sword across the line of the cut they already have prepped (something I talk about more in chapter 7).

Hunt The Debole

Here's a little game that can help take this from the theoretical and move it into the more practical. Each person should start by holding their sword out in front of them.[22] From there, it is the job of each of you to try and hunt the other person's *debole* (the weak of their blade) and finding it with your sword. If you have the other person's *debole*, congratulations! If your *debole* has been found, now you have to get your sword into a new position that allows you to find theirs, by going around their blade or going through it. Once you've done this for a little while, start to add in footwork as another option to help you with your finds.

Finally, once that's all settled in, it's time to move on to the final stage of this drill. Thrust! More specifically, if you've successfully found their blade and the opportunity presents itself, move on to trying to gain their blade and then strike them with a thrust. As you may have guessed, this is just fighting, just limited to winning through mechanical advantage and only hitting with thrusts. As with any drill, all we've done here is to build a slow on-ramp from having a structured game that on its own is decently removed from a fight and then we slowly progressed to just short of the real thing.

The Three Advantages

Yep, they're back. Thankfully it's just the same exact three we learned during the chapter on cuts. However, they do work a tad bit differently here. With cuts we learned that the advantages, in descending order of importance, are **true edge, leverage**, and **crossing**. Here, that order is going to get flipped around. If two swords meet while they're both thrusting, the thing that matters the most is going to be **crossing**, followed by **leverage**, and with **true edge** coming in last. The reason for this is largely that you're pushing a lot less down the axis of the edge of your sword while you thrust as opposed to when you cut.

---

[21] Some authors will also refer to this as forming a counterguard.
[22] Guy Windsor, *The Swordsman's Companion*, 157.

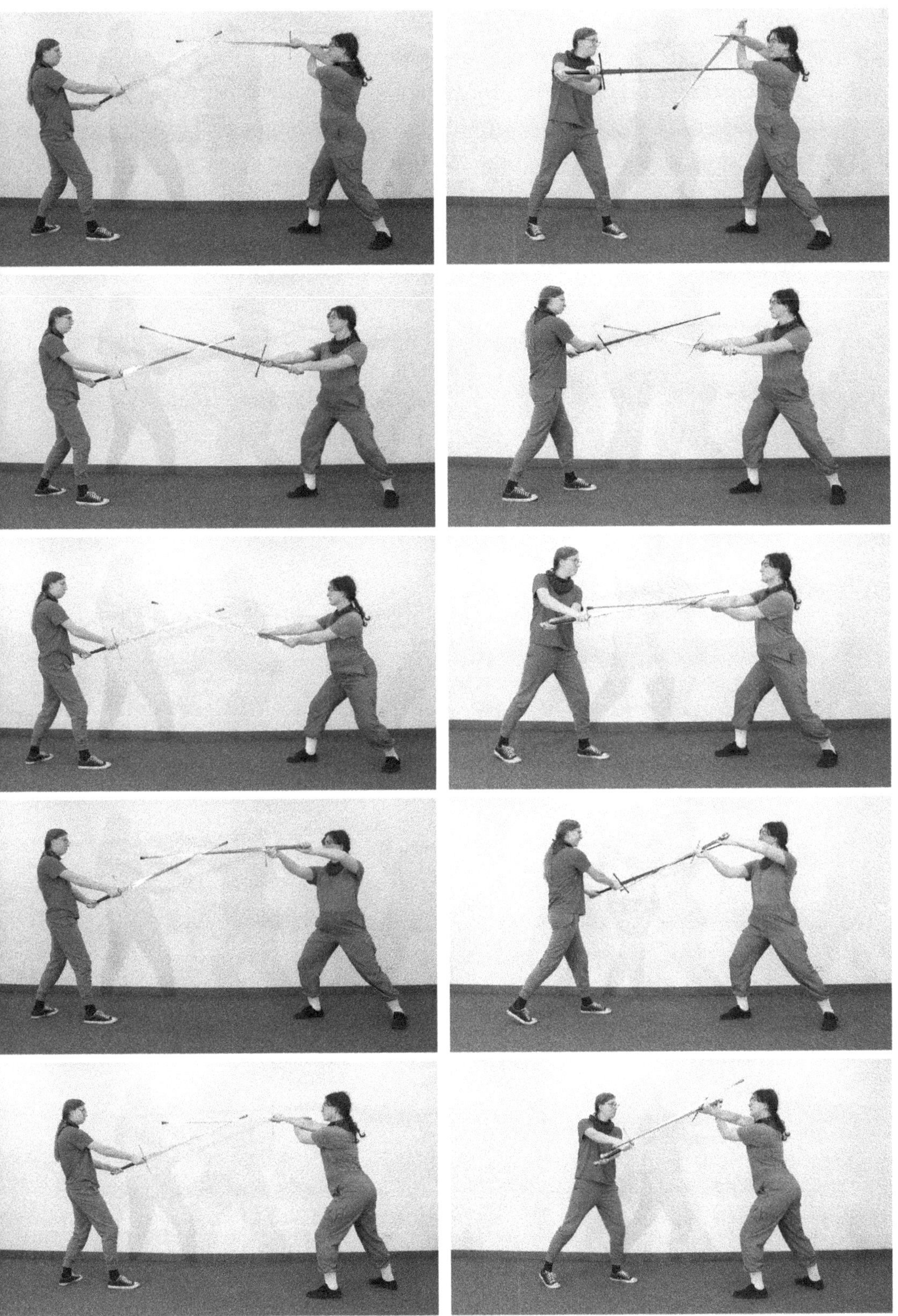

Hunt the *debole*

As I mentioned earlier, one of the most common mistakes with thrusts is creating a weak angle as they come in, making it relatively easy for their opponent to counter by just pushing through their line, crossing over their sword, and going through. The other is people taking their point off from the line of their opponent's, having it no longer point across where their opponent's sword is heading, generally trying to strike center mass but forgetting to control the threat of their opponent's blade. This is a great way to ensure that double kills happen. While you don't need to be touching your opponent's blade with yours, if you cease putting your sword in between their sword and you, they're going to take the hint and strike. There are some exceptions we'll get into later, but generally speaking the best plan is to always go through the line of your opponent's sword, ensuring that you're safe before coming in to strike.

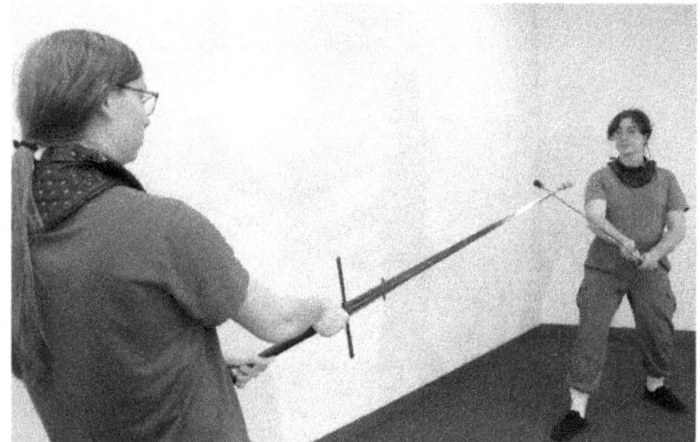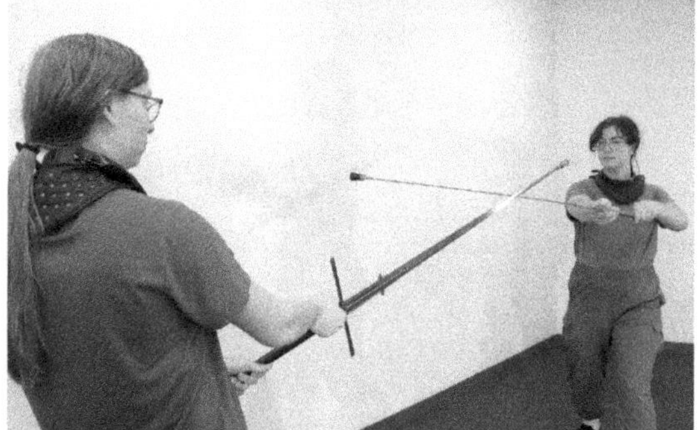

Point coming off line

Different Kinds of Thrusts
So now that we've learned how to thrust, it's time to learn the different lines your point can attack. The first option is what's called a *stocatta*: this is a rising thrust, done from either the inside or outside lines. For reference, if you hold your dominant hand out as if you're going to shake someone's hand, the side of your body your palm is facing would be considered your "inside" line whereas the back of your hand would be facing your "outside" line.

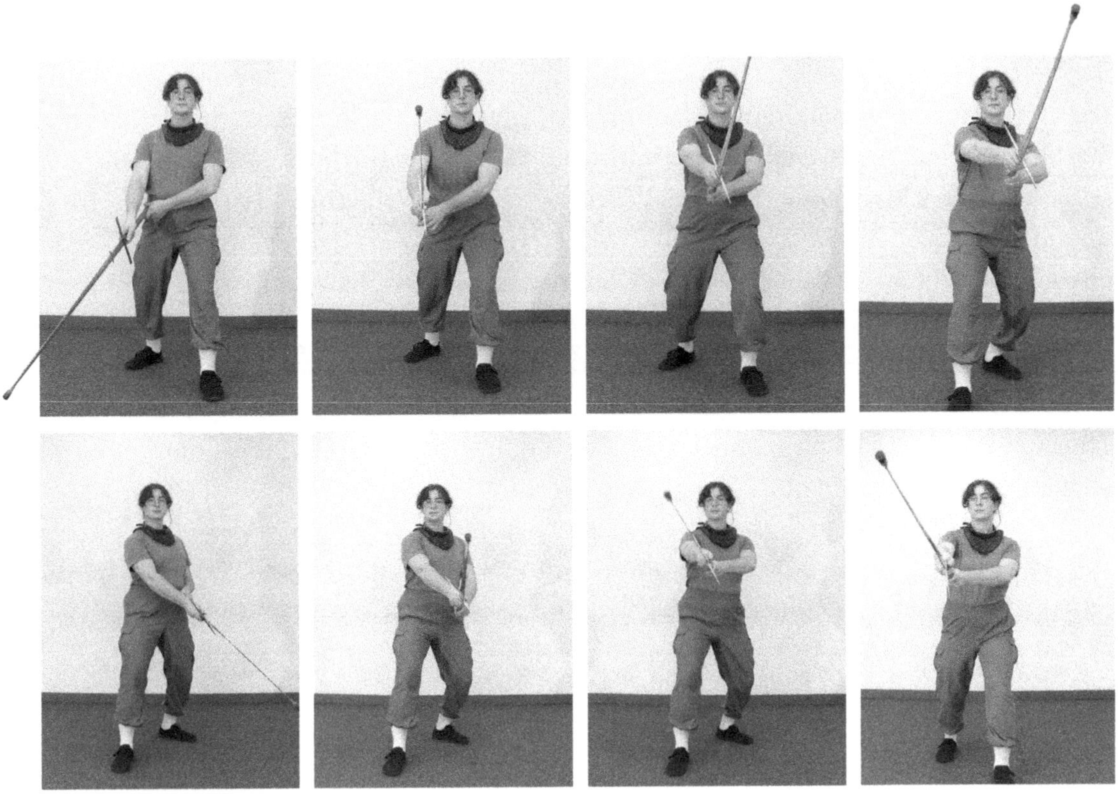

Stocatta

A similar option is referred to as a *punta ferma* (firm thrust): this is essentially just a *stocatta*, but performed just by stepping in and without moving the arms. This could be due to your arms having already extended for a previous action or because you find yourself fighting in close enough that you don't need that extra reach in order to strike.

Punta firma

The next option is called the *punta dritta* (thrust from the right). There are two ways of performing this thrust. The first is by pointing the true edge to your outside and then push through their sword with your true edge and deliver a thrust. The second option is to perform this as a yield, giving way to the pressure from your opponent's sword. For instance, you might be trying to perform a *stocatta* and your enemy strongly pushes against your sword toward your right side. Instead of trying to overpower them, just turn your sword so that your false edge points at their true edge. If you do this at enough of an angle and they're pushing strongly enough, their blade will just ride down into your quillons handing you the advantage of **leverage**. This is also a great way to set up a *presa* (a grapple), as your off hand is now in a nice spot for grabbing a hold of their arms.

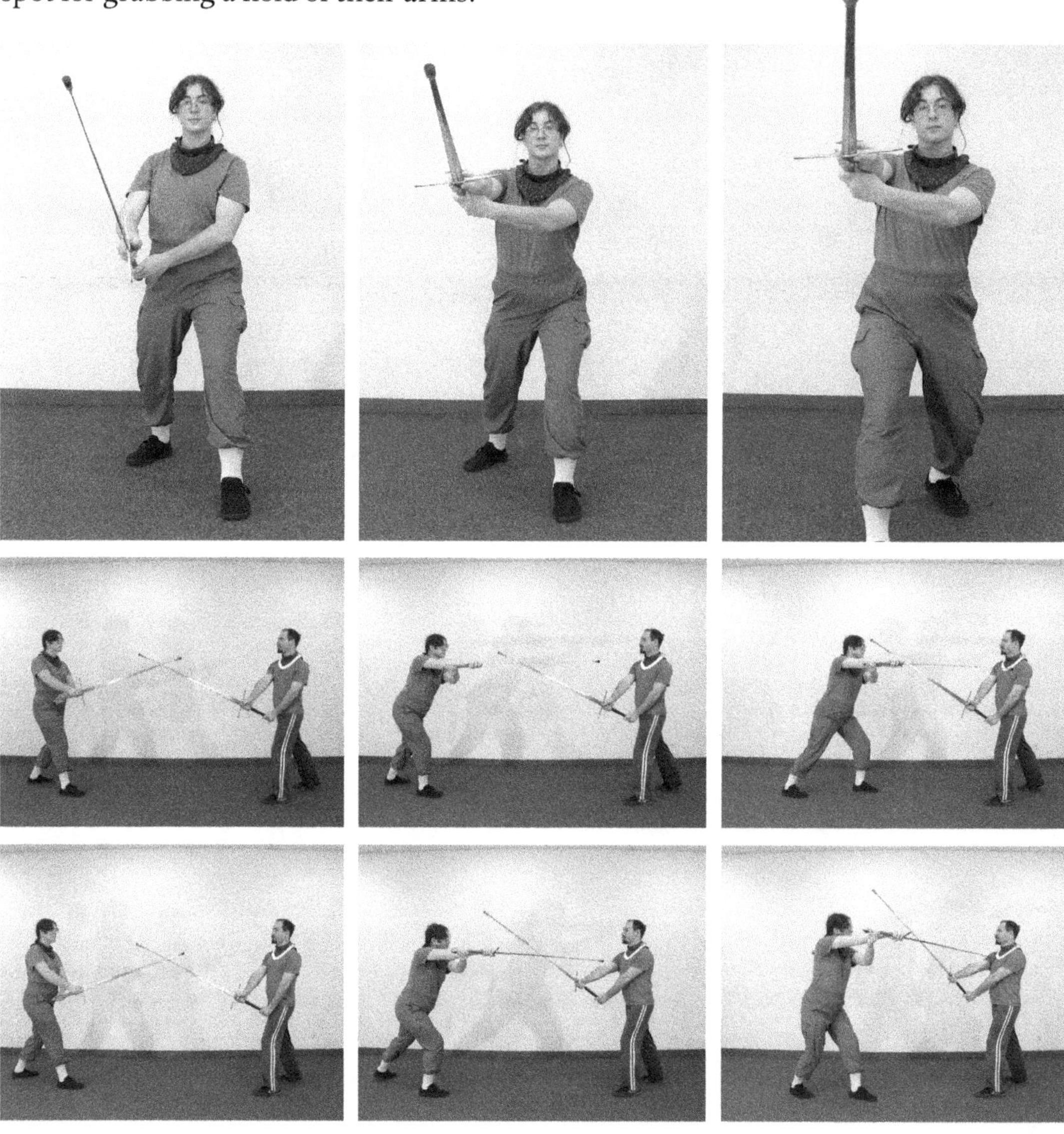

Punta dritta

After that comes the *punta roversa*. This is the same exact thing, but from the other side. Again, you have both the true and false edge versions available to you. As a note, the false edge version here often has a tendency to come up a bit higher in order to come around your opponent's sword and poke them right in the corner of their chest.

Punta roversa

Next, we have the *imbrocatta*. This a descending thrust delivered from either side. That said, the term is more generally used to describe a thrust from the right (assuming your right hand is on top). There are two ways to perform this from either side. First, you can just extend your point down from one of the high guards, keeping the true edge of your sword pointed up. Alternatively, you can rotate your blade in an almost drilling action as your point comes down, ending with your true edge pointed down. Both options work, it just depends on what your goal is and where your opponent's sword is. If their sword is above yours, you want your true edge pointed up. Alternatively, you can make an *imbrocatta* with the true edge turned up to get around your opponent's sword instead of pushing through it. If their sword is below yours and is proving a more active threat, the other option would be to drill down by rotating your wrist and pushing into their sword with your true edge as you bring gravity around to your side.[23] Some teachers use the terms *mandritto imbrocatta* and *roverso imbrocatta* to indicate whether your thrust originates from your dominant or nondominant side. **Imbrocatta**

Finally, we have the *punta infalsata*, which isn't a thrust from any particular direction, but is instead a way in which any of the other thrusts can be performed. The default, when thrusting, is to have your true edge facing your enemy's sword. However, there are times, either to just get around their sword or as a yield, that it's to your strategic advantage to thrust with the false edge pointed toward their sword instead. This is most commonly done with a *punta dritta* or a *punta roversa,* but could be done with any other thrust as well.

How To Collapse a Hard Thrust

Always remember that we never want to break our friends. It's okay to show them what we could have done had the swords been sharp, but it's always best to avoid doing so to the point that anyone is actually injured. I know that early in my career I used to look at bruises all over my chest and arms as points of pride. As I've gotten better and become more aware, the more I see them as indicators of when things went wrong. Swords are sharp and you don't need to hit a person particularly hard for them to go straight through. So, let's try and keep that in mind as we try and poke each other.

There are generally two main reasons a thrust came in hard. The first is striking order. If you go with your arm and foot at the same time, you're now hitting your opponent with all of your body at once. Instead, if you go arm, then body, then foot, you're reducing how much of your body is moving toward your opponent at any given time. If I decide to put on gloves and get in a boxing ring I have to switch gears as just touching someone with my glove won't make much of a difference, so now I have to generate force. With swords, though, the point itself does all that work for us. We just need to get it there.

---

[23] Performing a drilled thrust is what the Bolognese authors sometimes refer to as a *trivallatto*.

Imbrocatta

The other issue is measure. If my opponent is close enough that I only need to reach out my arms in order to touch them, but instead I do a full out lunge, now all that force is going to be absorbed right into them. Having a decently flexible blade can help a bit, but only so much. Here's an exercise I put together in order to help students train the safety aspect of measure control.

STEP 1: Start by putting your hand out, moving it slowly forward and back. While you do that, have your partner poke you in that hand with a thrust. You'll be able to feel if they came in too hard, but the advantage here is that your hand can just be pushed back safely in a way your ribs cannot.

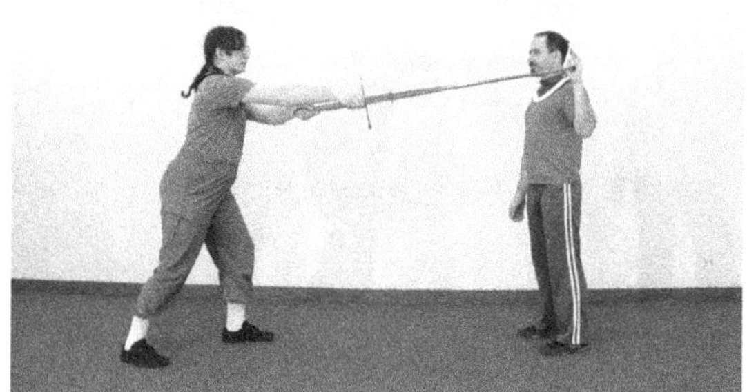

Thrust against the hand

STEP 2: Now slowly start to increase the speed of your hand as well as the frequency with which your partner strikes.

STEP 3: Try and get both of you to move faster than you're likely to see in any given fight. It's always better to be over prepared than under. When you do this, make sure to hold your fingers together. Otherwise, their point is going to slip straight through.

STEP 4: Once you and your partner have that down, switch to having them poke you in the chest as both of you move around.

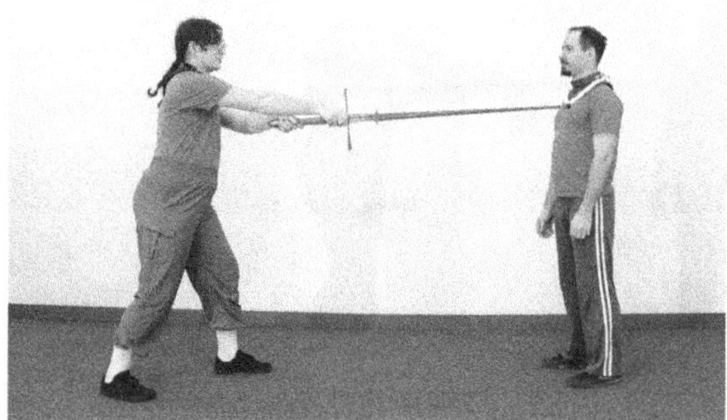

Thrust against the chest

STEP 5: Start to add in some blade engagements. You're going to be trying to find each other's swords, but only they will be actually striking.

STEP 6: Once that feels comfortable, start switching it up between being aggressive as opposed to defensive.

STEP 7: Finally, switch to regular sparring, but with a concentration on hitting well instead of necessarily trying to win. What we're doing here is slowly upping the intensity of the drill in order to ease the other person into performing well under stress instead of just throwing them into a fight.

On top of the psychological aspect, there's a mechanical aspect that can help as well. Ask yourself, out of the three major joints of the arm (shoulder, elbow, wrist), which one has the largest range of motion? Feel free to try this out and see how many degrees each can move for yourself. Okay, think you have an answer? Great. Here's hoping you were thinking "shoulder". If you think about it, your elbow has a little under 180 degrees it can move through. Your wrist moves even less, just in a wider variety of directions. That shoulder joint, though, lets you swing your arm around in a 360 degree arc. Now, if you had to choose one of these joints to use to collapse a shot, which would you go with?

What I have personally seen most often, is people relying on their wrists to do this work. Not only do you have very little space in which to cushion your shot using your wrist, but by raising up and collapsing your wrist, you increase the chances of injuring your own joints. Instead, if at all possible, try and collapse a shot by swinging down with the shoulder. If that doesn't work, particularly for an *imbrocatta*, try pulling your whole arm upward. You can go out to the side, but you're going to have a lot less flexibility in that direction, so be careful.

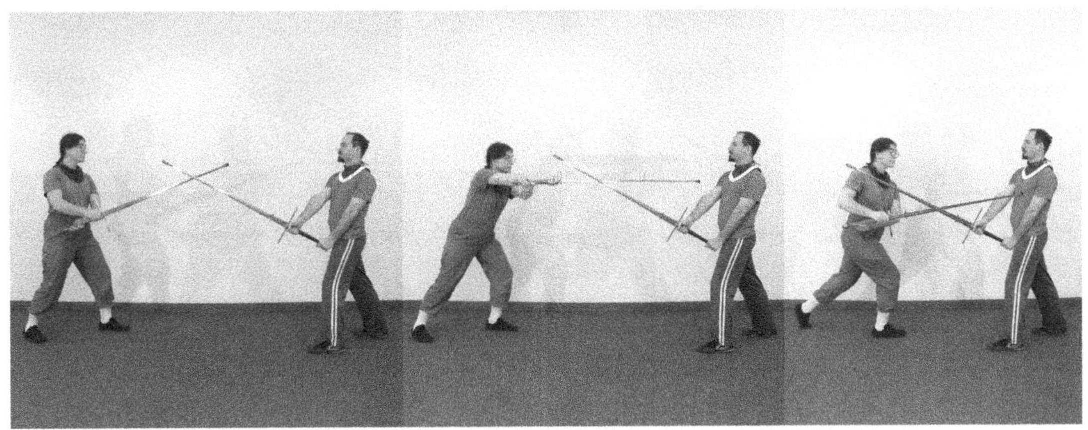

Breaking a thrust with the shoulder

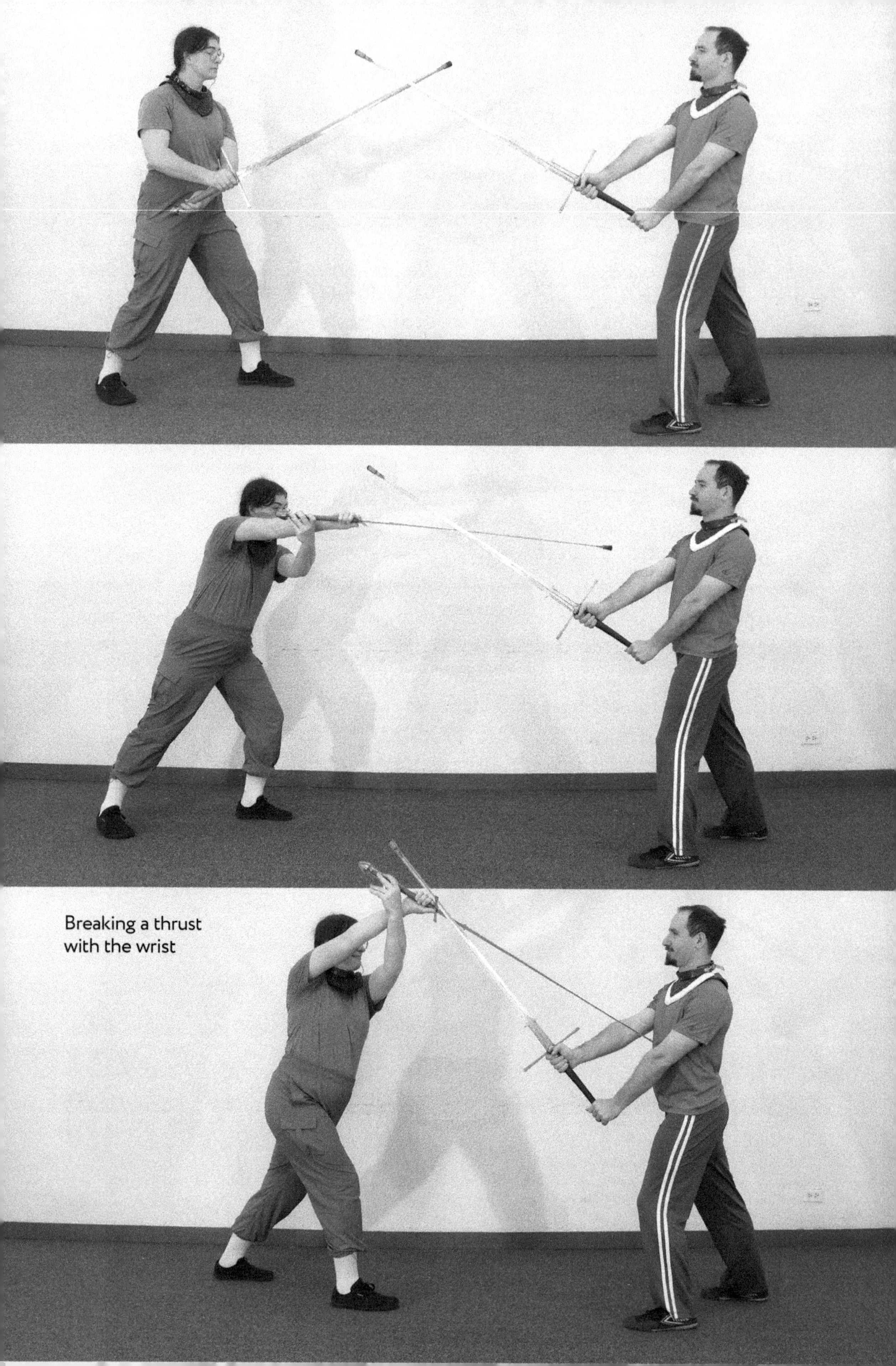

Breaking a thrust
with the wrist

Thrusting Patterns

Here are a few examples of how you can string some thrusts together. Please do not take these to be an exhaustive list. Instead, treat these as a starting off point for your solo work and from there figure out what patterns you can create that will help you train to have the fight you want to have.

1.Thrust a *mandritto imbrocatta*
Turn your sword and thrust a *punta roversa* as you step forward.

2.Thrust a *stocatta*
Rotate your blade and thrust up into a *rovero imbrocatta*.

3.Thrust a *punta dritta*
Turn your blade up and continue with a *mandritto imbrocatta*.

Prepping A Cut or A Thrust

So now you know how to cut and how to thrust, but how do you get into position to use these techniques in the first place? Glad you asked. Let's explore a few different possibilities.

To start, if you want to thrust and you're starting in a point-forward guard, you've already done most of the work—stab away! If, however, you find yourself starting your action from any place that doesn't involve your point aimed directly at your opponent, you're going to have to throw a cut to get there. As an exercise, try starting in different positions and see which of the cuts you would need to throw from there to end up being able to deliver the thrust of your choosing.

If your goal is to end with a cut, you're going to find yourself with the shoe on the other foot as compared to thrusts. If you start with your point on line, there's no direct route to throw a cut, so you're going to do some sort of preparation to get there. If, for instance, your goal is to throw a *mezzo mandritto sgualimbratto* to your opponent's hand, but you're starting with your point out in front, try preparing the action by first raising your tip by throwing a *falso manco*. Alternatively, you could try thrusting wide to set you up your next cut. Play with it a bit and see what combinations you can find.

At the end of the day, your options boil down to throwing a cut and then a thrust, a cut then another cut, a thrust and then a cut, or a thrust and then another thrust. While that might not sound like too many possibilities, try going through it with all the different cuts and thrusts we've laid out so far. Also try throwing a *falso* to another *falso*, or a true edge cut to a *falso*.

7: Guards

As a warning, this is by and far the most vocab-intense part of this book. I have a friend who only learned the guard names by giving his kid a sheet with the pictures and names of all of them and then having the kid call a name out and see if his dad got the answer right. It takes a bit of time for it all to click in, but once it does it makes describing what you're doing so much easier. Something to remember is that guard is just a named point along a trajectory. You can stop there or keep going, at the end of the day they're just a tool that helps us to explain where we are in space. Marozzo teaches us that "there is no blow that can be thrown that doesn't end in a guard."[24] To help you understand not just how to form each one, but also how it might be used, I've attached a few example plays for each of the guards listed.

Inside vs Outside

We talked about this in regard to line in chapter 6, but it's worth reviewing here. Inside and outside aren't guards, but knowing what they mean is going to make the rest of this chapter make a whole lot more sense. Take whichever hand you put on top when you hold your sword (as opposed to the pommel hand) and hold it out like you're going to shake someone's hand. Do you see how your palm is facing one way? That's what we call your "inside line". Now see how the back of your hand points the other way? That's your outside line. Now pick up a sword and have it point across your body. Your sword is now covering your inside line. Next, point the tip of your sword the other way where it goes past your body. That's you having your outside line closed.

24 Marozzo, 80.

Closing the
inside line

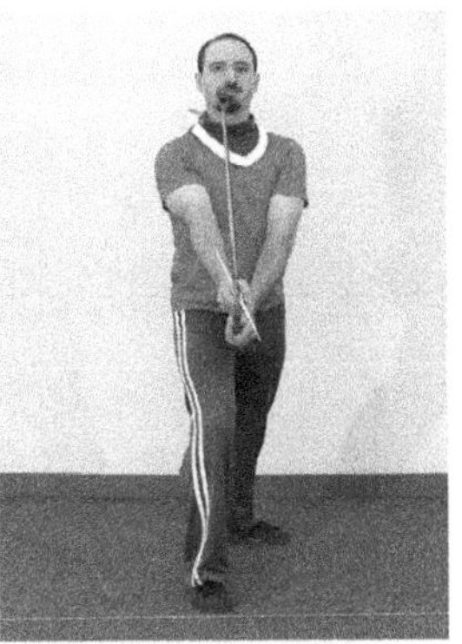

Poorly covering
the inside line

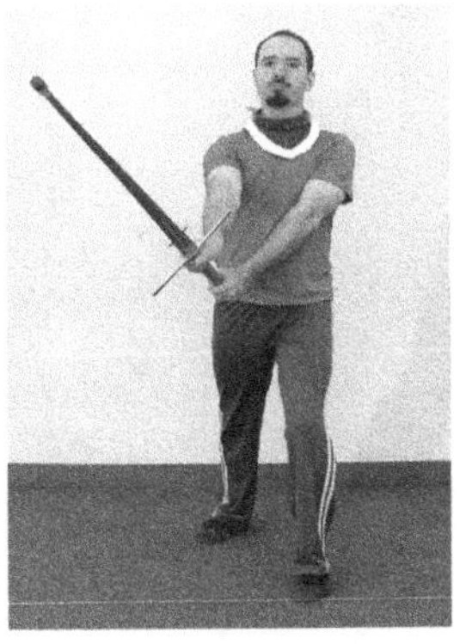

Closing the
outside line

Poorly covering
the outside line

High vs Low

The terms here are a bit more obvious than inside and outside. Still, I wanted to bring in a bit of Manciolino where he gives us a nice overview for the guards we're about to study. He explains, "The objective of the high guards is to attack and then to follow with a parry; that of low guards is the opposite—to parry first and then follow with a strike."[25] Now of course you should always make sure you're safe before striking your opponent. That said, high guards have the benefit of having gravity on their side, making their attacks an inherently larger threat.

Manciolino goes on to tell us, "If you want to strike your opponent in his upper body, you should begin your action below; similarly, if you want to strike him below, you should begin your operations above. This is because as one defends the parts being attacked, he necessarily creates openings elsewhere."[26] We often focus on the direct line of attack, but at the higher levels, your first intention is almost never what ends up winning you the fight. Getting your opponent to move out of their initial guarding and hitting them where they were once closed off, though, is a winning strategy if there ever was one.

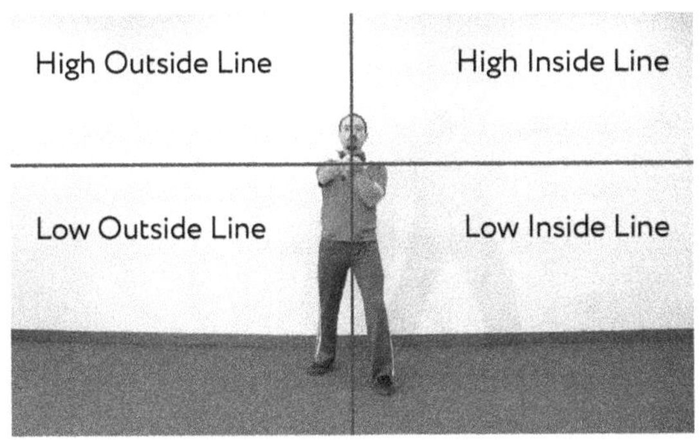

Right-handed

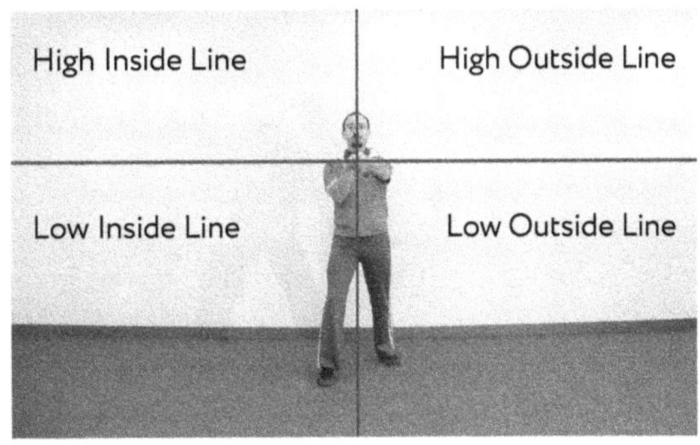

Left-handed

[25] Manciolino, 74.
[26] Manciolino, 75.

Guardia alta

Poorly formed *guardia alta]*

Guardia alta is a nice neutral guard in that it doesn't start on one side or the other. It can be a really intimidating position to assume because not only is your opponent uncertain as to how easily you can reach them, but they also know that your sword is coming straight down onto their head and they're going to have to do something about it and fast. When you form this guard, you can have the tip of your sword either point straight up or point slightly backward. We see both portrayed throughout the tradition. Plus, if you're in a training hall without particularly high ceilings, it's useful to have a way for your sword not to get caught on the rafters. Also, when forming this guard, make sure that your elbows aren't coming in front of your face. Oftentimes we'll use this guard as a way to pull our arms out of the way of an oncoming cut in order to prep your next attack, and if you leave your arms hanging out there, you're going to be reminded of the importance of elbow pads.

The clear and obvious option for this guard is to cut straight down into your opponent with a big *mandritto fendente*. Your opponent is likely going to be able to see through this master plan of yours, but if you never execute it then it won't be much of a viable threat.

Mandritto *fendente* from ***guardia alta***

Another option is to cut a *mandritto ridoppio* from this guard. Your opponent is likely tensed up waiting for you to come crashing down and it's going to take them a second to catch up when they realize the cut is coming from the opposite direction than they expected.

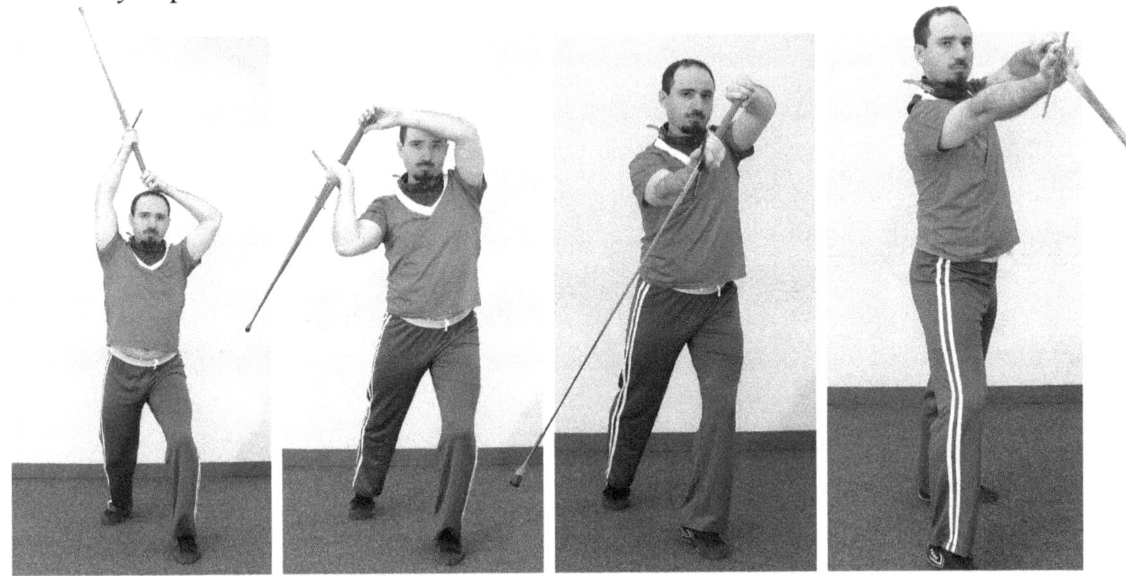

Mandritto *ridoppio* from ***guardia alta***

A third option, which I personally gravitate toward, is to throw that same initial *mandritto fendente*. This time, though, instead of connecting, pull the cut short and disengage underneath your opponent's sword and pop up with a *stocatta* on the other side.

Cutting short to a *stocatta*

Defensively, this guard leaves open the entirety of your low line and then some. People probably aren't going to throw a *fendente* that comes down on top of your head when you're standing in *guardia alta*, but otherwise it leaves you open to most any initial attack. The good part is that regardless of what your opponent does, you've narrowed down your own decision tree to be able to just crash down on top of whatever they're doing.

Guardia d'Intrare (guard of entering)
With this guard you have a nice way to threaten from up above without having to take your point offline. You form this guard with the pommel hand held at head height and with your dominant hand held at shoulder height, with your sword held in line with the shoulder of your pommel hand, and with your tip aimed toward your opponent's chest.[27] It's a little easier to form this guard with the right foot forward (left foot forward for lefties), but you can really do it with either foot in front. Some things to remember for this guard are to keep your arms extended and to keep your point out so as not to create a weak angle. If you think you have your upper left quadrant (upper right for lefties) covered, but then find out that your opponent was able to push through and fold you in half like a pretzel, you're going to go home a tad bit disappointed. Remember here to keep your blade extended and try to line up your handle with the forearm of your pommel hand.

---

[27] This guard is given a much more ambiguous description when it comes to the single sword with the earlier authors. Dall'Agocchie's version, which he only shows us with the single sword, is completely different and is formed with the true edge of your sword pointing to your outside line with the blade oriented parallel to the ground.

Guardia d'intrare

The obvious first move from this guard is to strike with an *imbrocatta*. Especially if you drill down so that your true edge ends up crashing down into your opponent's blade, it's a great way to clear a large section of your body while simultaneously striking into your opponent.

Imbrocatta from *guardia d'intrare*

Another option would be to unwind down into a *roverso sgualimbratto*. This can be a really powerful cut from this position, so make sure to mind your calibration.

Roverso sgualimbratto from **guardia d'intrare**

A third option that I go for a lot is to get your opponent to try and bind with you in one of the lower guards, and then loop up around into *intrare* while they least expect it and strike them in the chest with that same *imbrocatta* from earlier.

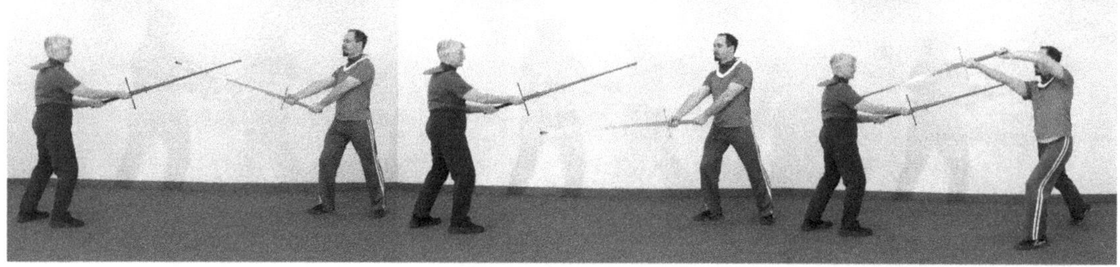

This guard does a great job of covering one of your upper quadrants. This means it's vulnerable to attacks thrown to the other side of your head. It technically leaves you open to low-line attacks, but those are going to be incredibly risky as geometrically you have a shorter distance (assuming you're both the same height) to their face than they do to your waist. Beware, though, of leaving your hands open. Also, if your point dips too far down your opponent can just put their sword on top of yours and continue forward.

For the longsword specifically, Marozzo (and only Marozzo) further divides this guard into *guardia de intrare non in largo passo* (guard of entering in a narrow stance) performed with the dominant foot forward, and *guardia de intrare in largo passo* (guard of entering in a wide stance) performed with the non dominant foot forward. I tend to skip over this in my own pedagogy, but feel free to get as detailed in your teachings as you would like.

Guardia di Croce[28] (guard of the cross)

Guardia di croce

Poorly formed *guardia di croce*

The name of this guard has a lot less to do with Christianity and a lot more to do with the fact that your arms are crossed. Overall, this guard is much the same as *intrare*, but just on the other side and a little more awkward. As well, this time your handle should be lined up with the forearm of your dominant hand. Thrusting around your opponent's blade is a little harder with this guard, however, and because it's inherently more awkward, other people are going to shy away from it. So, if you can figure out how to get really good at it, you're going to have an advantage. Oh, and if you ever see a German fencer lining up in this guard, chances are they're about to try and hit you with a false edge *mandritto tondo*.

This guard has essentially all the same upsides and downsides as *guardia di intrare* with one of your upper quadrants being well covered with the other upper quadrant being less so. The only real difference is that this guard doesn't reach quite as far forward, but can unwind with a lot more power.

[28] The one-handed version of this is referred to as guardia d'alicorno (unicorn guard).

Becca Cesa

Becca Cesa

Becca Possa

Becca Possa

Our next two are variations on *di croce*. In *becca cesa* you have your arms crossed with the point now aimed downward and with your right foot forward. *Becca posa* is formed much the same way, except now with your left foot forward. Oftentimes when I'm teaching I'll just teach all three as one guard. However, these two do have their unique uses. Specifically, they're really good at inviting your opponent in to try and take control of your sword, which you can then respond to with either a *stramazonne* or a *molinetto* (something we'll touch on in the next chapter).[29] You can also transition from *guardia di croce* into either of these in order to fend off attacks to your abdomen, whether it's a cut or a thrust, without having to move particularly far. Another option would be to use either one of these to strike at a lower target.

[29] Both of these terms have multiple spellings in almost a "choose your own adventure" kind of way.

Each of these perform what later authors, such as the Anonimo Riccardiano,[30] refer to as *tutta coperta* (full coverage). With your point dipped downward, there likely isn't a clear single tempo strike your opponent can throw at your head or your body. At the same time, though, it leaves your hands open and it isn't that structurally sound of a position. As a result it can be easy for your opponent to gain your blade and step in if you don't respond quick enough.

Guardia di Testa (head guard)

Guardia di testa   Poorly formed *guardia di testa*

As you might have guessed, this guard does a great job of protecting your head.[31] To borrow another term from Fiore, I generally treat this one as an *instabile* (unstable/moving) guard. This is not something I really like to start the fight in, as it leaves my hands far too exposed. Instead, it's a guard that I'll move through on my way to something else. This of course could be done with any guard, but most of the other ones can also serve as *stabile* guards where I can set up from. To form this guard, you move the thumb from your dominant hand off from the handle and on to the flat of the blade. From there you push your hilt out in front of you such that your quillons line up roughly with your eyebrows. Some of the earlier Italian authors refer to this as *posta di corona* (crown position), so if the imagery of lining it up with your imaginary crown works better for you, go with that.

[30] The Anonimo Riccardiano is a late 16th century Florentine fencing manual, not to be confused with the Anonimo Bolognese or the even later Viennese Anonymous.

[31] This same task is performed differently with the single sword where instead of the tip pointing straight up you instead cock your hand out to the side and have the tip angle upward, almost forming a roof over your head. Dall'Agocchie uses the same term to accomplish a similar mission, but instead forms it with the tip pointing downward.

This guard works really well to stop a *fendente* or a *sgualimbratto* at your head. As we talked about earlier, this guard lets you respond with a really strong collection, allowing you to come in easily for a *presa* of your choosing. Alternatively, you can use this same motion to beat your opponent's blade away, clearing the path for you to move forward.

Collecting with **guardia di testa**

The two things this guard leaves open are your hands and your low line. Compared to the other high guards, this one provides less of a direct path to crash down on to your opponent's blade, so beware of being drawn up high so that your opponent can sneak in underneath. The nice thing, though, is that by having their blade on your quillons you've essentially maxed out the advantage of leverage, so it doesn't particularly matter which side of your blade (inside vs outside) their sword is on.

Guardia di Faccia (face guard)

Guardia di faccia

Poorly formed guardia di faccia

This is perhaps my favorite name given to any of the guards. To form this guard, extend your point forward such that your blade is parallel to the ground and so that the palm of your dominant hand points up toward the sky. It's really easy to form this guard up too high so it's important to remember to trust your geometry and that by holding the guard far enough out, you're going to create a ramp that deflects your opponent's cut and that you don't have to form this above your head. This guard can either be used as a way to deliver a thrust, or as a collection that affords you the opportunity to strike at the same time. Because you're using your quillons instead of relying on blade mechanics for this one, it works on either side of your blade. One thing to watch out for with one is that it's really easy to blast someone right in the face with it. It's a great guard, just be careful when you pull it out as we want to "kill" our opponent, not hurt them.

As with *guardia alta* and *guardia di testa*, inside vs outside doesn't especially matter. However, you are susceptible to an attack that moves into your low line.

Coda Lunga (long tail)

So, this is actually a collection of guards. It can be helpful, though, to think of them all as variations on the same theme. So instead of necessarily having to add three new guards to your list, it can be easier to think of it as the same guard but in three different places. Remember, that the thing that ties these three together is that they are all outside line guards.

We can think of all the *coda Lunga* guards as being outside line guards. This means that unless your opponent particularly likes making life hard for themselves, you are inviting them to try and strike you on the inside line.

Coda Lunga e Alta (high long tail)

Coda Lunga e alta

Poorly formed *coda lunga e alta*

This guard is set up to close out your high inside line and is formed by having your dominant hand out at shoulder height. The biggest mistake I see with this guard, as well as the following ones, is people letting their point drift toward the center.

At any given moment, you want to only present your opponent one option for attack at a time. If you leave both the inside and outside lines open, then you won't know which one they're going to go down and are going to have to start playing some catch up once they make their choice. If instead you only give them the one option, then you know exactly where their first move is going to be and can plan accordingly.

On top of keeping the one side of your head safe, there's a few other places this guard really shines. First and foremost, it sets you up really well to perform a *mandritto*. As the *mandritto* is inherently the stronger of the two cuts, starting your fight in *coda lunga* can be a really powerful opening. This guard also allows you to thrust into *guardia di croce*, *becca posa*, or *becca cesa*.

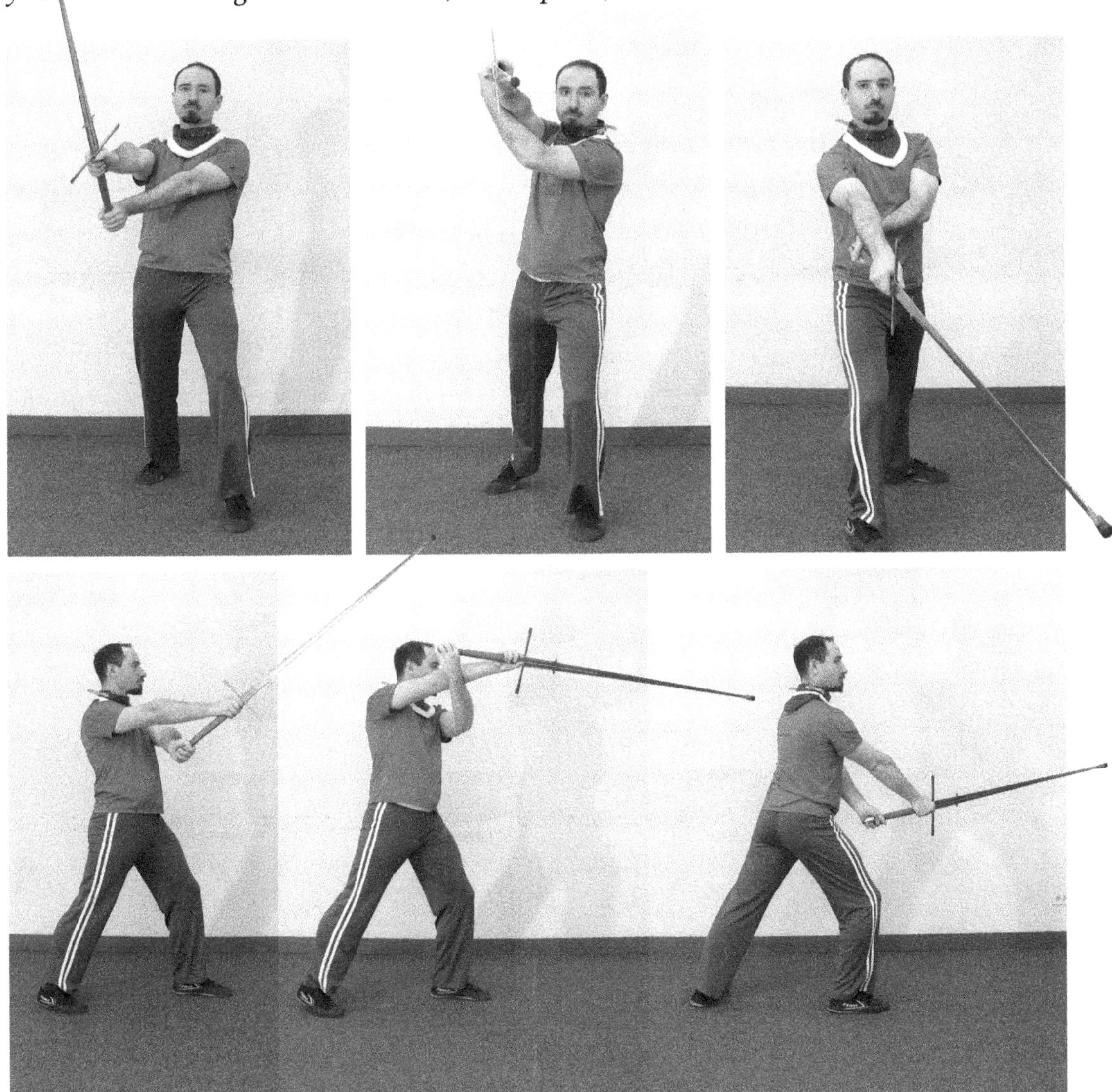

Imbrocatta from **coda lunga e alta**

By forming this guard, you are inviting an attack to your high inside line. While your low inside line is technically also open, you are really well set up to just crash right down into it, so people are less likely to try you over there. As well, if you're too rigid, people can hit you in the arm with a rising blow coming up from your low outside line.

Coda Lunga e Stretta (narrow long tail)

Coda lunga e stretta

This guard is just a slightly lower version of *coda lunga e alta*, but now with the nondominant hand in line with the hip. The major difference here is that your point is at the same height as your opponent. This means that you can just extend the guard forward and strike your opponent with a *stocatta*. Alternatively, you're really well set up here for a *mezzo mandritto* or a *mezzo roverso* into your opponent's hands. Another option from here is to find your opponent's sword on the outside and step in, leading to a whole world of possibilities.

Mezzo mandritto to the hands

By forming this guard properly, you are informing your opponent that this is now going to be a fight on your inside line. The only real exception to that is when it's a righty fighting a lefty, as people are often stronger forming inside line guards and can use that to push through an outside line guard.

Coda Lunga e Larga (wide and long tail)

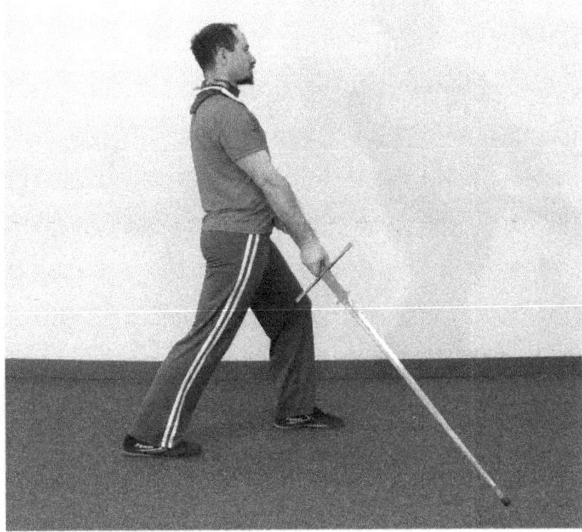

Coda lunga e larga

Poorly formed *coda lunga e larga*

Again, here you're going to stand with your sword point to your outside line. This time, though, your tip is going to be aimed toward the ground with your true edge pointing down and somewhat out. This guard might seem a bit foolish at first, seeing as you no longer have your sword between you and your opponent. That said, there's a lot of hidden strengths that it gives us.

First and foremost, fighting can be tiring and sometimes you need to give your arms a rest. The thing to remember here is that if you're going to relax with your arms down, make sure to do it well out of measure. If you think your opponent has a chance in hell of hitting you, go ahead and take another step back before you go into this guard. That said, rest and relaxation aren't the only things this guard gives us.

By standing in this position, we are setting ourselves up to be able to exploit a few different lines of attack. By removing our sword from presence, we've made it harder for our opponent to read what exactly our reach is. This is something you can use to your advantage as it can be awfully satisfying to try and get that strike in right when your opponent thought they were finally safe. Another option we're presented with here is the ability to easily throw a *falso dritto* either as a beat to our opponent's sword or as a strike into their hands. Finally, this guard sets us up to throw a low *fendente* just by pushing down on the pommel. This can be used to parry an incoming attack, find our opponent's sword, perform a beat, or to strike an exposed target.

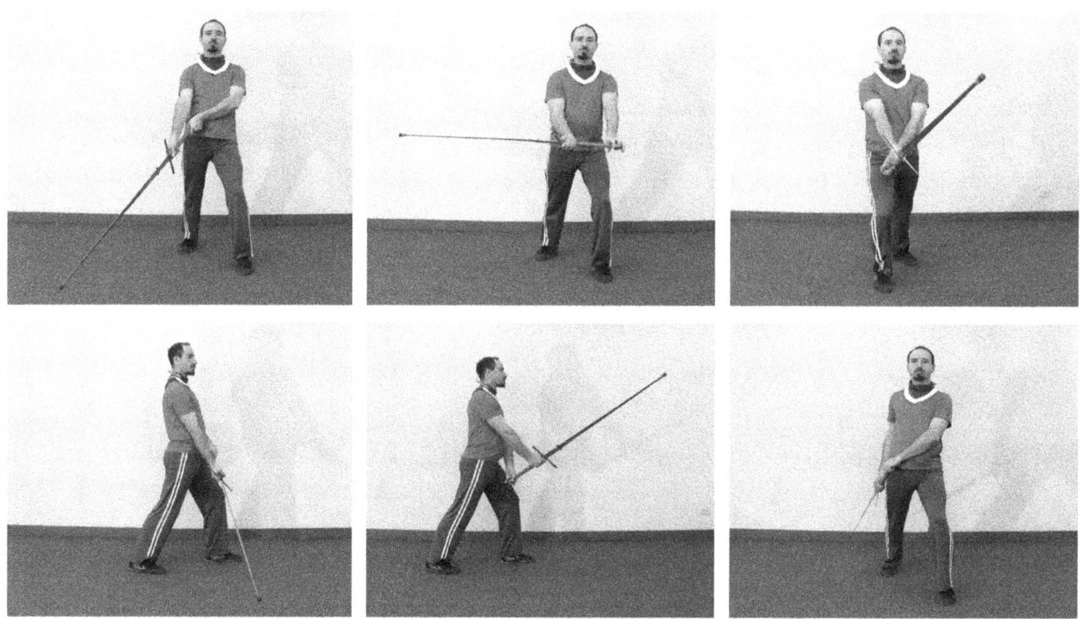

Low **fendente** from **coda lunga e larga**

While this guard does leave most of our body exposed, most everything can be responded to by us moving to our inside line. Your opponent is going to have to do a whole lot of footwork if they want to try and move to threaten your outside line here. As well, we can respond with what's often referred to as the "universal parry" which is just cutting a *ridoppio* that moves across the entirety of our body.

As a more general note, *larga* guards are really only suited for *larga* play, a concept we'll cover more in chapter 13. In short, there's a time and a place for them, but if someone is trying to bind up close with you and you just move your sword out of presence, you're likely going to get shanked.[32]

[32] Dall'Agocchie, 23.

Coda Lunga e Distesa [33] (extended long tail)

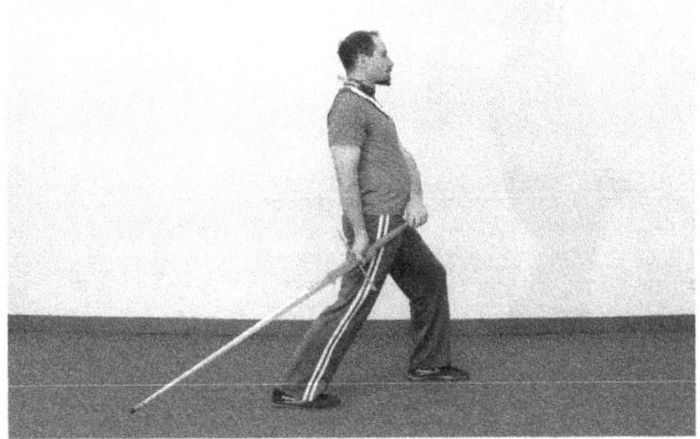

Coda lunga e distesa

This is admittedly one of the showier guards to start a fight from. To form this take *coda lunga e larga*, but now have your point trail behind you instead of pointing in front. As well, while the other *coda lunga* guards can be formed with either foot forward, we only see this one done with the left foot (right foot for lefties) in front.

The obvious move from here is a big *mandritto ridoppio*. However, it's also a fun place to throw an *imbrocatta* from, mostly because people won't see it coming. As well, you can also make a *mandritto sgualimbratto* from here in order to parry an incoming thrust. Mostly though, this ends up being what Fiore would call an *insatiable* guard, a guard you only move through as opposed to one you can safely sit in, for when you're making big, clearing cuts.

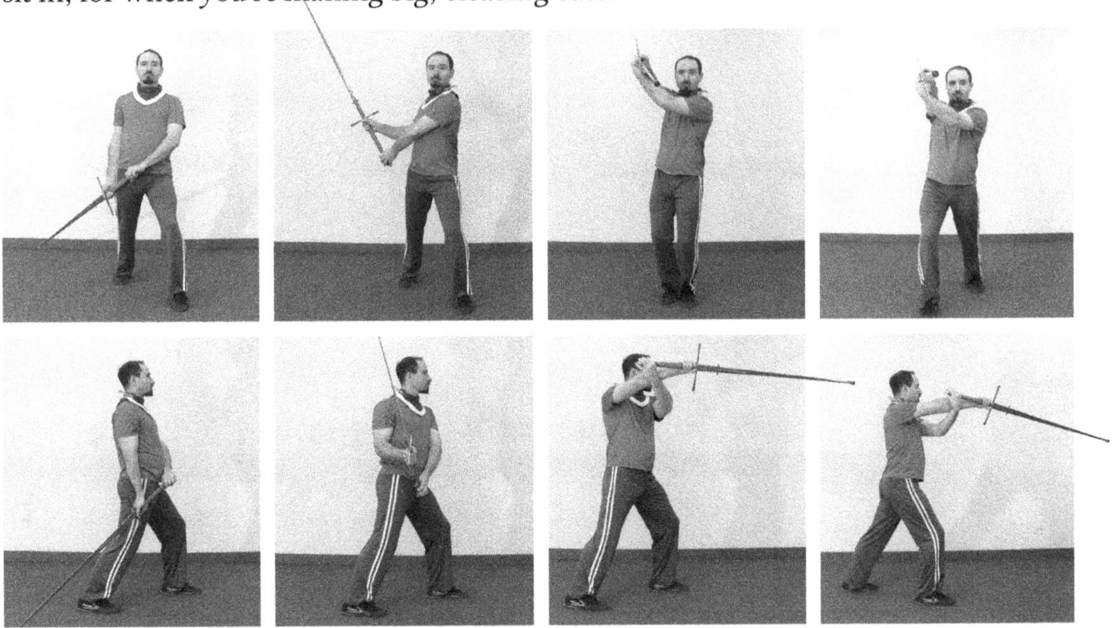

Imbrocatta from *coda lunga e distesa*

[33] The Anonimo Bolognese refers to this as "coda longa longa", but it's the same guard either way.

While it might seem that we are leaving everything but our hands open with this guard (which is true), it does also work to simplify our decision tree. Regardless of what our opponent throws at us, we know we can respond to it by throwing a *mandritto*. Every single thing is now just answered by us moving to our inside line.

Porta di Ferro (iron gate)

The *porta di ferro* guards are just the inside line corollaries to the *coda lunga* guards. People who like to fight a narrower game tend to use these a good deal as they're a great way to gain control over the inside line and nullify your opponent's sword. So by forming these guards, you are inherently inviting to your outside line. The other thing to note is that compared to the fairly squared up *coda lunga* guards, the *porta di ferro* ones are formed with your body being a lot more profiled. This both serves to extend your reach as well as reduce the amount of target area you have exposed. In order to do this, from your *coda lunga* stance I want you to turn on the balls of your non-dominant foot so that it's turned almost ninety degrees out as opposed to being pointing primarily straightforward.

The imagery used in the guard's name harkens back to the notion that a sturdy iron gate is something that is going to take a whole lot of work to batter down.[34] Similarly, by forming these guards, you are shutting off your opponent's path of entry.

34 Dall'Agocchie, 9.

Porta di Ferro Alta (high iron gate)

Porta di ferro alta

Poorly formed *porta di ferro alta*

Much like *coda lunga e alta*, this guard is formed with the dominant hand in line with the shoulder and overall does a great job at keeping the high inside quadrant safe. Again, one of the major issues I see here is people drifting with either the point or the hilt toward the center. Doing this will either provide your opponent with a weak angle to exploit and or will give them the opportunity to choose which side they attack down as you're left scrambling.

From a properly formed *porta di ferro alta* you've got a pretty wide array of choices available to you. One option might be to drop the point in and thrust an *imbrocatta* in *guardia d'intrare*. Another option would be to throw a *roverso sgualimbratto* at your opponent's head. You could also, depending on where you're standing, feint a *mandritto fendente* and then go around their sword.

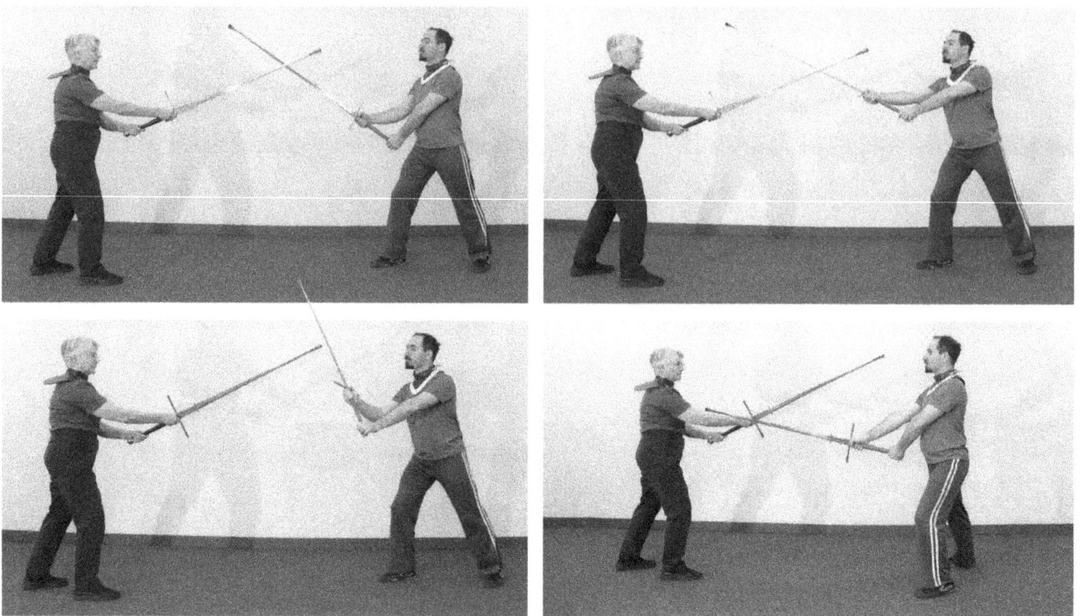

Feint *mandritto fendente to the head, mezzo roverso fendente* to the hands

The primary opening here is to your high outside line. While your opponent could try and shoot for the low line, doing so means they're going to be fighting against gravity as your crash down on them.

Porta di Ferro Stretta (narrow iron gate)

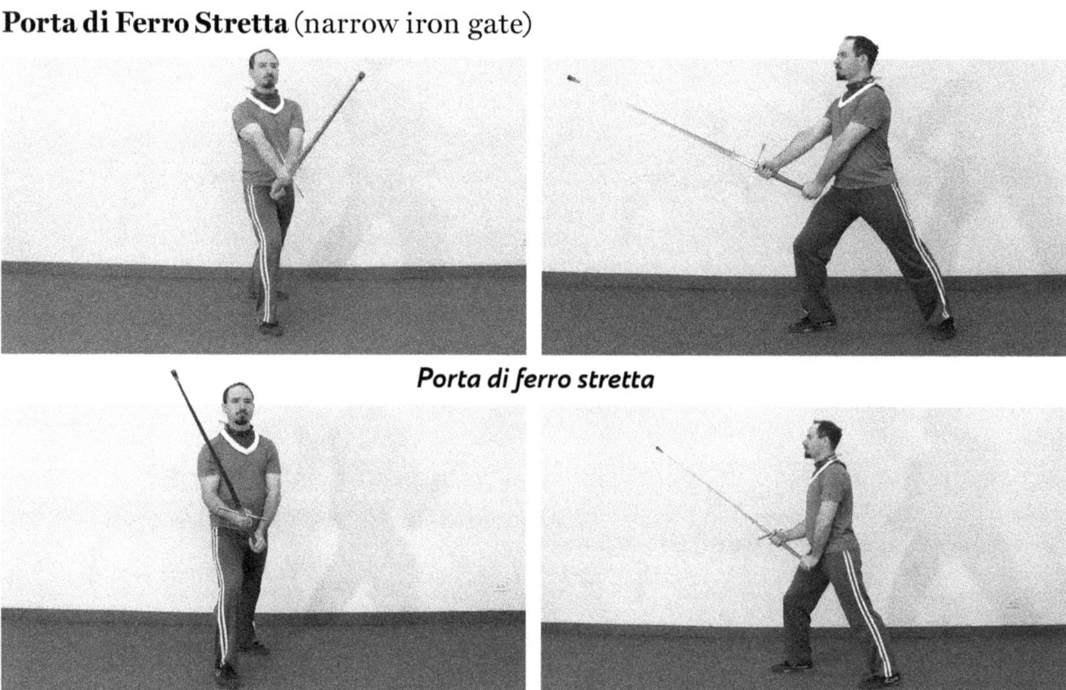

Porta di ferro stretta

Poorly formed *porta di ferro stretta*

This guard is again fairly similar to its *alta* sibling, but this time your pommel hand should rest in front of your hip. If you and your opponent are fighting same handed (right vs. righty or lefty vs. lefty) you're going to find yourself spending a lot of time in this guard as you fight over that inside line. It's also an incredibly powerful tool against the high guards as it cuts off that big initial cut they're set up to do so well. However, it leaves open your outside line. So, when you form this guard, do so expecting your opponent to disengage to the other side.

Porta di Ferro Larga (wide iron gate)

Porta di ferro larga

Porta di ferro larga is the more specialized sibling to *coda lunga e larga*. You have more of your body in the way when standing in this position, but it sets you up for a really fast *falso manco* that you can use to your advantage. As well, you can come out and disengage really quickly in order to find your opponent's extended sword on the inside line. By forming this guard, you know that whatever your opponent does, you can answer it with a *roverso*. So although you're more exposed, you've simplified your choices a lot

Cinghare Porta di Ferro Alta (boar's high iron gate)

Cinghare porta di ferro alta

Poorly formed *cinghare porta di ferro alta*

Unlike the *coda lunga* guards, which don't really care which foot is forward, which foot you have in front makes a bit more difference for the *porta di ferro* guards. With this guard, not only is your left foot forward (right foot for lefties), but you're also going to your hands in front of your left knee (right knee if you're left handed). The imagery here comes directly from boar hunting, something that was quite popular back when these books were being written. When a boar comes in to attack you it'll charge straight on, but because of the placement of its tusks it changes its trajectory at the very last moment in order to come in and gouge you at an angle. In the same fashion, the Bolognese *cinghare* guards are set up primarily to come in with angled strikes as opposed to coming in straight forward.[35]

[35] Fiore also has a guard called posta dente di cinghare. Both are pulling from the same imagery, but the end result is different. Fiore is focused on pulling the hands to the hip whereas the Bolognese are more focused on which foot is forward as well as having the hands in line with the knee. In general, the Bolognese authors have a tendency to take all of Fiore's guard names, throw them into a blender, and use whatever comes out.

This means you'll see both a lot of the *falso manco* being thrown from these guards, as well as a lot of thrusts thrown as a *punta infalsata*. From this guard in particular, it's really easy to threaten a thrust going into *guardia d'intrare*, or to crash down on to your opponent's sword with your false edge. Again, this guard leaves your high outside line open, so plan accordingly.

Cinghare Porta di Ferro Stretta (boar's narrow iron gate)

Cinghare porta di ferro stretta

Poorly formed *cinghare porta di ferro stretta*

This guard functions similarly to its *alta* sibling. Again, make sure you're only offering either the inside or the outside line to your opponent. Particularly with these two guards it can be really easy to let that point drift in toward the middle. From this guard in particular I'll use the *falso manco* a lot as a beat to my opponent's sword. Alternatively, I'll feint a *punta roversa* and then either strike my opponent or disengage in response to their parry.

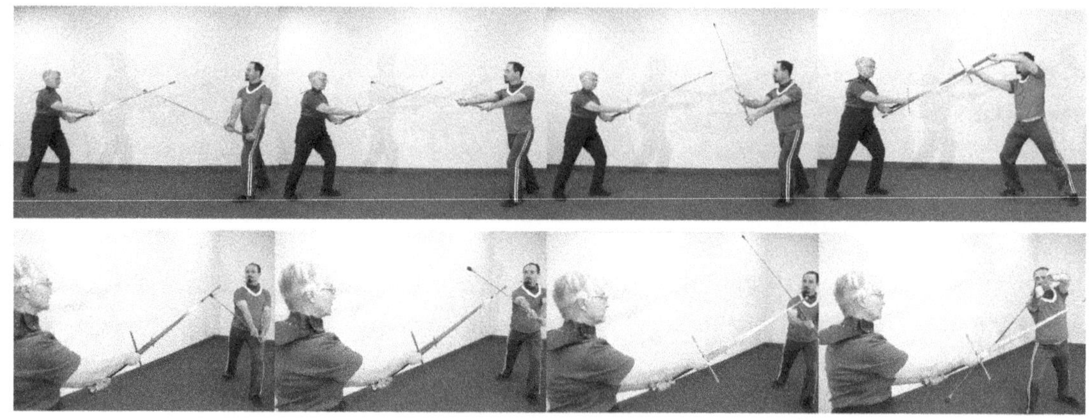

Feint a punta roversa

Just like *porta di ferro stretta*, forming this guard leaves your outside line open. The nice thing about the *cinghare* version, though, is that it's even easier to spring forward with that false edge.

Cinghare Porta di Ferro Larga (boar's wide iron gate)

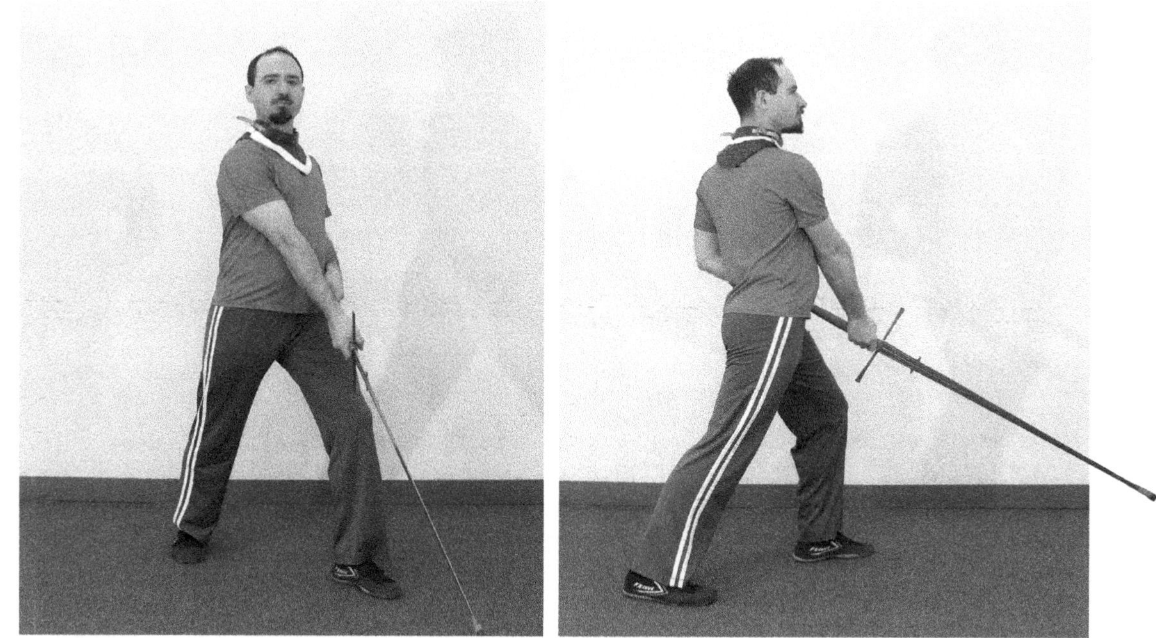

Cinghare porta di ferro larga

Hand snipe city, baby! This guard is a great way to harass your opponent's hands, as well as mess with their sense of measure as your sword isn't out in front for them to visually measure from. If you really like off-line shots, this guard could easily be one of your favorites. As well, setting up here means you can respond to pretty much everything with a *roverso*, even if they try and hit you with a *mandritto* of their own.

Guardia di Fianche (guard of the hips)

Guardia di fianche

Poorly formed *guarda di fianche*

This is a guard that often gets glossed over, but does still have its unique uses. In essence, it's essentially just *porta di ferro stretta*, but more structurally supported. With keeping your pommel braced against your hip, you have to rely a whole lot less on your arm strength. You can use this both as a way to block incoming blows to your inside line or as a way to deliver a really structurally sound *punta ferma*. As well, you can use this guard to lie a bit about how far you can reach. So, if you like playing measure games in particular, this guard is one for you. Just be mindful that when your arms launch out that you don't gack anybody.

Again, by forming this guard you are inviting your opponent to your outside line. Also, because it's held so far back you're encouraging your opponent to come in with a descending blow. At the same time, though, there isn't a lot for them to try and strike up into so your low line is pretty well taken care of.

This one isn't so much a guard as it is a position to start from where you can kick your sword up and begin to impress the gender of your choosing with all your fancy flourishes. Not particularly helpful for winning tournaments, but is a great way to add a bit of pizazz to your fight. We also don't have a picture or a good description of this guard in any of the treatises. Instead we just have the name and a very small amount of context cues. As such I tend to leave this one out when I'm teaching, unless someone specifically asks how they can walk into a fight being as showy as possible.

As a note, we do see a few other guards vaguely alluded to for the longsword (but only by Marozzo). That said, we aren't given descriptions for them and they pop up so rarely that I decided not to include them in this book. If you are interested and want to dig deeper though, the other guards are *guardia di gombito, guardia di consentire, guardia di spalla*. We are also given a clear guard for using a longsword against a polearm, but polearms are a topic for another book.

Choose Your Guard, Any Guard

Here's an exercise I like to use to help people start figuring out their decision trees as opposed to me handing ones to them.

STEP 1: Grab a partner and have one of you choose a guard to start from.

STEP 2: After Fencer A chooses a guard, Fencer B chooses a guard of their own. This can be the same guard, or something entirely different, doesn't matter.

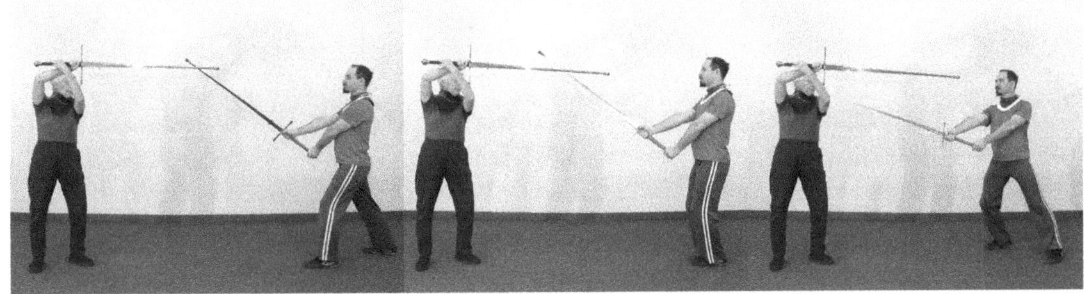

STEP 3: From here, Fencer A is going to throw a strike into Fencer B's opening.[36] Do that a few times to get the movement down.

STEP 4: Now try it again, but this time Fencer B gets to make a move of their own in response. This doesn't necessarily have to happen all the way after Fencer A finishes their attack, but you should still leave enough time for Fencer A to begin their move first without Fencer B anticipating it and firing before it's time.

[36] You made sure to just have one opening, right?

STEP 5: Once you've done that a few times, Fencer A gets to make a second move, but Fencer B is stuck only making their one.

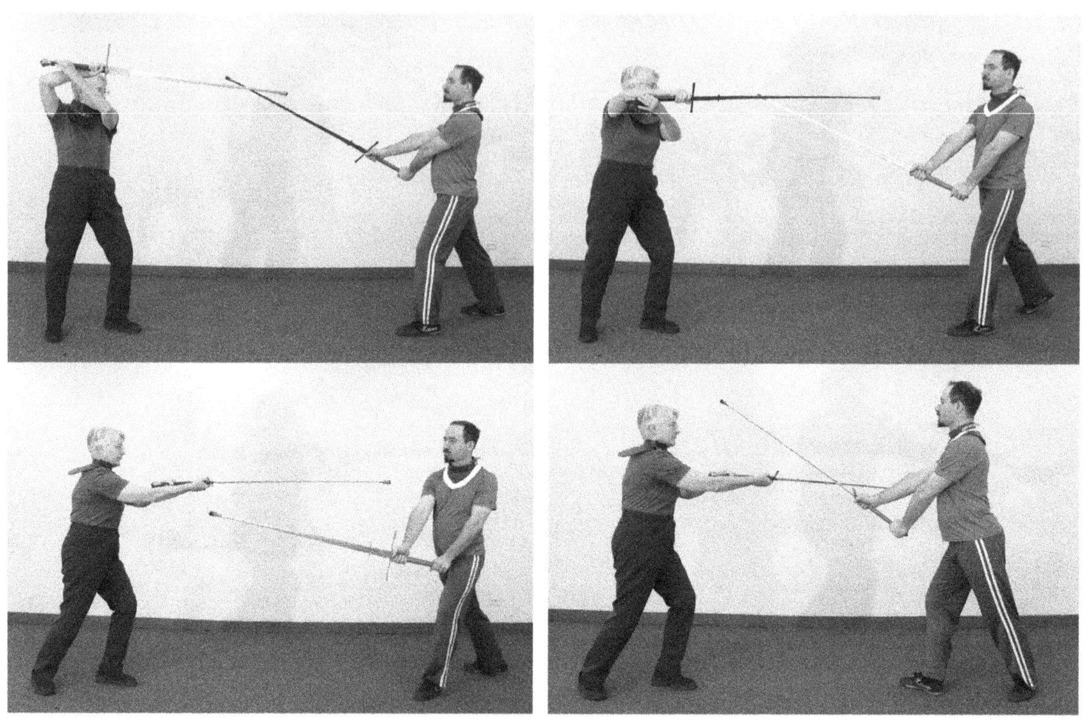

STEP 6: After a few more times, Fencer B gets to make a second move of their own.

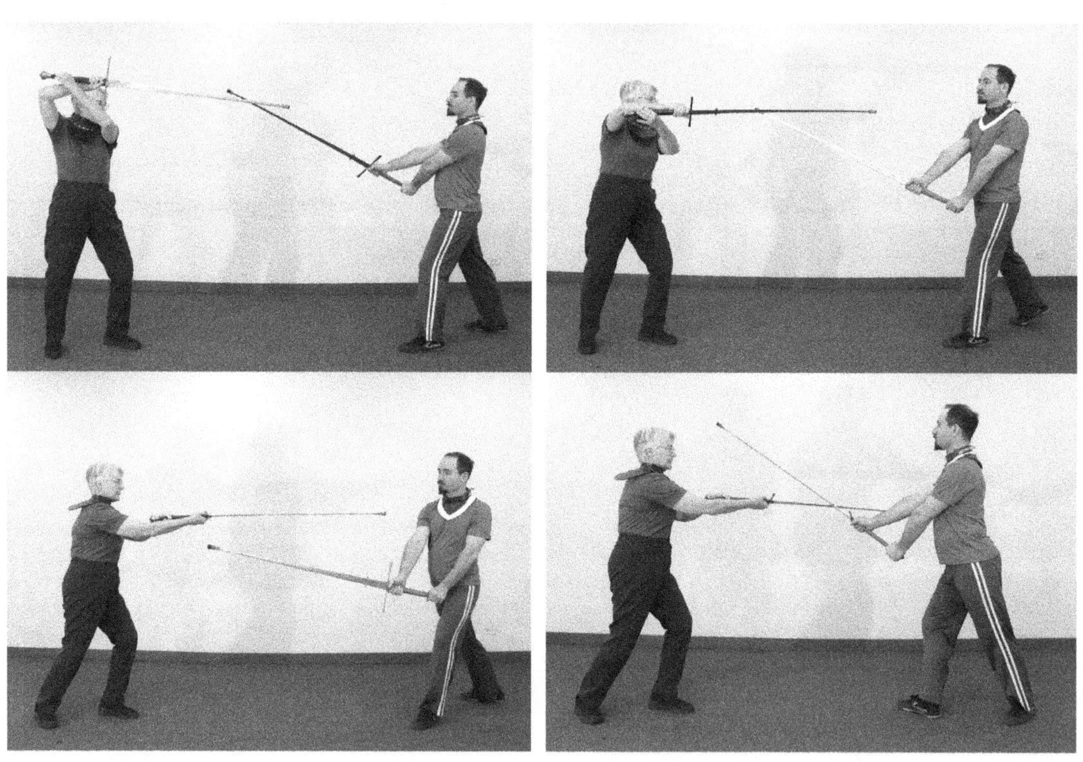

You could theoretically have this go for an infinite number of steps on each side, but to keep the drill realistic I tend to only go until two or three moves on each side. Instead of moving a bajillion different times, after both fencers get comfortable two or three steps in I have them both pick brand new guards and then switch who gets to go first. Overall this is a great way to explore in a controlled environment what moves come naturally to each person, as well as what possibilities there might be that folks haven't thought of. The great part is that you as an instructor don't need to think of any of the plays beforehand. You're just handing your students the pieces and seeing what they come up with. If your group has the fairly common issue of all the students fighting just like their instructor, this is a great way to start and break out of that.

Throw Every Blow

If you're on your own and are looking for a way to explore how each and every guard could be used, this one is a particularly helpful exercise. Pick a guard and figure out how you could throw each of the cuts, both true edge and false edge, we discussed from that position. Next, try and figure out how you might perform each and every thrust we went over. Once you've done that, go on to the next guard. Keep doing this until you've tried every guard with every cut and every thrust. Dall'Agocchie teaches us that to master the art we must both know how to both attack our enemy and defend ourselves from each and every guard.[37] Overall, this exercise serves as a way to illuminate the various possibilities you're presented with at any given time. Especially if you've hit a rut in your fencing and aren't sure what you can do to change up your game, this is a great way to explore your options in a low pressure space. It's also just a great way to keep yourself busy while waiting for your next match.

Four Corners Drill

Here's a neat little exercise that can help you explore how a few specific guards really work well together. The first iteration of this is what I like to think of as the *larga* version. That's a term we'll get more into later, but for the moment just think of it as starting with guards that don't have the point forward and using attacks that end by passing all the way through instead of stopping in presence.[38]

---

[37] Dall'Agocchie, page 7.
[38] Anonimo Bolognese, 70.

STEP 1 - Have Fencer A start in *guardia alta* and Fencer B start in *coda lunga e larga*.

STEP 2 - From there, Fencer A is going to throw a *mandritto sgualimbratto* that Fencer B is going to have to figure out how best to not get hit by.

STEP 3 - Now do the same thing, but with Fencer A throwing a *roverso sgualimbratto* instead.

STEP 4 - Next, have both fencers start in *coda lunga e larga* but this time have Fencer A throw a *mandritto ridoppio*.

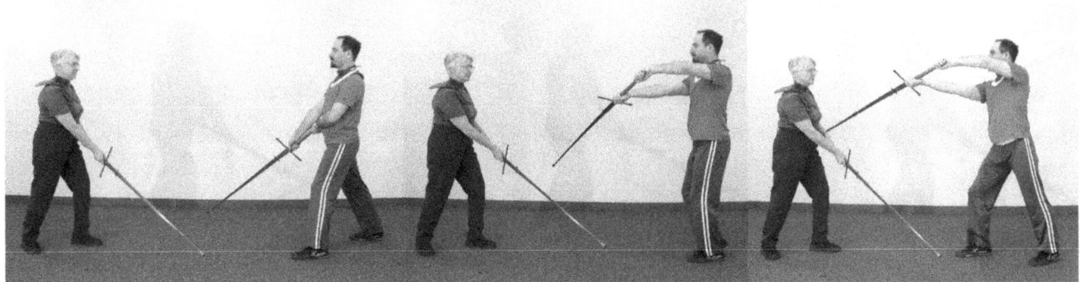

STEP 5 - Once that's done, have Fencer A do it all again, but starting from *porta di ferro larga* and have them throw a *roverso ridoppio*.

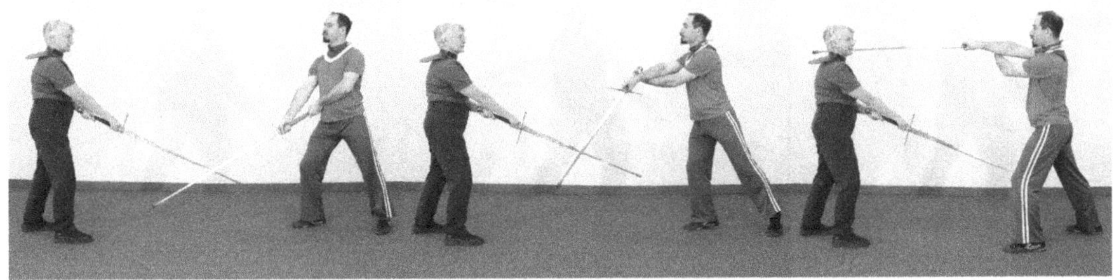

STEP 6 - After that, do the whole thing again with Fencer A throwing attacks from the three different guards I've listed here, but this time have Fencer B start in *porta di ferro larga*.

STEP 7 - Once you're finished, do it all again. This time, though, Fencer B gets to start in *guardia alta* for all of it. Once you're done, switch roles.

STEP 8 - If that doesn't seem challenging enough, try this. Instead of throwing the cut that feels natural from any of the guards, try and see if you can throw one of the other ones. So, if you're Fencer A and you find yourself starting in *guardia alta*, see if you can't threaten your partner with a *ridoppio*.

STEP 9 - Same thing with the low guards, except this time you're going to try and figure out how to throw a descending cut from there toward your partner's head.

STEP 10 - Finally, try throwing a full *roverso* starting from your right side (left side if your hands are switched) or a *mandritto* from your left side. As well, if you haven't already, see what changes if you throw any of these with the other edge. Rising cuts are often done with the false edge whereas descending cuts are generally thrown with the true edge, but that doesn't mean it always has to be so.

At the same time, if you're Fencer B try and see which blade actions you can do from where and against which cuts. Play with your parries, collections, and deflections from every quadrant. See what happens.

Once you've gone through all of that, it's time to try the *stretta* version. **STEP 1** - For this one, Fencer A is going to start in *guardia di croce* and fencer B is going to start in *coda lunga e stretta*.

STEP 2 - From here Fencer A gets the choice of attacking with either an *imbrocatta* or a *mezzo mandritto sgualimbratto* and Fencer B has to figure out how to intercept it.

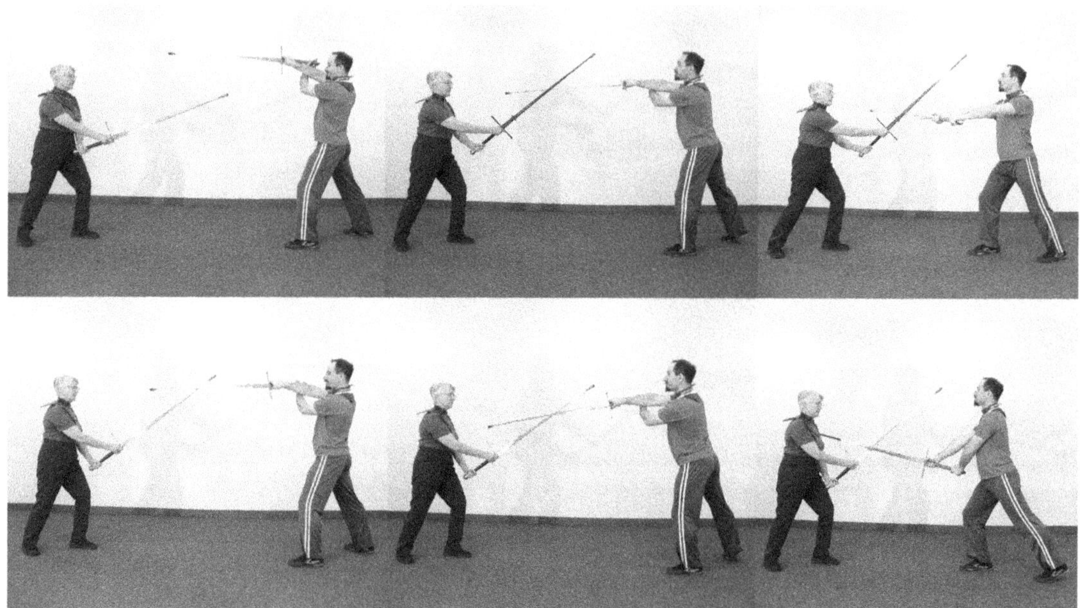

STEP 3 - After that, try it with Fencer A up in *guardia di croce* with Fencer B in *cinghare porta di ferro stretta* with the false edge of their blade pointed toward Fencer A's sword.

From here, Fencer A should try striking both with an *imbrocatta* and with a *roverso sgualimbratto*.

STEP 4 - Next try it with Fencer A starting in *coda lunga e stretta* and throwing a *stocatta* or a *mezzo mandritto sgualimbratto* against Fencer B's *guardia di croce.*

STEP 5 - After that try it with Fencer A starting in *cinghare porta di ferro stretta* and throwing either a *stocatta* or a *mezzo roverso sgualimbratto* against Fencer B's *guardia di intrare.*[39]

Just like we did with the *larga* plays, now try throwing all the other blows that seem just a bit less straightforward from the four different guards.

[39] You could also throw in cinghare porta di ferro larga if you wanted here, but it's the same cuts either way.

Commit to Your Guard!

This isn't a drill, but instead a piece of advice that never stops being helpful. One of the most common issues I see in people's fencing (including my own), is under-committing to a guard. I don't mean that you need to swing for the fences every time you throw a blow, but instead I want you to think about whatever line a guard is supposed to close off and fully commit to doing so. If you under-commit your guards you're not only weakening your structure, making it easier for your opponent to blow straight through, but you're also giving yourself choice paralysis. Let's look at a few examples.

Look at the above photo. If this is how your opponent lines up against you before you even enter measure or commit to a guard of your own, how many openings do you see right now? Think about it for a minute or two and then keep reading.

I see at least two lines of attack, each with a few different ways of seizing on it. The clear option is attacking down the inside line. You could do this with a *mandritto sgualimbratto* to their head or a thrust right down the center in *guardia di faccia*. It's not as open, but you do also have a bit of an opening to go down on the outside line. Here you could hit their dominant arm with a *mezzo roverso* or possibly push through a thrust in *guardia di croce*. Not only is the way their guard set up structurally weak, but it also leaves you with multiple ways of coming in without a way for them to know which one you're going for. Now there's no perfect guard that covers everything, even plate armor has gaps in it. What you want a guard to do is provide one clear option for your opponent to take so that you can have your response ready to go. It doesn't even matter all that much if they come down that line with a cut or a thrust. All you really care about is clearing that trajectory before stepping in. If you give your opponent two options though, you now have to play catch up and now you're in what later authors would call "obedience". Let's look at another example now.

To start with, what line is this supposed to be closing off? I'll give you a minute to flip back to the page we first talked about this guard. Alright, you ready? It's the inside line. Good job! Now what line is the guard in this picture actually closing off? It takes away a small bit of the inside line, but really the answer is "neither of them." The point comes across enough to begin to close off a small bit of the outside line, but wouldn't take a maestro to get around it. As a result, someone forming their guard like this just doesn't have a good way of predicting where you're going to go. You could either push through and collapse their weak angle on the inside line, or you could fairly easily come around and strike them on their outside line. Instead, when you try and form a guard, make sure you're committed to closing one line off entirely or suddenly you're going to start getting hit in places you thought you had locked down. Now let's look at one final example.

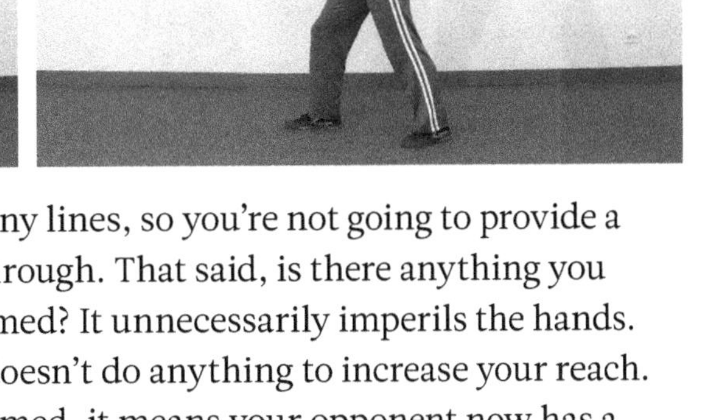

Guardia alta doesn't really close off any lines, so you're not going to provide a weak angle for your opponent to push through. That said, is there anything you notice about how this guard is being formed? It unnecessarily imperils the hands. Moving your hands a few inches closer doesn't do anything to increase your reach. However, the way this guard is being formed, it means your opponent now has a closer target they can hit. So, if the guard you're making doesn't put your point in front of your hands, don't have your hands any closer to your opponent's sword than the rest of your body.[40]

---

[40] *Guardia di testa* is the one exception we have to this, but it also doesn't sit still.

8: Blade Actions

So, it turns out that there's more you can do with a sword besides just cut or thrust. While those will almost always be the end goal, sometimes we need just a little bit of help getting there. In order to make some sense of this, I would like to present to you the following.

The Three Turns of the Sword

If your sword is pointed one way and you need it to go somewhere else, there's only really three options to get it there.[41] As a heads up, the language used for these isn't consistent across the different Bolognese texts, so I'm going to be using the schema given to me by one of my teachers.

Option one is what we call the ***volta stabile*** (stable turn).[42] Let's say that you've come in and found your opponent's sword to one side, but suddenly they go around and pop up on the other side. Simply take your point and aim it across the other direction while turning the true edge of your sword in just a bit in order to help you out.[43]

Volta stabile

---

[41] While some of these are technical terms in the Bolognese texts, none of them break it down to this same degree. I got this taxonomy from one of my teachers and have found it incredibly useful in my own teaching, but it's not strictly something that's "Bolognese".

[42] Boorman, 106.

[43] Many of the Bolognese sources will instead refer to this as a mezza volta, but unfortunately the language isn't consistent. Here I have used the terminology that was taught to me, but feel free to use whatever suits you and your students.

As an exercise, try coming in against a partner and have them bring their sword around any which way in order to try and hit you on another line. See how many of these can be answered with a *volta stabile*. You might be surprised how versatile a tool it can prove to be.

The next option is what we call a ***mezza volta*** (half turn).[44] This involves disengaging your blade around theirs, but without bringing the point so far back that it goes behind your hands. This technique is generally used when you see that your opponent is coming in to take your line and you need to get to the other side quick. Ideally this means that you get your sword out of the way before your opponent is able to make contact, forcing them to play catch up when they realize your sword is no longer there. Another thing to note is that this technique can be performed either by going over their sword or under it. As we'll talk a bit more about in just a minute, going over the top is going to be easier the steeper the angle of their sword is. However, the straighter they hold the point out there, the easier it will become to disengage underneath.

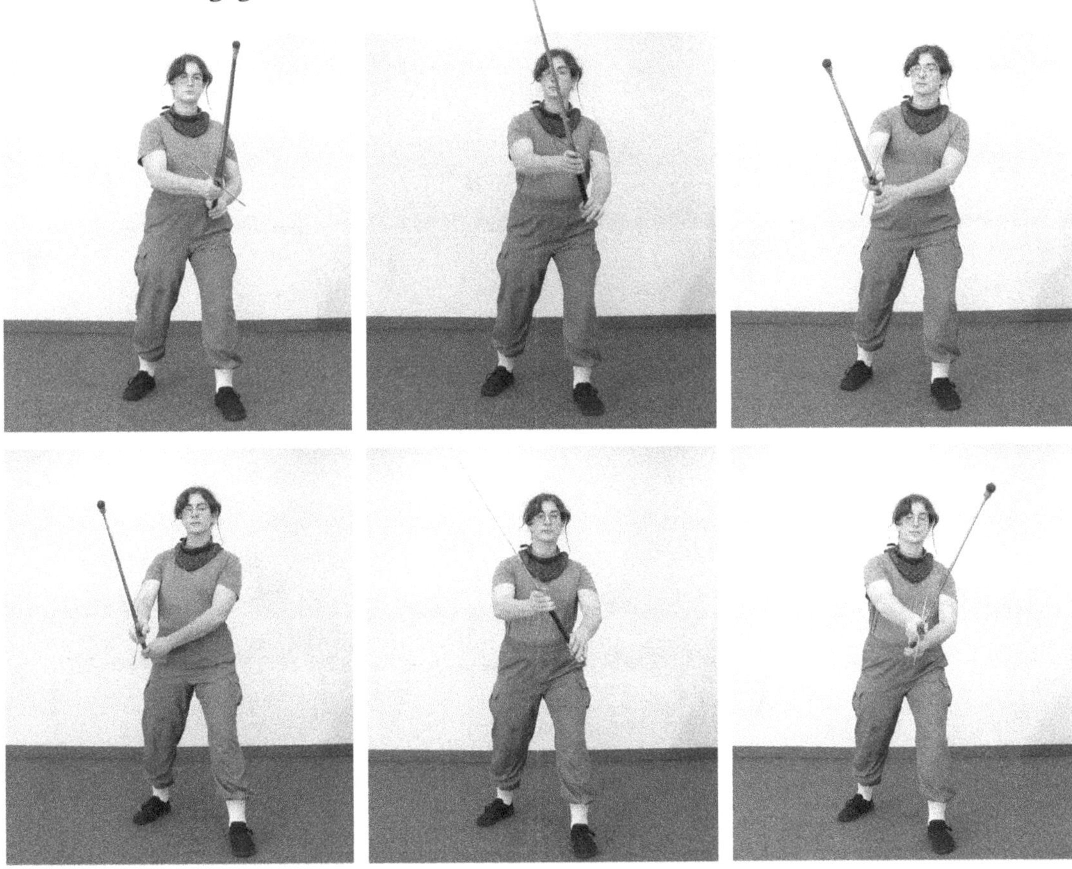

Mezza volta

[44] Again this term is used differently by different sources. I'm just using the version taught to me by my teachers, but feel free to stick to any particular book's vocabulary if you see fit.

Another term for this technique we see used by the Bolognese authors is referring to it as a ***sflasare***. Fencers coming in to this from the later rapier traditions might also know it as a *cavazionne*.

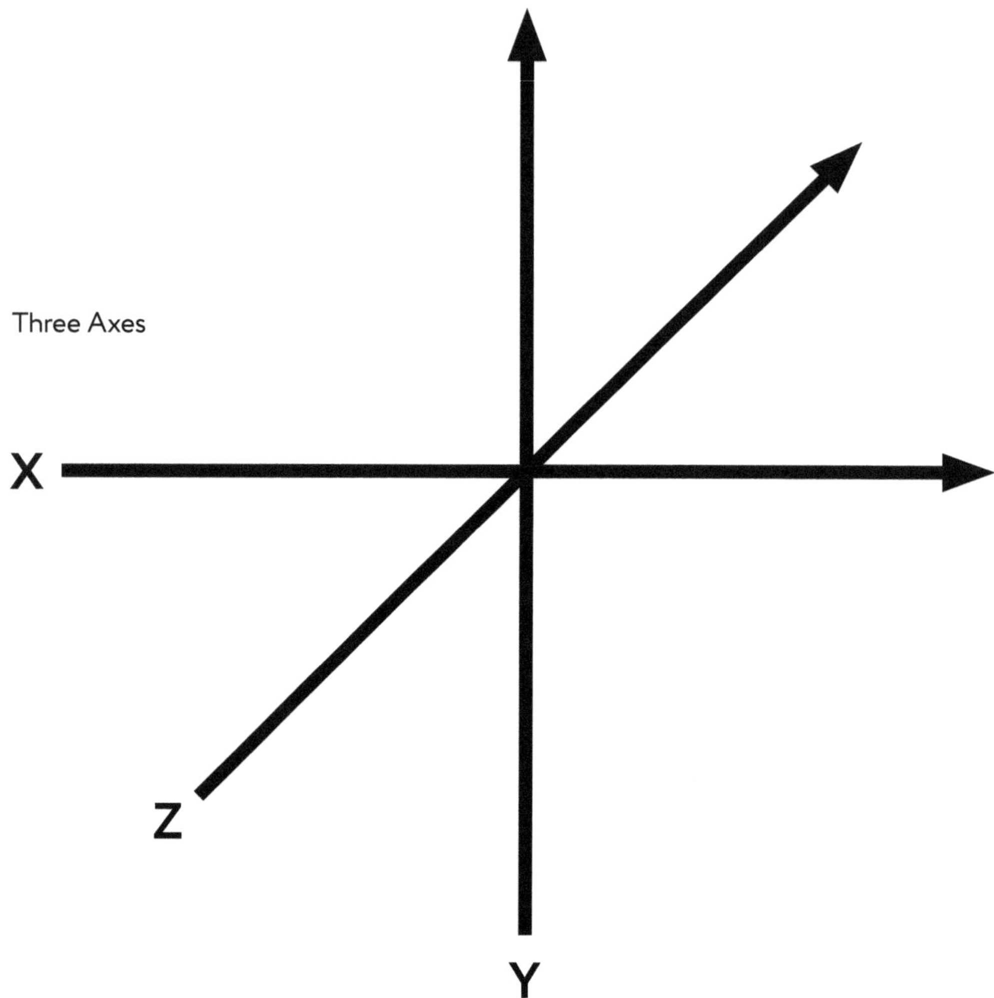

Proportion

There are three factors that dictate how large a *sflasare* has to be in order to get it around your opponent's sword, which overall come together to form what we call **proportion**. The first is what we call **penetration**.[45] Another way of thinking about this is that you're just moving your sword along the z-axis. As an exercise, have one person stand there with their sword held straight out as the second person stands there performing an infinite number of *sflasari* around their partner's sword. Now have the first person slowly take a couple steps forward and then a couple steps backward. As you'll quickly see, as the two of you get closer and closer the more sword there is to go around, making the *sfalsare* take that much longer.

[45] Boorman, 145.

Penetration

The next factor is what we call **angulation**.[46] Another way of thinking about this would be to say that you're affecting where your sword is along the y-axis. To explore this take the same setup as before. However, this time instead of having one person step in and out, have them slowly change the angle of their sword. As that angle changes you'll quickly notice that there's suddenly way more/less sword to get around. Think about this when you set up your guards as the longer a path you can force your opponent to take, the more time you'll have to act.

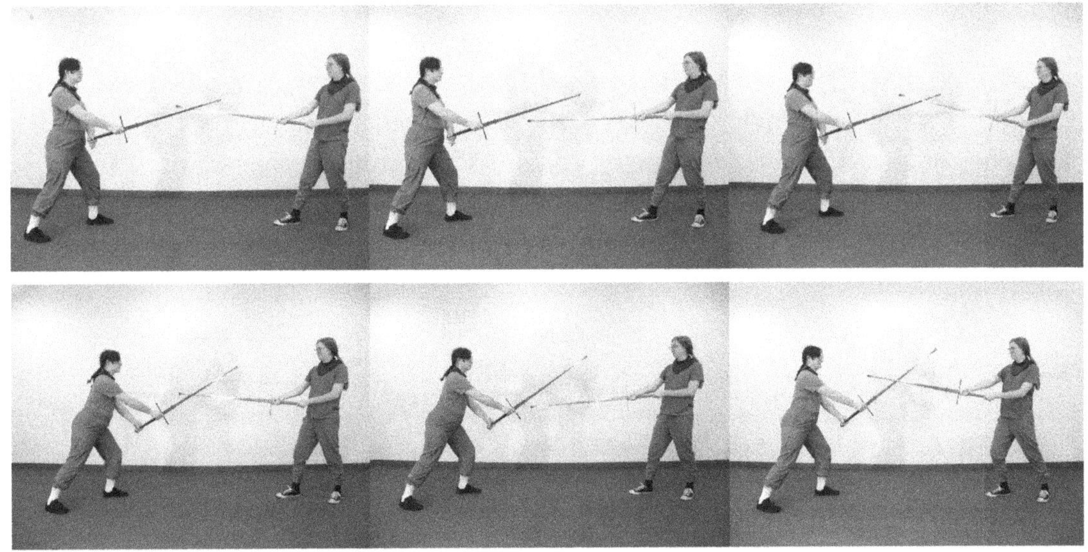

Angulation

46 Boorman, 144.

Our final factor is what we call **breadth**. This is really just changing where your blade is along the x-axis. For this one take the same set up again, but now have the one person move their tip from side to side, bringing in some off-line footwork if they want. Something you'll notice here is that going around one way is going to feel really easy, while trying to go the other is going to feel like running through quicksand. Again, remember this sensation as you're fighting and try and use this to put your opponent in as uncomfortable a position as possible.

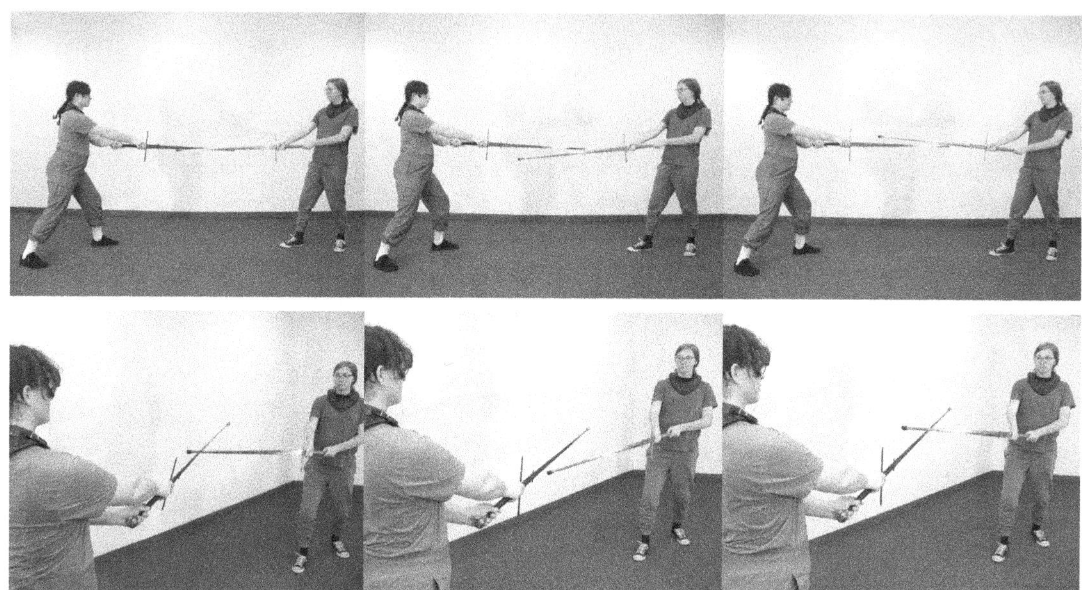

Breadth

Once you have tried all three of these options on their own, see if you can create some more compound angles by combining all three to varying degrees. As some of you might have already picked up on, these three factors correlate directly to the three axes of three dimensional space. **Penetration** is just moving along the z-axis, **angulation** is changing things along the y-axis, and **breadth** is just making adjustments along the x-axis.

I'll talk about this more in chapter 12, but all of this is also what dictates how large or small of a tempo your opponent's next move is going to be in relation to your action.

Returning to the broader subject at hand, the last of the three turns is what we call a ***tutta volta*** (full turn). This is differentiated from the ***mezza volta*** by the point coming back behind your hands. Generally speaking, this technique is used either when you're at the far edge of measure and can more easily pull off grandiose actions, or when you're pressed in close and you're trying to get in to strike your opponent as you come in bringing your body past their point.

Tutta Volta

There are two specific versions of the *tutta volta* the Bolognese authors give us, namely the **strammazone** and the **molinetto**.[47] Again the usage (as well as the spelling) of these isn't wholly consistent across the various Bolognese authors, so I'm going to give you the versions I use in my personal teaching but feel free to base yours off of the author of your choice. The *strammazone* is a "wheel-like" action that involves you yielding to the inside line and generally coming back with either a *mandritto* or a *roverso*, having the entire action happening as a wrist cut of the dominant hand.

The *molinetto* is the same thing but done to the outside and as an elbow cut of the dominant hand instead. The key here is to have your blade pass by as close to your head as possible without giving yourself a haircut. These can both be used to help you transition from one guard to another, helping you prep your attack on the way in, or can be used as a way to yield to a greater force and go around it to the other side. I personally find them the most useful as feints (something we'll talk more about in chapter 15), as they really catch someone's eye without necessarily requiring you to come in as close as you might with any other kind of feint.

The following is a drill I've found serves to not only help introduce the idea of the three turns of the sword, but to also use that concept to work on starting to build decision trees.

---

[47] Across the different treatises you will occasionally see both of these spelled differently. Also note that while these are both full turns of the sword, they can still be used as a part of *gioco stretto* (see chapter 13).

STEP ❶ - Start with both fencers in a point forward position.

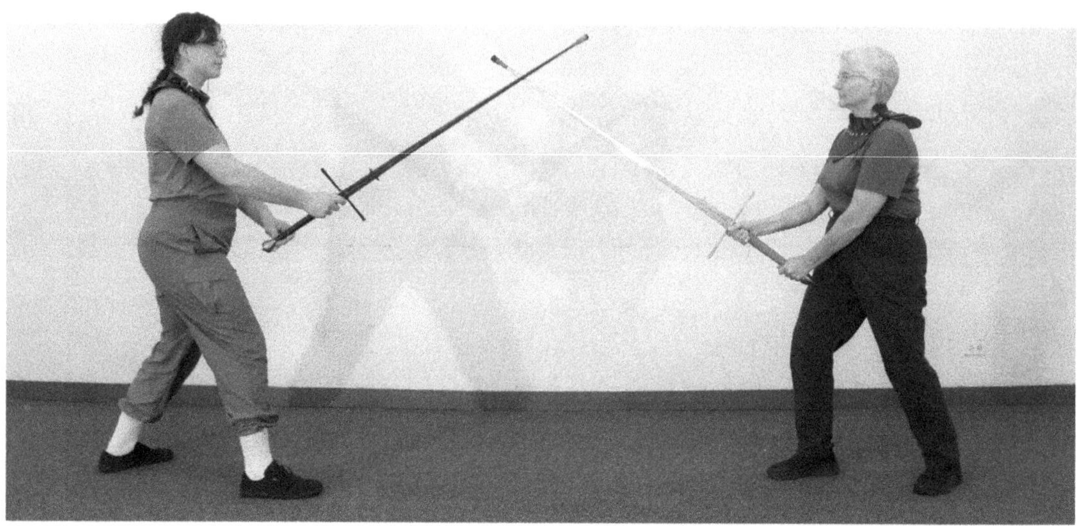

STEP ❷ - From there have Fencer A step in to try and find Fencer B's sword. In response, Fencer B is going to perform a *sfalsare*, disengaging their sword around their opponent's.

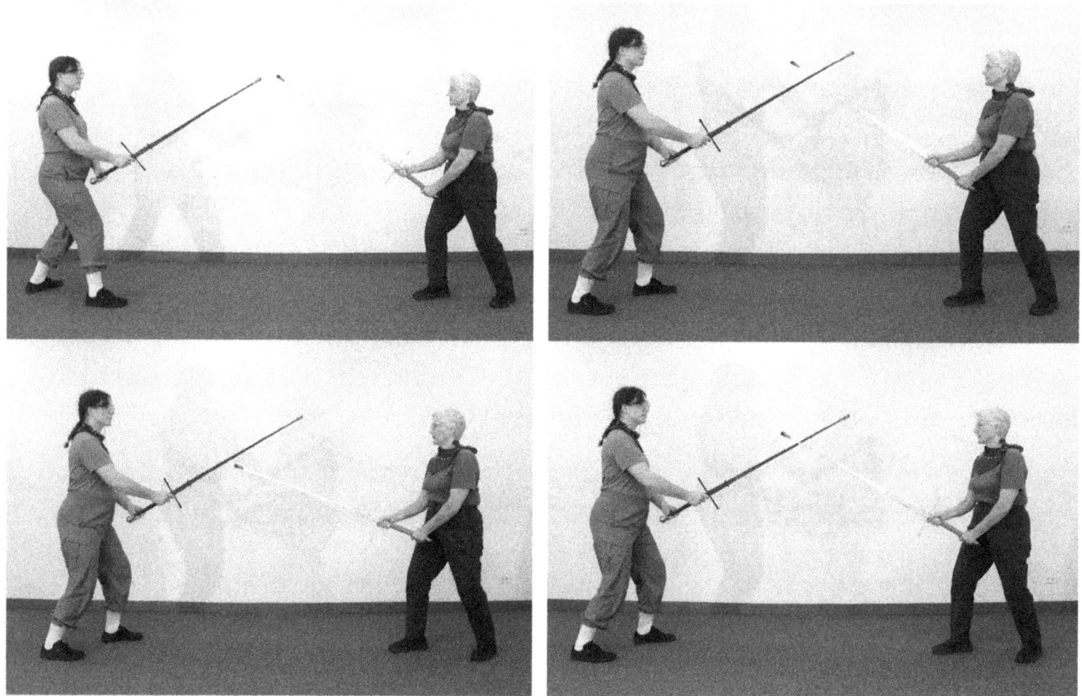

STEP ❸ - Depending on how close this puts the two parties, Fencer A will want to go with one of two options. If, after Fencer B has moved, the crossing of the blades happens more than one *palmo* (handspan) down Fencer A's sword, then Fencer A is going to want to perform a *volta stable* and then come in with a thrust.

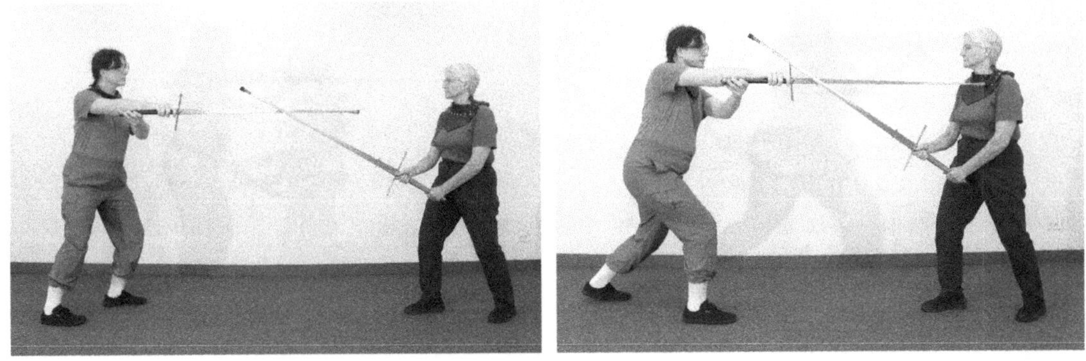

If, instead, the crossing happens further out, Fencer A is going to want to go with a counter-disengage, performing a *sflalsare* of their own, and then proceeding to thrust into their opponent.

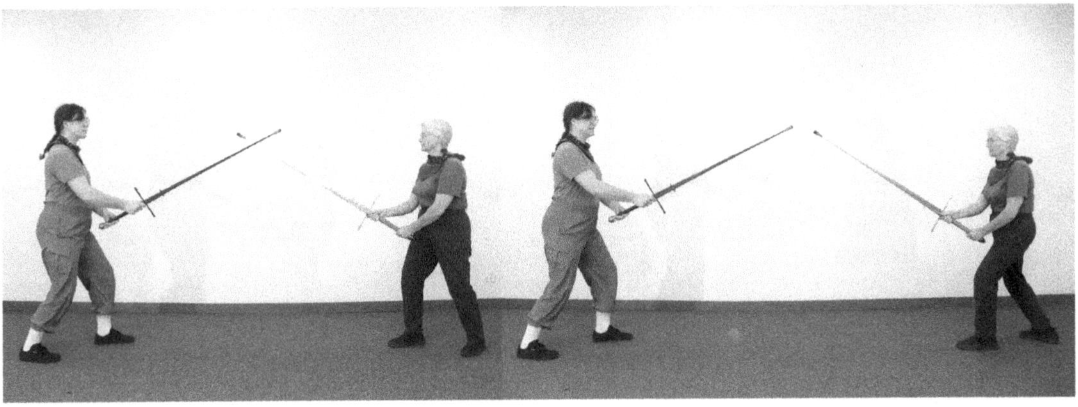

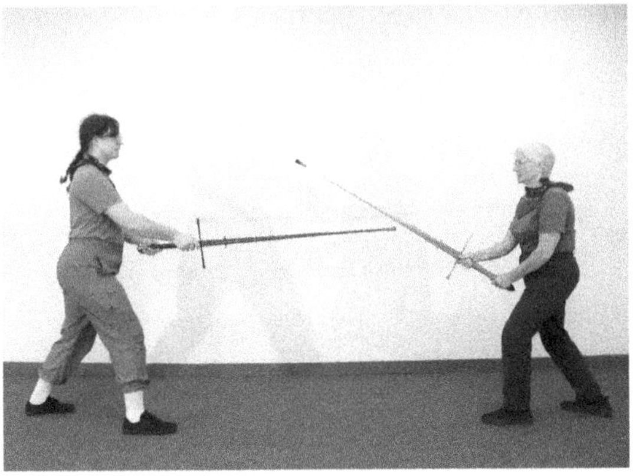

The reason for this is, as we just learned, the closer the two fighters are and the more Fencer B has penetrated into Fencer A's guard, the larger Fencer A's *sfalsare* is going to have to be. In contrast, the *volta stable* remains the same sized action regardless of how close the two fencers are. So, if Fencer A only has to move a little bit to disengage their sword, that's going to be the faster option. However, the closer they get, the more the *volta stable* becomes the economical choice.

For the next drill, we're going to look at the dynamics choosing between the *mezza volta* and the *tutta volta*. With this we are going to start again with our points extended.

STEP 1 - Fencer A is going to step in to find and Fencer B is going to have to figure out which option to go with.

STEP 2, OPTION A: If Fencer A steps in just a bit, Fencer B should respond by coming around with some version of the *mezza volta* and should use that to end with throwing a cut into their opponent.

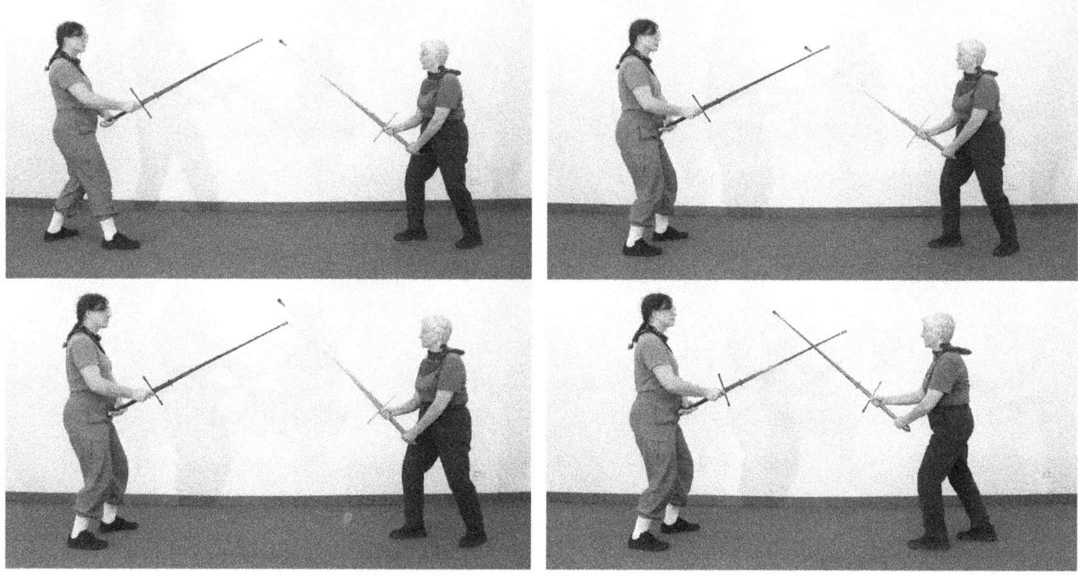

STEP 2, OPTION B: If, instead though, Fencer A takes a large step in and their opponent hasn't reacted fast enough, the answer now is going to be for Fencer B to respond with a *tutta volta*.

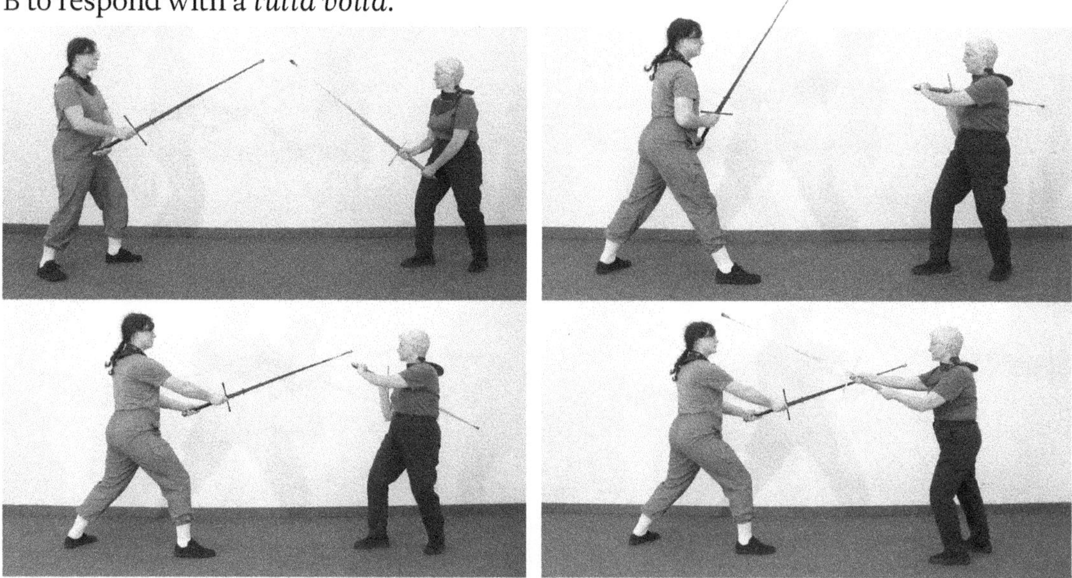

STEP 3 - Try this on both the inside and outside lines. As well, play with how big your steps are to try and figure out where exactly the line is for you between the two options.

Neither of these drills are meant to be exhaustive explorations of how the turns of the sword work. Instead, treat them more as jumping-off points. Once you've played around with them a bit, feel free to try and create your own scenarios and see where each turn of the sword might fit best.

Counter-Finds

Earlier we talked a bit about how to find and then gain someone's blade. That method works fine and dandy if they don't have control of your sword and you just get to come in and take theirs away from them. Oftentimes, though, our opponents have spent time reading the same books we have and will likely be trying to do the same to you, much like we saw in the "hunt the *debole*" drill. As we just talked about, if your opponent finds your sword, one option might be to perform a *sflasare* and go around. Another option is performing a **counter-find**.

A counter-find is simply responding to your opponent's find with one of your own. This is generally done in response to a poorly formed find, but can also just come from turning up the intensity dial when your opponent least expects. You may have both been fighting with a certain level of give and take being expected from both sides. If you suddenly disrupt that rhythm and come in way harder than they're expecting, you can give yourself a little bit of an edge using the element of surprise.

Returning back to the mechanical side of things, there's three ways to perform a counter-find and hopefully regain your opponent's blade. Just like with the ideas of penetration, angulation, and breadth, these correspond directly to each of the first three dimensions of space (we'll get to time later). The first option goes along the z-axis. If someone comes in to find your sword, particularly if they step fairly far in, you can just pull back in order to place the crossing of your two swords closer to their *debole*.

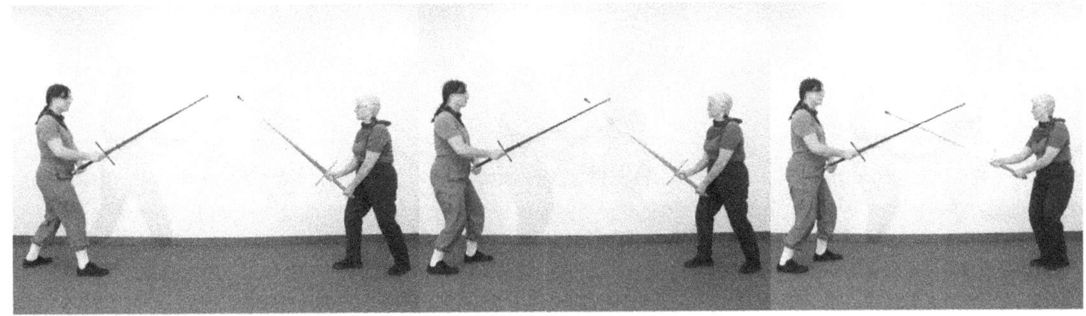

Counterfind along the z-axis

Generally, I recommend doing this either by leaning back of the upper body or a small step back with the front foot. You could theoretically do it by pulling your arms in, but that opens you up in a lot of ways that the other two options don't.

Option number two, just like with affecting angulation from earlier, goes down the y-axis. If your opponent steps in to find your blade, you can respond by raising the tip. This time, instead of moving things closer to their *debole*, you're moving the crossing closer to your *forte*.

Counterfind along the Y-axis

While this may make it harder for you to riposte with a thrust, it does set you up nicely to drop a half cut into their mask. With this option you're going to have to put a little bit more bend in your elbows, but again try not to pull too far back as at that point you're setting your opponent up to easily disengage around.

Finally, with option number three, just like when we were messing with breadth from earlier, we can affect the intersecting of our two swords by changing how they relate along the x-axis. This option requires you to push through more than the other two do, but it also makes it harder for your opponent to disengage in response. All you're doing here is increasing your advantage of crossing. If anything, this means there's now more of your sword to get around as compared to our other two options.

Counterfind along the X-axis

Something to think about is that none of these three options are mutually exclusive. Depending on where exactly your two swords meet the best move might be to use some combination of two or even all three options. Each axis operates independently, so moving along one doesn't prevent you from moving along one of the others at the same time.

Stringere

We talked about the idea of *stringere* a bit in chapter 6 when discussing how to properly execute a thrust. Now that we've laid down a bit more of the theoretical groundwork down, let's revisit the subject to look at it in more depth. There are three components to *stringere*, most of which we've covered already. The first is the idea of **constraint**. The way you constrain someone's blade is by using the three advantages. For the thrust this means having the advantages of crossing, leverage, and the true edge. With a cut it's the advantage of the true edge, leverage, and then crossing.

The next component to *stringere* is that of **invitation**. A sword exists along a straight line and will never be able to close off all of your lines at the same time. As a result, every guard and every action inherently bring some sort of invitation. If I constrain your sword to my inside line by moving to *porta di ferro stretta*, I am inherently inviting you to perform a *sfalsare* and attempt to strike me to my outside line. It can be really easy to get caught up thinking you have complete and utter control over someone's sword. A better way to look at it is that you are safe to move for that one tempo, but that your opponent is likely about to move into wherever you have invited them in the next tempo.

Finally, there's **proportion**, which we just talked about a few pages ago. The way in which you *stringere* your opponent's sword will affect the proportions of how large their follow up move will have to be.[48] Remember that wherever they end up going, you're going to want to have your next move be proportionally smaller than theirs.

The Three Choice Problem

Now, we've already learned nine different cuts that could be done with either edge, at least four different thrusts, and a whole bunch of other moves in between those. This can all be pretty overwhelming, particularly during the din of a fight. The good news is that at any given moment, your choices are actually a lot simpler than you might think. If someone's blade comes to meet yours, there's only three options for you in that moment of the fight. What's even better is that 95% of the time it's only going to come down to two of those.

Option one is to go through. If both of your swords meet and you have the advantage, go forth and stab. Or, as my old kung fu teacher likes to say, "If the way is clear, go forward." Alternatively, your opponent might come to try and find your sword, but does a poor job of it. I see this a lot with fencers who work almost entirely inside of fully cooperative drills. They get really used to it being one person's turn to go and for their partner to never try and stop them. Don't do this. If someone comes in with a bad find, you can just counter-find their sword and push on through.

Option two is to go around. If they have the line and you know that you're not going to be able to go through it, it's time to go around. There's two ways of doing this.

The first, and more popular option is to disengage and get to the other side. This is generally done with some sort of *sfalsare*.

---

⁴⁸ Boorman, 135.

The trick here is to remember not just to move your point to the other side of theirs, but also to use that opportunity to gain yourself some sort of advantage, either by finding their sword or by striking them. If you just change lines without improving your situation, you're just handing your opponent an empty tempo. Also, if they were threatening you and then you went around their sword without then closing off the line, that threat is still there.

The other way to go around is by performing a **yield** where instead of either meeting force with force or performing a *sfalsare*, you instead stay in contact with their blade (at least for the first part) while simultaneously letting their force continue along its original path.

Again, there's a few ways of doing this. One option would be yield without changing lines. This is generally done when your opponent puts a lot of pressure on your blade and instead of pushing against it with your true edge, you yield to that greater force by turning into a *punta dritta* or a *punta roversa*. Particularly with the *punta dritta* it can be helpful to take your off hand from your pommel and use it to sandwich their blade into yours while you also thrust. Be warned that this is something you need to be fairly close to your opponent in order to pull off.

Another way for you to yield is to go around their sword. Again, this is done when they press strongly into your blade and you then use that over-commitment to your advantage. Typically, this is done either via *stramazonne* or *molinetto*. With either one of these, you'll also like have the opportunity to make a *presa* and do something like push their blade out of the way with your hand or to wrap your off arm around their arms or grab one of their arms with your hand, clearing the way for you to do whatever you want with your sword.

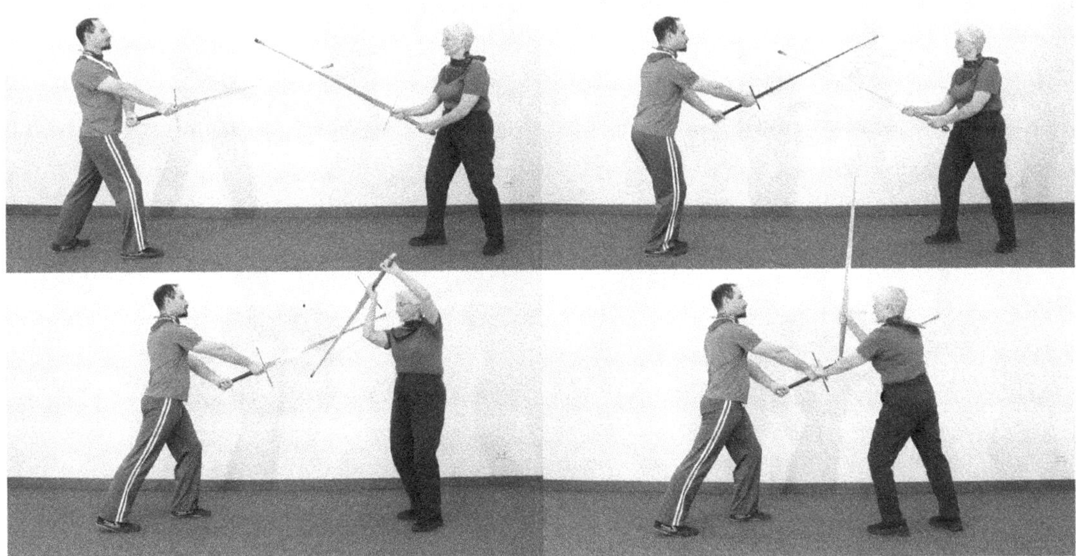

Yielding into a *molinetto* leading to a *presa*

Option number three is to stand there and do nothing. This generally happens when one person freezes and is thus something you have to drill against, lest you run your face into a sword that you could have sworn was supposed to be somewhere else. However, it is also something you can use to your advantage. The Anonimo Bolognese, for instance, is quite fond of telling us to just stand there and ignore any bad feints our opponent throws our way. There are times to use that opportunity to seize the tempo, but sometimes doing nothing is just the best course of action. It's also a great way to freak out an opponent who always expects you to move every time they do, allowing you to hit them off-rhythm.

Half-Swording

As a note, I'm using the modern English terminology here. This is derived from the German tradition's *halbsbschwert*, but it's become so standardized across the historical fencing world that I thought it would be easier not to swim against the current just this one time. The Bolognese masters use a couple different terms for this kind of action, with the one I am most fond of being *spada in armi* (sword as in armor), which is derived from how you use a longsword when both of you are in armor. The term *mezza spada* while literally translating to "half sword" would be better understood as a meeting of the swords at the middles of the blade.

All half-swording (*spada in armi*) means is that you take your nondominant hand off of your pommel and use it instead to grasp the blade of your own sword. This is an action we see pop up a lot in the Anonimo's longsword section, using it to set up a strike your opponent's blade away with either the quillons of your sword or the lugs on your blade.[49]

49 Anonimo Bolognese,
   198, play #462.

Covered vs Uncovered Attacks

These are less specific blade actions and more a way to contextualize what it is you're doing with your sword. A **covered attack** is just any kind of strike that ends with your sword in between your sword and theirs. This might mean finding their sword, gaining, and then proceeding to strike them with a *stocatta*. It could also mean throwing a *sgualimbratto* and then compassing out, all while you keep your guard up, preventing their sword from hitting you in a single tempo.

An **uncovered attack** is just the opposite. If they thrust at you in *guardia di faccia* and you respond by beating their sword with a *falso manco* and then striking them with a *mezzo mandritto*, that would be an uncovered attack as the thing that is keeping you safe in that moment isn't your sword physically blocking theirs out. This doesn't mean that uncovered attacks are inherently a bad plan, but they do come with an inherent risk that covered attacks don't. You're relying on the size of your opponent's action, footwork, and/or your ability to beat their blade in order to keep you safe. If you know your opponent's blade mechanics far surpass your own, you might use an uncovered attack in order to avoid having to bind with them. That said, the difference between the two largely comes down to what's available at any given moment in time.

Double Cuts

These are a great way of not only fitting more attacks into the same space, but also changing the kind of cut you're doing without having to change the line. Start in *guardia di croce* and begin by throwing a false edged *mandritto sgualimbratto*, then, as your sword is still moving down, perform a *stramazonne* and finish with a true edge *mandritto sgualimbratto*.[50] Try the same thing from *guardia di intrare* but this time with *roversi* and a *molinetto*. If you want, you can also try these starting from *guardia alta*.

Once you've figured out how to do it cutting downward, try doing the same thing but by cutting upward. Start in *coda lunga e larga*, cut a *falso dritto*, perform a *molinetto* and finish with a true edged *mandritto ridoppio* ending in *guardia di intrare*. After that try starting in *porta di ferro larga*, cut a *falso manco*, perform a *stramazonne*, and finish with a true edged *roverso ridoppio*, ending in *guardia di croce*.

Double cuts

On top of teaching you how else you might be able to move from guard to guard as well as how to change up your attack mid-movement, there's one other major thing it gives us. It's deceptively easy to view both the *stramazonne* and *molinetto* as actions that only occur as a part of descending cuts. Really, though, they're both just ways of getting around someone's sword, regardless of which direction your sword is coming from.

Punta Infalsata

This blow is one of the more hotly debated techniques these days. The way I think about it is as a trajectory, as opposed to thinking of it purely as a thrust or a cut. The *punta infalsata* is a descending blow where the false edge leads. Think about striking down from either *guardia di intrare* or *guardia di croce*. Sometimes it ends up being a descending *falso*, whereas other times it's just an imbrocatta.

Cutting/Thrusting Patterns

Rarely will you be asked to only throw cuts or only throw thrusts. Lots of people can get caught in the trap of thinking of the longsword as purely a cutting weapon, but seeing as the point is at the very end of the sword it inherently has more reach. So not only should you mix up what kind of blow you're throwing more generally, but it's also really fun when you do so in a way that catches your opponent off guard. To help you with that, here's a few examples of solo patterns involving both cuts and thrusts. While I could have included this at the end of the chapter on thrusts, I decided that it would be a bit difficult to explain how to get from any one position to another without going through all of the blade actions first.

1. • *Stocatta* to *roverso ridoppio* *(mezza volta)*.
   • *Stocatta* to *mandritto ridoppio* *(tutta volta)*.
   • *Stocatta* to *roverso fendente*.
   • *Stocatta, tutta volta* around the head, *mandritto imbrocatta*.
   • *Stocatta, tutta volta* around the head, *mezzo mandritto fendente, mezza volta* into a *roverso*
   • *fendente*.

2. • *Stocatta, mandritto ridoppio, mandritto sgualimbratto. Stocatta, roverso*
   • *ridoppio, roverso sgualimbratto.*
   • *Mandritto imbrocatta, mandritto sgualimbratto, mandritto ridoppio. Roverso imbrocatta, roverso.*
   • *sgualimbratto, roverso ridoppio.*
   • *Mandritto sgaulimbratto, mandritto ridoppio, stocatta. Roverso sgualimbratto, roverso*
   • *ridoppio, stocatta.*
   • *Mandritto ridoppio, mandritto sgualimbratto, mandritto imbrocatta. Roverso ridoppio, roverso*
   • *sgualimbratto, roverso imbrocatta.*

3. • *Punta dritta, mandritto tondo. Punta roversa, roverso tondo.*
   • *Punta dritta, roverso tondo. Punta roversa, mandritto tondo.*
   • *Start in porta di ferro larga. Cut a roverso tondo* (falso), *roverso tondo* (true edge), *mandritto imbrocatta.*
   • Start in *coda lunga e larga. Mandritto tondo, mandritto tondo, roversa imbrocatta.*
   • Start in *porta di ferro larga.* Cut *roverso tondo* (falso) to beat, *roverso tondo* (true edge), *punta dritta.*
   • Start in *coda lunga e larga. Mandritto tondo, mandritto tondo* to miss, *punta roversa.*
   • Start in *porta di ferro larga.* Feint *punta roversa,* feint *roverso tondo, mandritto sgualimbratto.*
   • Start in *coda lunga e larga.* Feint *punta dritta,* feint *mandritto tondo, roverso sgualimbratto.*
   • *Start in porta di ferro larga.* Feint *punta roversa,* inside yield, *mezzo mandritto tondo, roverso sgualimbratto*
   • Start in *coda lunga e larga. Pundta dritta,* outside yield, *mezza roverso tondo, mandritto sgualimbratto.*

9: The Shitty Parry Drill

This is a drill I created a while back that helps illustrate a few of the major concepts we covered in the last chapter. As well, it's a particularly helpful drill in order to help students make that jump from being intermediate to being advanced fencers. I'm certain other people have created this drill on their own using their own descriptions, but this is what I personally have found works to communicate these ideas to a fair number of fencers.

To begin, in drilling we often practice as if both fencers are making ideal choices at every turn. One person might do one thing and if the other person executes a certain technique the proper way, the first person has to change and do something else. Quite often, though, even the top end fencers are less than perfect. This drill helps folks to identify when that is happening and what they can do to exploit it.

Walking in, both fencers should have a good idea of how to find an opponent's sword, proceed to gain their blade, and execute a proper strike. None of this has to be perfect, but if that foundation isn't there, this drill won't be of any use. We should always strive to build off of a fundamental conception of proper mechanics before we move on to anything fancier.

So, here's the drill itself:

STEP ❶ - Fencer A finds their opponent's sword, steps in, leans forward to gain their blade, and then steps forward to strike.

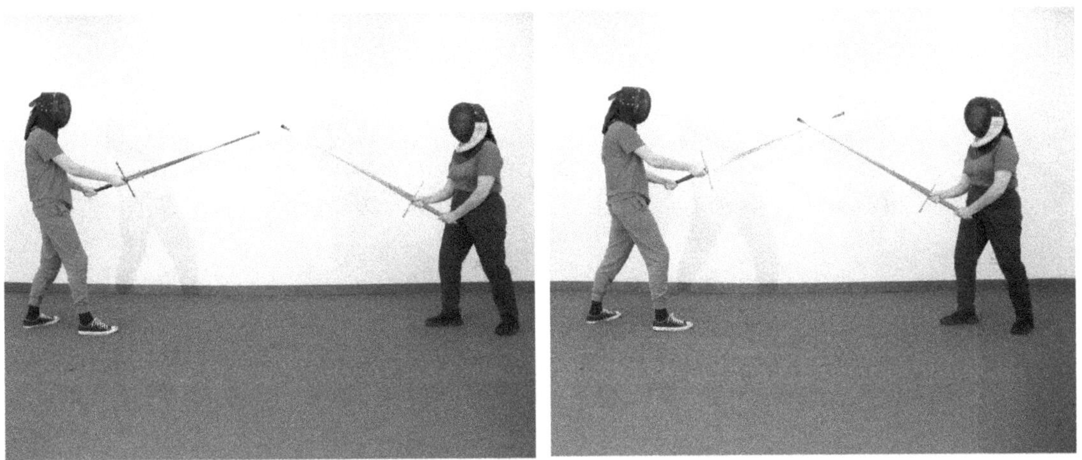

STEP ❷ - Fencer B, upon being attacked, moves to parry.

STEP ② - OPTION A: If Fencer B performed a good and proper parry, Fencer A disengages and strikes to the other side.

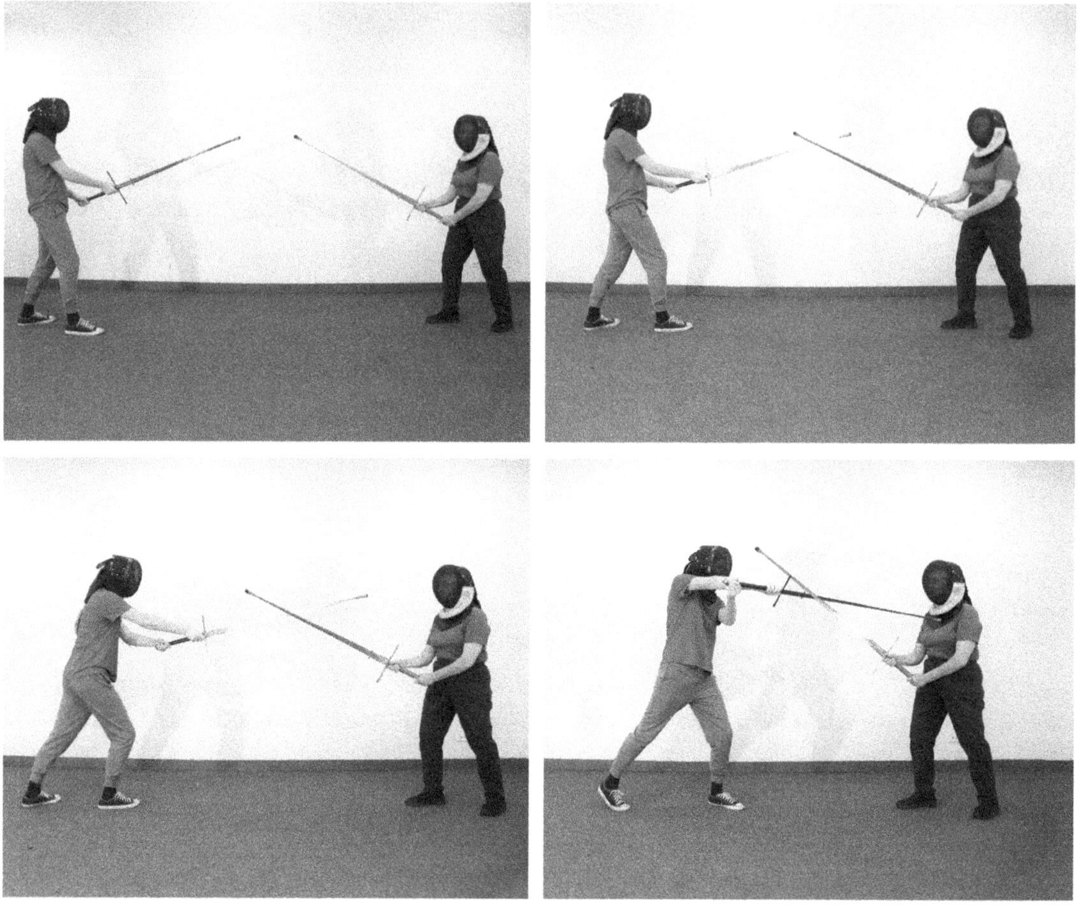

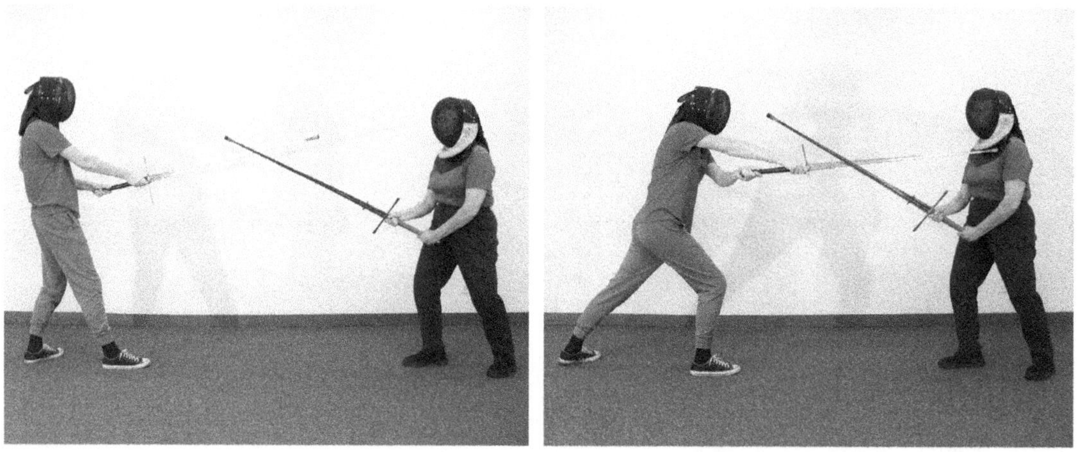

STEP ② - OPTION B: Alternatively, if Fencer B performed a shitty parry, Fencer A should push on through and strike along their initial line without disengaging.

Here's another version for you focusing on approaching with a cut.

STEP 1 - This time, start a little closer and instead of going "find, gain, strike" have Fencer A come in with a *mandritto fendente* to Fencer B's head.

STEP 2 - **OPTION A**: If Fencer B parries poorly, they get bonked on the head.[51]

STEP 2 - **OPTION B**: If Fencer B parries well, Fencer A should perform either a *sfalsare* over the top or a yield of some sort, depending on how close the two fencers end up being.

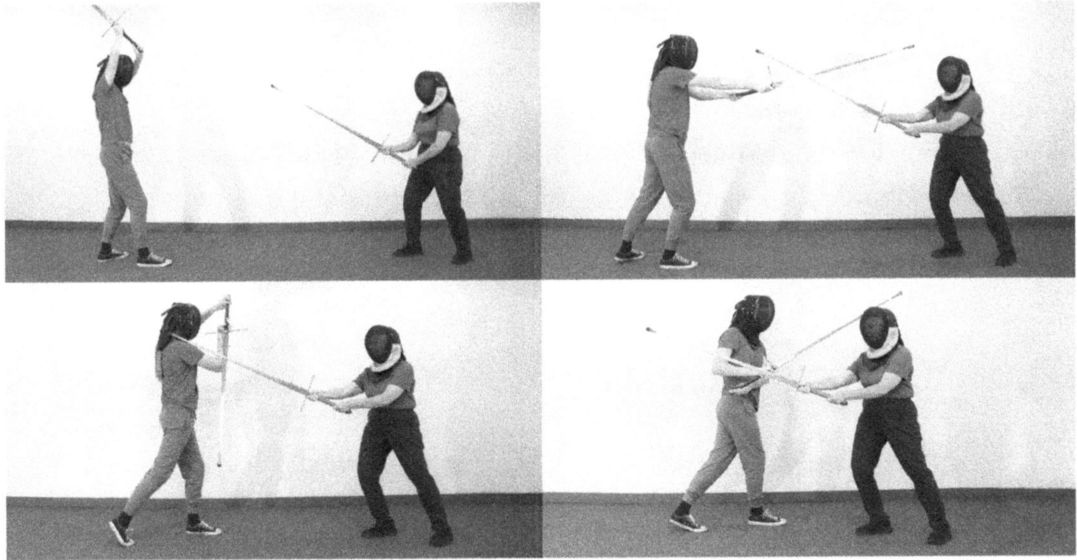

[51] Alternatively, I'll often do this with the cut aimed at the gorget as that's where I'm more armored and am happier to receive a stiff shot. That said, if your gorget doesn't cover your collarbone, then this won't help much.

Once you've done it one way with both partners getting a chance to attack, try doing it again, but this time with a *roverso fendente* instead.

How do you know if it's a proper parry or a shitty one? Simple. Did you get hit? As long as Fencer A throws a committed attack and doesn't do anything fancy like try and yield their blade, their attack should go straight through any shitty parry. If Fencer B performs their parry correctly, Fencer A's lunge should end up off-target, resulting in Fencer B standing there untouched.

The overarching point here is to teach Fencer A that just because their blade has been acted upon, doesn't mean their opponent now has the advantage. Sometimes in a fight people make the wrong move. More often, they go to make the right move but execute it poorly. So if you have control of a line and your opponent fails to regain control or threaten a different line, you have no reason why you shouldn't continue along your original plan as the line is still yours.

The point in a student's learning I typically introduce this drill is when they start to develop good mechanics, but don't yet trust them. Sometimes this manifests as students coming in, but then backing out before they have the chance to strike. Other times it's when they come in but consistently throw their shots short of the target. Alternatively, the fighter might consciously know they have the ability to control their opponent's blade, but are worried that it's going to slip out somehow, but they're just not sure how or when. What this drill does is get that feeling of "Now you have their sword. Go!" into someone's bones, giving them a tactile sense of when they do and don't have the line secured.

Hopefully this helps you and those around you get a better understanding of when the right time to strike is, as well as works as a way to help make that transition from mid to high- level fighter all just a tad bit smoother.

Once you have the fundamental drill down, here are a few dials you can play with to help folks get an even deeper understanding of the subject.

So far, we have given two options to Fencer B. Either parry well, or parry poorly. To mix things up a bit, feel free to add in a third option of not parrying at all. You'd be surprised how often people will just stand there, frozen in place, after you make your initial move. For Fencer A the response here should be the same as with the shitty parry; just stab them down the line you're already on. Even though mechanically an opponent doing nothing is the simplest thing to deal with, psychologically it's often the hardest. We're so hardwired to think that after every time we move a piece on the board our opponent is going to do the same, so it throws people for a loop when their opponent just does nothing. Thankfully this is a scenario we can train for by just adding it in as an option to all of our choice-based drills once students have figured out the initial version.

The second thing you can play with is when Fencer B performs their parry. Remember that Fencer A's attack comes to us in three parts: the find, the gain, and the strike. This means that there's three different points in time when Fencer B can decide to act (or not).

OPTION 1 - Fencer B can move to parry the instant their sword is covered.

OPTION 2 - Fencer B can move as their opponent is leaning in and taking control of their blade.

We often conceptualize this all being one continuous motion, but you'd be surprised by how much changing when you parry can affect things. People are generally used to their opponents moving to parry at only one part of the process, so changing when you act can really make a sizable difference.

Finally, remember that this can be applied to any strike that goes down straight down a line and isn't limited to one-handed swords. Whether it's a thrust from a spear, a cut from a longsword, or a punch from a closed fist, the drill will remain essentially the same. So, if you have a student studying multiple styles, feel free to run it through with them using a wide variety of tools.

Feel free to take this drill and make it your own. I look forward to seeing what all this can bring you.

10: Footwork

The thing to remember here is that if your footwork is perfect, you get to win every fight. I know a few fencers who don't have a particularly high-level understanding of blade mechanics, but no one can touch them because they know how to be in the right place at the right time. More traditional fencing schools, and martial arts schools more broadly, will often spend the first year or two focusing exclusively on footwork. I like to get a sword into people's hands as fast as possible as I figure that's what brought them in the door in the first place, but more footwork is always a good thing.

Out of everything there is to cover in regard to footwork, there's two specific themes that really stand out to me. The first of course, is distance, or as fencers often refer to it, **measure**.[52] The thing to ask yourself about measure is at any given point can your opponent hit you and can you hit your opponent.[53] I put the two of those in that order for a very specific reason. In a real swordfight with sharp blades, just hitting your opponent doesn't get you very far. Your goal is to get in and out while incurring the least amount of damage possible. If you landed that sweet shot, but one of your lungs now has air coming out of it through a different hole, you're going to have a bad time. It might not be much time, but it's not going to be good.

So, when you walk into a fight, the first thing I want you to size up is your **defensive measure**. This is defined by where your front foot is (and to a lesser degree where your head and arms are). Think of it as the border between your space and your opponent's. You and your opponent are inherently going to have different measures. This is affected by height, wingspan, flexibility, and how big your swords are. After you put this book down for a bit and go on your afternoon stroll, try figuring out at what point could anyone who passes you by reach out and touch you with a single action. If you get really good at this, you'll find that you now have the fun power move of being able to walk up to an opponent and tell them how tall they

---

[52] Dall'Agocchie, 15.

[53] Measure, or "misura" in Italian is a concept that the Bolognese masters clearly understood, they just don't spend much time talking about it in detail and don't really use the word as a technical term. It isn't until the later rapier authors that we really get a lot of ink spilled explaining the idea of measure.

are and how long their blade is. If you get really good at this, you can also tell them their inseam.

Next is your **offensive measure**. If your main attack is a lunge, then this is defined based on where your back foot is. If you prefer to attack with a pass, then it's set by your front foot. Overall, your offensive measure is just how far you can reach in a single tempo. The other factors that go into this are how long your limbs are, how flexible you are, and how long your sword is. As a sneaky little trick I've used on occasion, while my opponent and I are both moving around during the fight, I'll gather my back foot up to my front foot and suddenly add a foot or two to my offensive measure. Be warned though that by narrowing your base, it's going to be harder for you to react defensively if your opponent throws something unexpected and it'll be easier for them to push you off balance.

To try and hone your sense of your offensive measure, try the same exercise from before, but instead ask yourself if you could reach the other person.[54] If you want to test this a little bit more, try it but with inanimate objects. I used to do this at parties when I would get bored where I'd pick something like a table leg and see if I could reach it just by extending my arm, using my arm and leaning forward, etc. How well my perception of what my reach was lined up with reality also served as a nice little test of how drunk I was. The issue, though, is that the better you get at it, the less helpful of a test it becomes.

If you want to try doing this drill a little bit more seriously, pick a spot in your apartment and try reaching out to see if you can touch it, all while attacking in proper order. Once you have that down, try walking around a little bit and then firing so that you aren't shooting from the same distance every time. If you want to take it up another notch, try having something randomly cue when you fire. This could be a bass line in a song, or even throwing something metal into your washing machine along with your laundry and firing every time you hear it clang.

The next thing to think about with footwork is **balance**. At any given time during a fight, you should only be moving one foot at a time.[55] In order to move that foot, you're going to first need to take all the weight off of it. So much of whether I advance my front foot forward or pass with my back foot at any given point is defined based off of where my balance is at that given moment. If you find you prefer one footwork option over the other, make sure you're shifting your weight to the right place in order to make that happen.

[54] Please do not just pop out and start trying to touch random passersby on the street.
[55] Every once in a while it might be helpful to jump back with both feet, but generally speaking having both feet in the air is going to leave you incredibly vulnerable.

The other place balance shows up a lot is right after your attack misses. Throwing yourself all the way out there can definitely help to extend your reach, but if you can't recover quickly from that position, you've just made yourself a sitting duck. You can extend how far you can step with training and some folks have incredibly deep lunges that they can recover from with absurd speed, but that's something they've specifically drilled thousands of times. If you get stuck off balance, there isn't a ton you can do in that moment to give yourself any sort of advantage over your opponent as you're mostly just going to be trying to stand back upright. This matters even more if you're fighting on slippery surfaces (recently waxed floors, wet grass, etc.). Not only do you want to avoid pulling a groin muscle and having to sit on the bench for the next couple months, but falling on your ass is just not that helpful of a tactic. I've done it more times than I would have liked and knowing how to fall properly can definitely help cushion the blow, but falling down because you were off balance is certainly not going to win you any fights.

Okay, one more thing before we dive into the specific footwork actions. BEND YOUR KNEES. This is one of the most common things I end up saying to students. Think of your legs as a set of springs. In order for those springs to launch, they need to be loaded up a bit. If you stand there with your knees straight, they're going to have to unlock before you can move anywhere. You don't need to have the world's deepest stance, I know I don't, but if you don't bend your knees you're handing your opponent some free time for them to do whatever they please before you have a chance to act.

Footwork Actions

As a heads up, there's going to be a bunch of these. The good news is that a lot of them should seem fairly familiar. Mostly we're just giving specific names to things you're likely already doing so we can talk about them more easily.

Gather

There are three different gathering steps. The first is what I refer to as "gathering together." This is just bringing your two feet together. This could be the front foot pulling back or the back foot coming up to meet the front one. The great thing about this is that it means you can go anywhere. You could step to the side, go backward, go forward, any which way you like. As a note, make sure you stay level as you do this. If you bob up and down every time you gather your feet, it's going to make it a whole lot easier for your opponent to see what's coming. We generally see this used to help support either a parry or to help you prep a blow. I could, for instance, parry their *mandritto fendente* by going into *guardia di faccia* while gathering my feet together.

Alternatively, I could use the gather together to help me beat their blade away with a *falso manco* from *guardia porta di ferro larga* in order to then step again and strike with a *mezzo mandritto*.

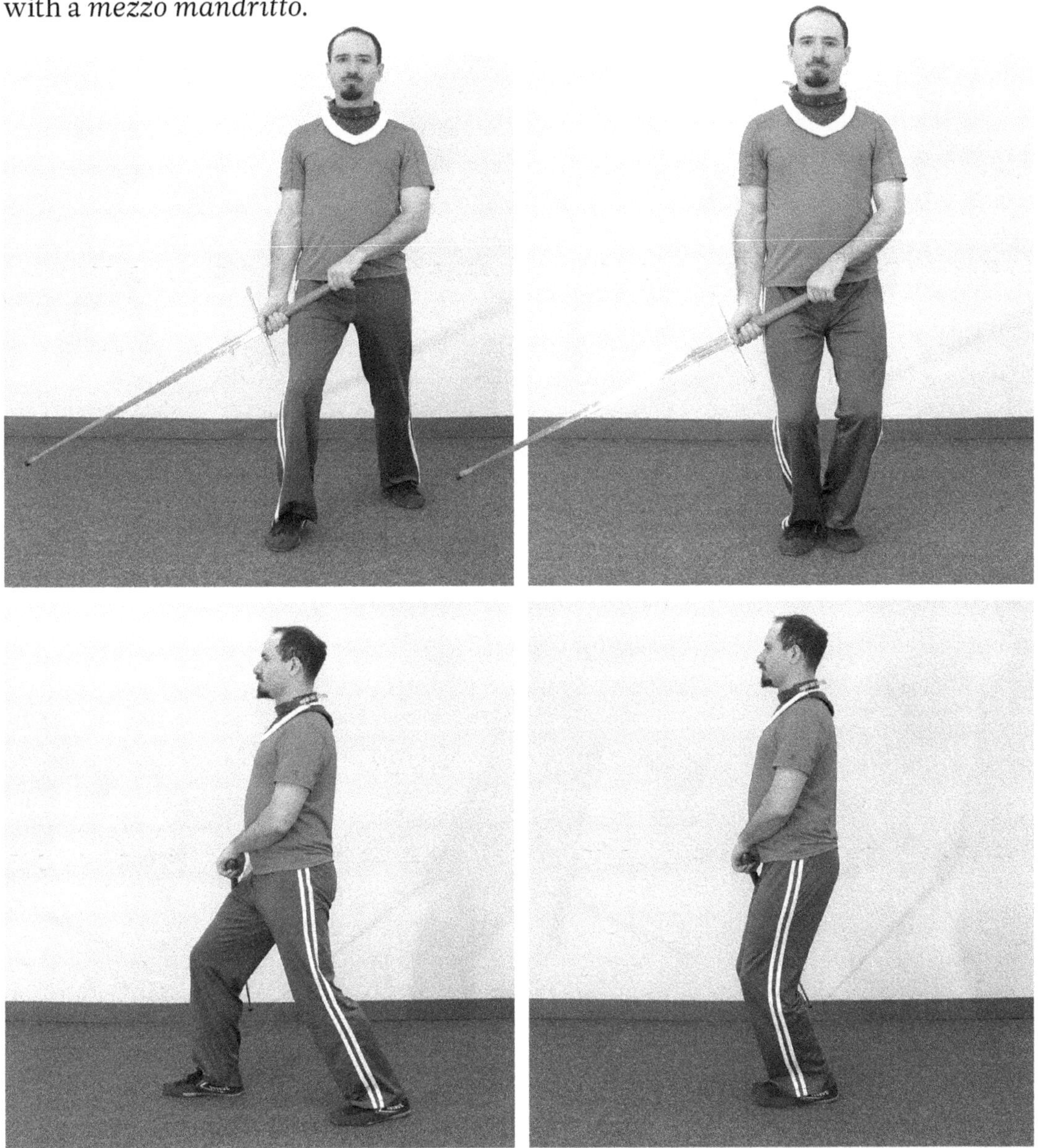

Gathering together

The second option is to "gather forward.". For this you just start with your two feet apart. From there you bring your back foot up to meet your front foot and then, as we just saw in the last example, step forward with what started out as your front foot. This affords us the opportunity to get a read on the situation as our feet come together before committing too hard to stepping in to our opponent's measure with the front foot.

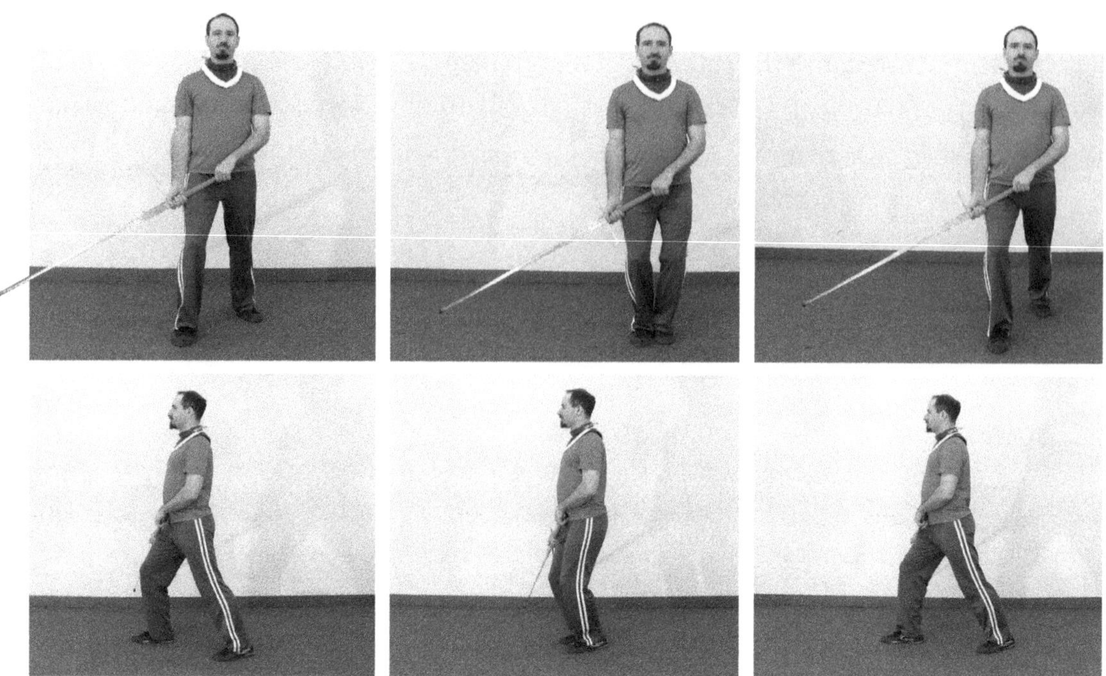

Gathering forward

Finally, we can "gather backward.". This is the same thing we just did, but in reverse. Here you gather your front foot back and then step back with your back foot. This technique works particularly well against leg cuts as it prioritizes getting that front leg away from danger instead of forcing it to wait for your back leg to finish up.

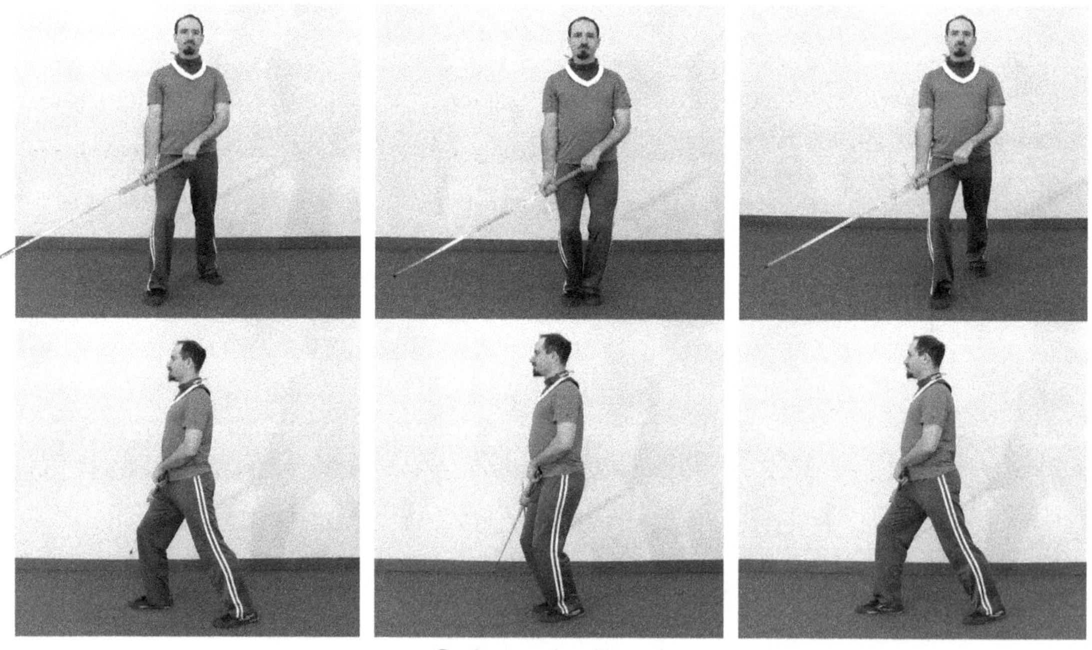

Gathering backward

Pass

This is perhaps the most common footwork action we see throughout the system. All it means is that you take one foot and step it in front of or behind the other one. While you could perform this by just swinging your leg all the way around, I generally advise bringing your foot along a C-curve, almost as if you're gathering forward or back. Your foot doesn't necessarily need to touch down in the middle, but this way it's easier for you to change your mind along the way and also makes it harder for your opponent to swoop in with a single leg takedown.

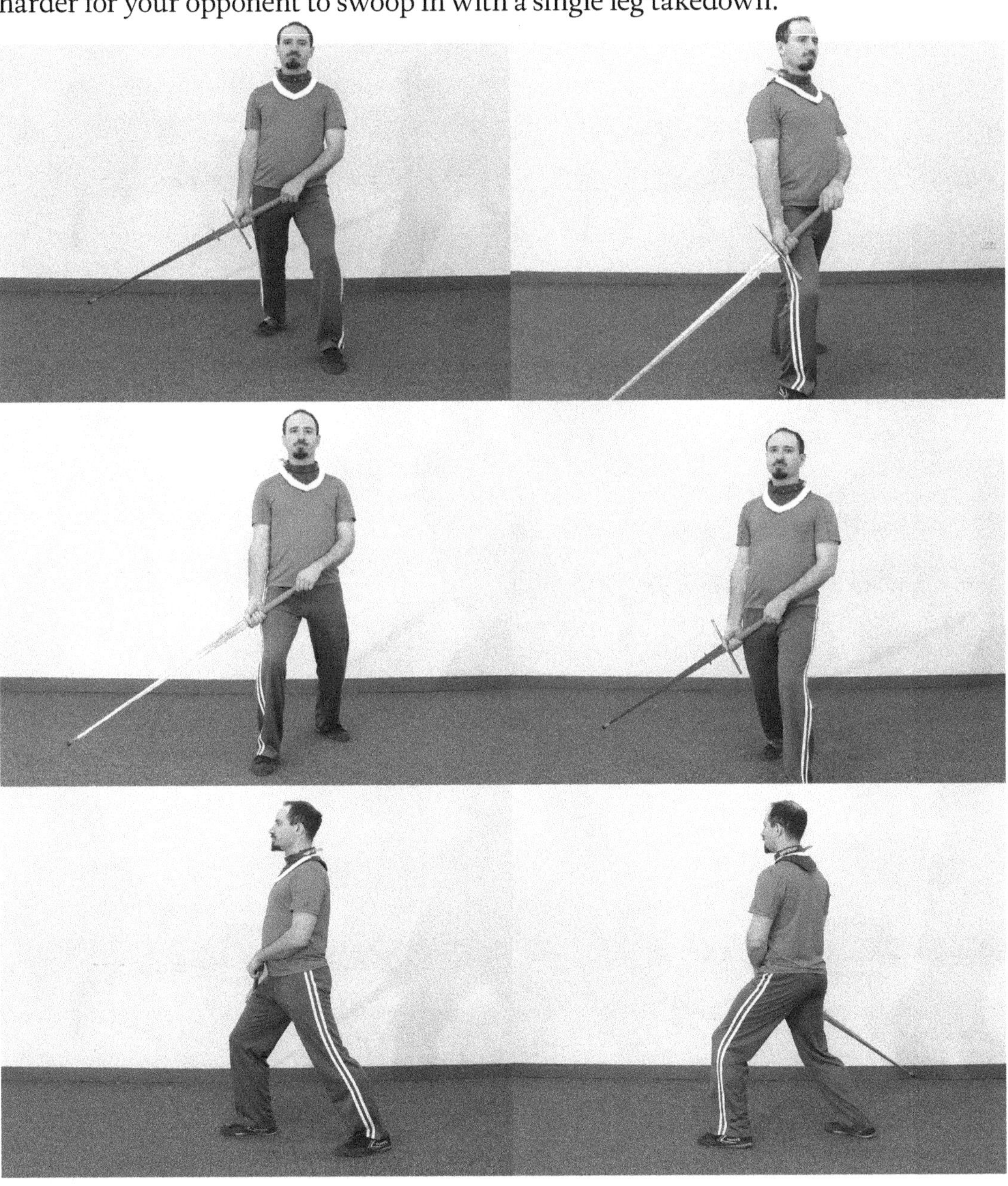

Passing step

Advance

This serves as an alternative to the gather. To go forward, instead of starting with your back foot, this time start by moving your front foot forward and then having the back foot step forward once the first foot has landed.[56] This isn't a technique that's given a specific technical name in the original sources, but we see it performed nonetheless. As such I've gone with the modern phrase of "advance," but other instructors might describe it in different terms.

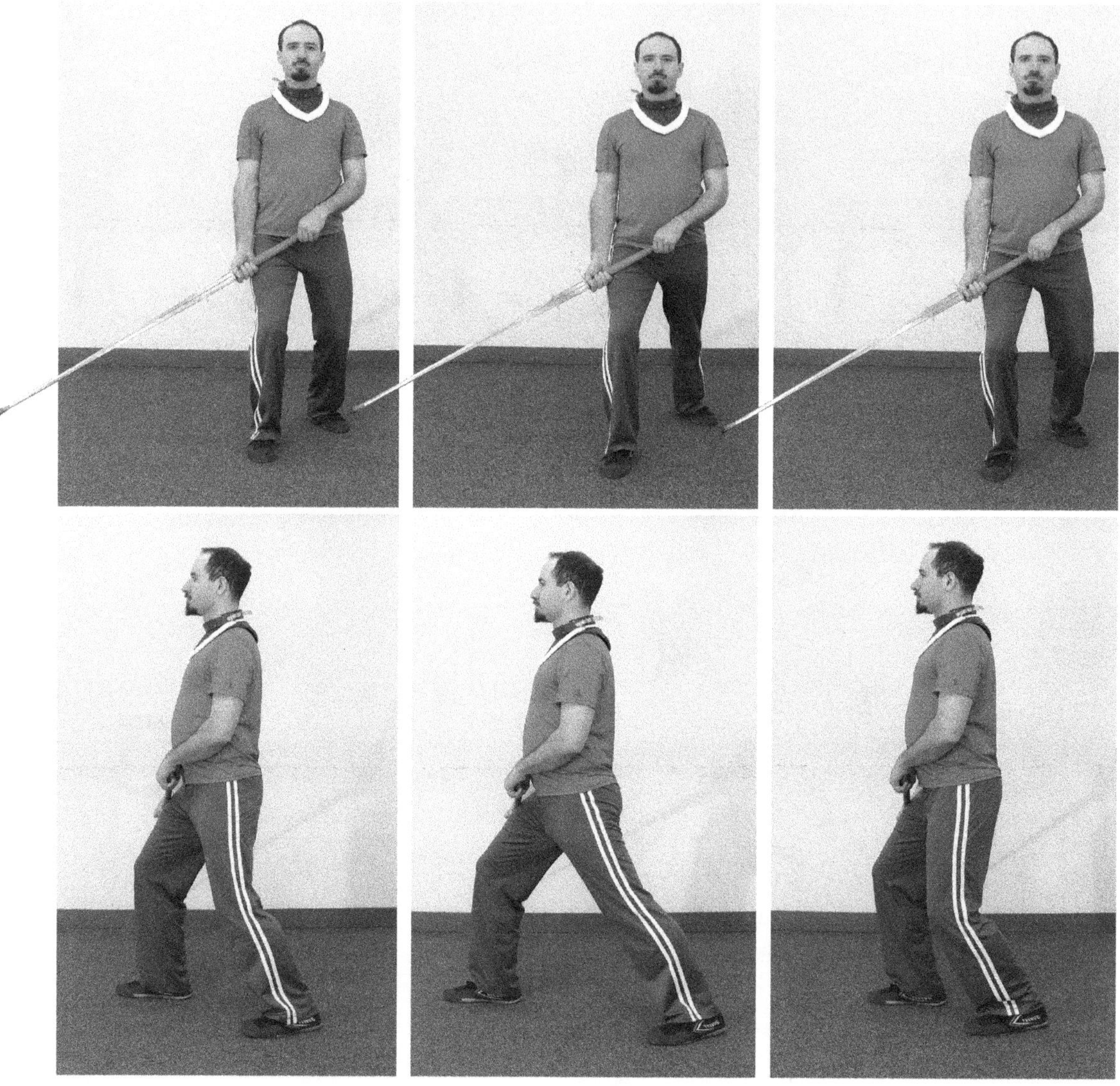

Advance

56 Dall'Agocchie, 12.

Retreat

This is just the backward facing corollary to the advance. To perform this, just move your back foot back and then have the front foot follow.

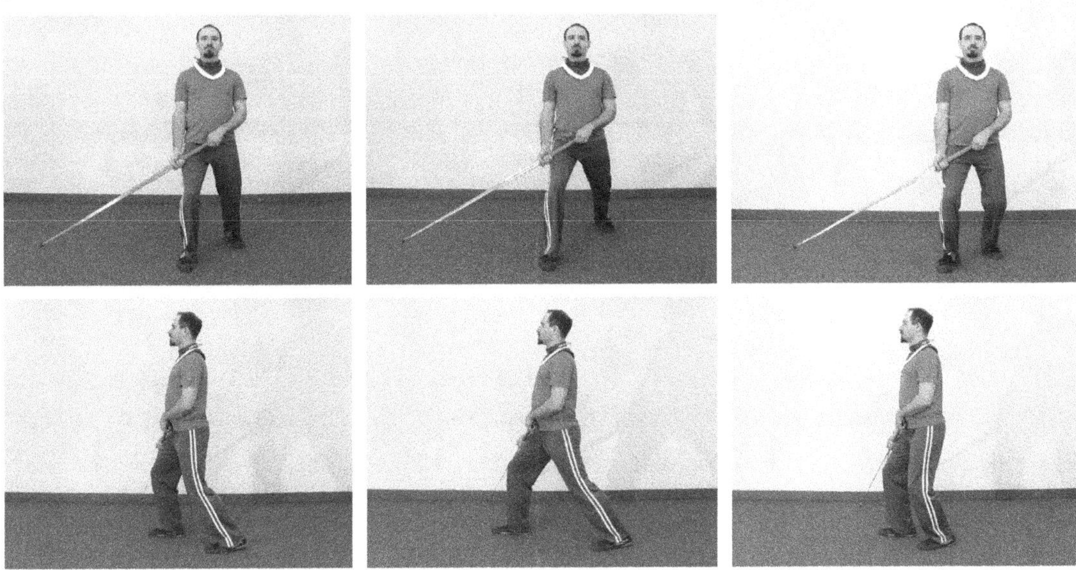

Retreat

Lunge

We talked about this a bit earlier in more general terms. More specifically it's just an advancement of the front foot without the back foot following.[57] Generally, this is accompanied by a recovery of the front foot back to its original position.

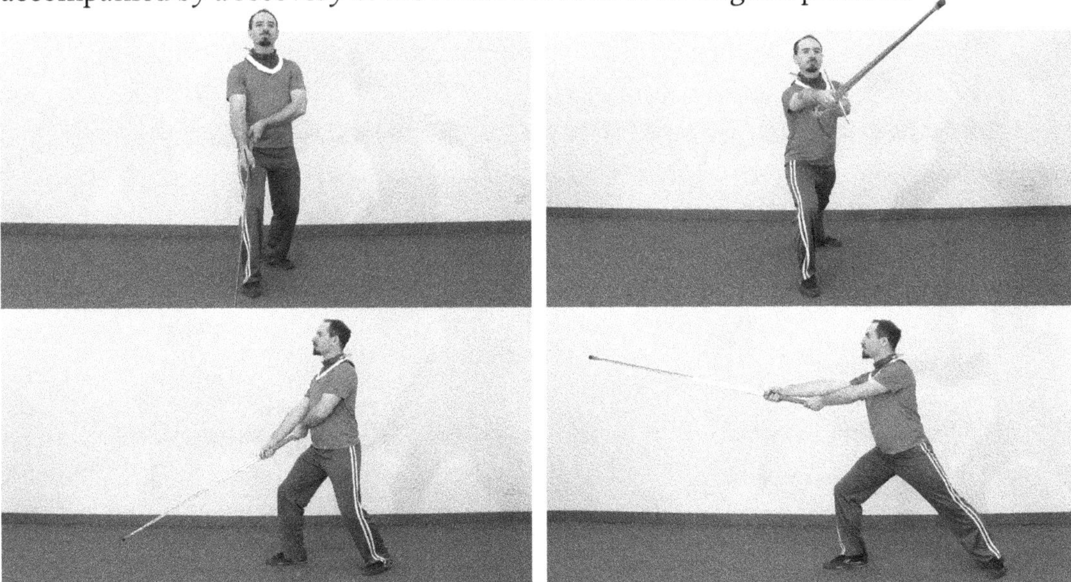

Lunge

[57] Both Fiore in the beginning of the 15th century and Capoferro in the beginning of the 17th both use the exact same word *"accrescimento"*, here. So if anyone ever gives you grief for lunging with a longsword, ask them to suit up and then lunge away.

Triangle Step

For this one, imagine that your feet are positioned on two points of a triangle. So, if your right foot is in front then that foot would be at one corner of the base of the triangle while your left foot is at the top. Now just move your left foot to the other point on the triangle and once it's landed have your right foot move to the empty point at the top. After that, try it the other way. The triangle step is a great way to incorporate angled attacks into your game as well as help you point your hips across your opponent's sword, giving you a stronger structure and helping you with the advantage of crossing.

Triangle step

Replacement Step

This is essentially just a cross between a gather and a triangle step. This can be done either with your front foot gathering to meet your back foot or the other way around. All you do is just step one foot so that it meets the other and then send the other foot to its corresponding point on the triangle. So, if you bring your right foot back to meet your left, your left foot would now step forward and to the left. Alternatively, you could bring your left foot up to meet your right and then take your right foot and step it back and to the right. Replacement steps are a great tool to use while performing feints as they let you change how you're set up without your front foot having to move any closer toward your enemy.

Replacement step

Compass Step

This is generally done not as an initial action, but as a way to help you get out cleanly after either you finished your attack or in response to your opponent barreling toward you. To do this, you're going to take one foot and use it to draw a semicircle on the ground. Try doing this with both your front foot as well as your back one. The important thing here is that you should end up still facing your opponent, even if they're no longer facing you.

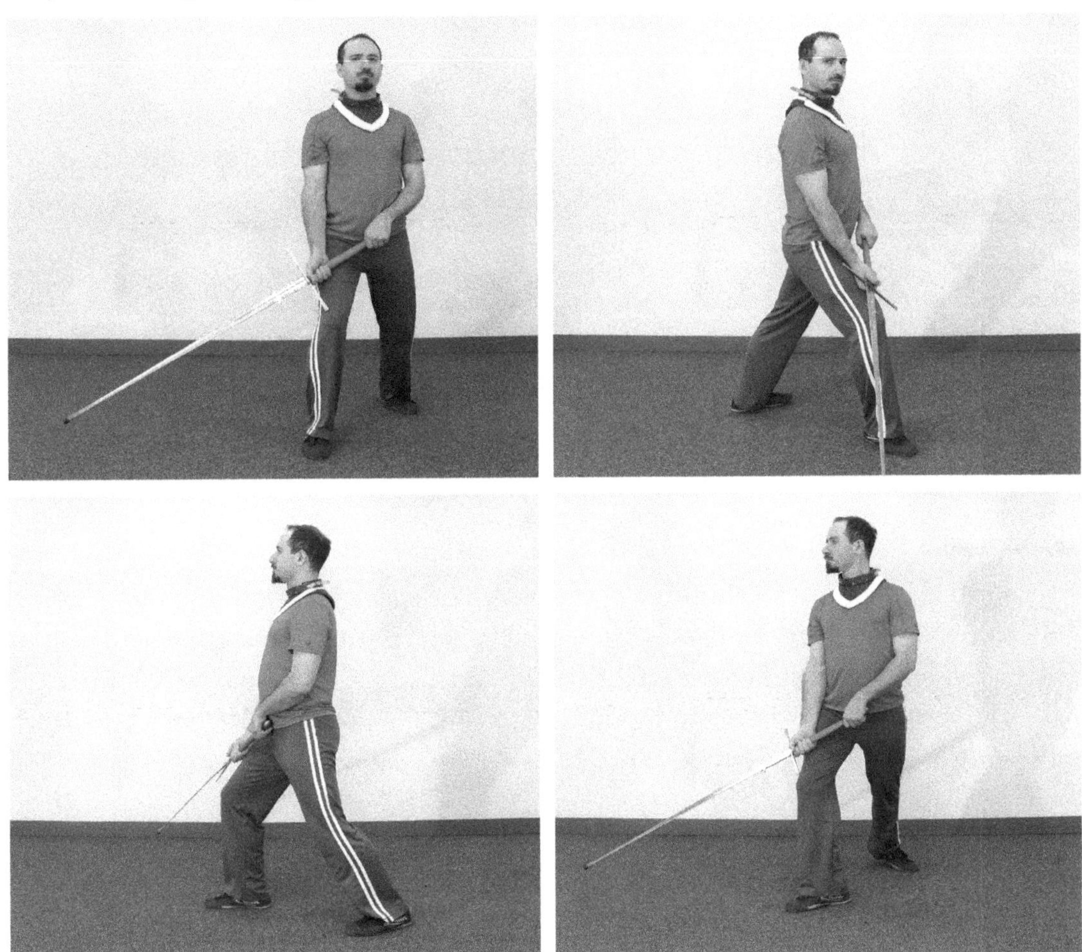

Compass step

The Three Turns of The Feet

In the same way as we had the three turns of the sword, we can look at footwork in much the same fashion.[58]

---

[58] The three turns of the feet are actually from Fiore as opposed to the Bolognese authors, but I've had multiple teachers use them in their Bolognese classes and I find them useful for my own practice as well. That said, if your aim is to be a Bolognese purist, then feel free to skip this part.

Volta Stabile (stable turn)

This is done by lifting your heels and then pivoting on the balls of your feet without lifting them off of the ground. Lots of the time we just need to make small adjustments in direction but that don't necessarily require us making a full step. The important thing to remember here is to turn one foot at a time. If you try and do both at once, you won't have the structure to receive any incoming blows and your opponent is going to be able to knock you off balance.

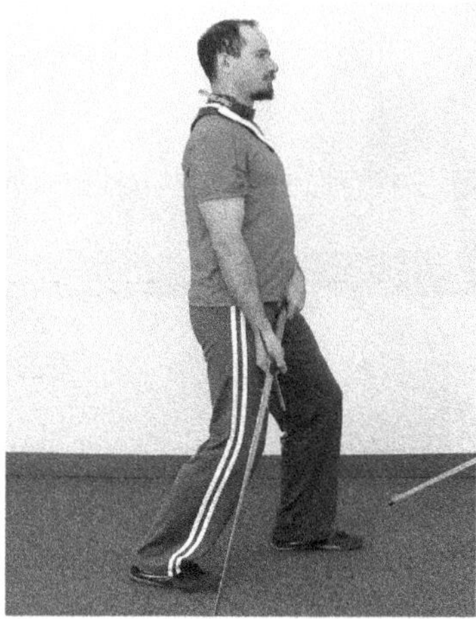

Volta stabile

Mezza Volta (half turn)

This is just another way of thinking of the passing step we mentioned earlier. The only real difference is that a pass is often used to describe a linear step, whereas a *mezza volta* comes in at more of an angle. Mostly, though, it can just be helpful to have a larger schema to attach our ideas on to instead of just memorizing a bunch of independent moves.

Mezza volta

Tutta Volta (full turn)

There are two things that really define the *tutta volta*. The first is that it involves a crossing and uncrossing of the legs. The second is that it ends with you turning almost 180 degrees. This is generally used as a way to power a large throw, but can also be helpful when taking on multiple opponents.

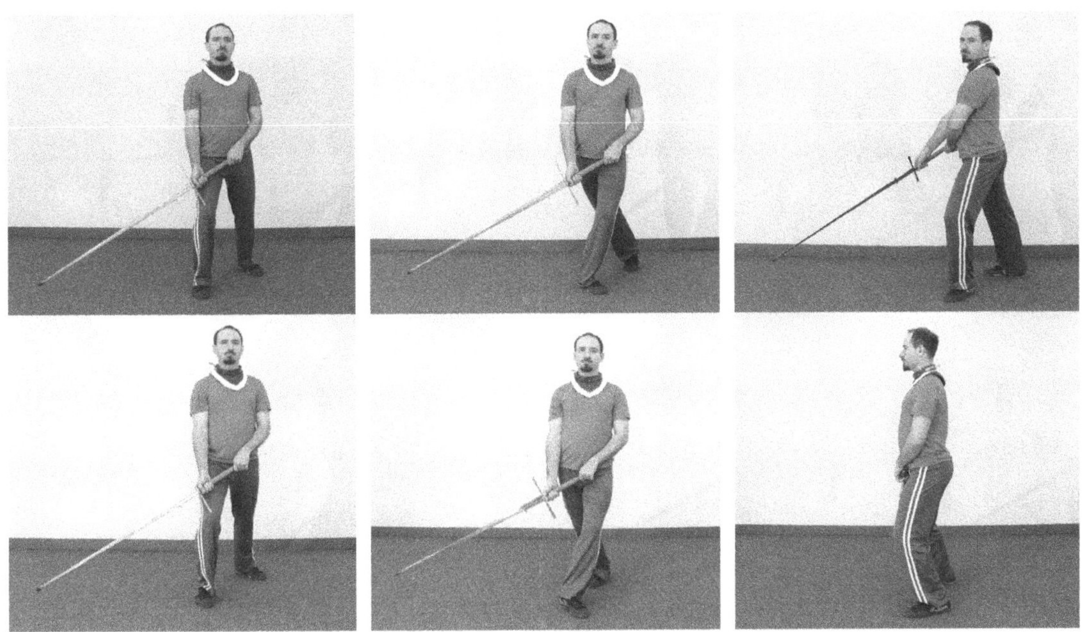

Tutt*a Volta*

Concordant Action/Guard

A concordant action is any action of the sword (cut, thrust, parry, etc.) that's in agreement with the action of your foot. That alone can be a bit of a confusing concept, but all it boils down to is that your leg and your arm are getting along and the way you're moving feels natural. Concordant actions are likely what you're doing already. For instance, if I'm right-handed and I want to throw a *mandritto*, in order for it to be concordant I would need to step forward with my right foot. Alternatively, if you wanted to throw a concordant *mandritto* as you retreated, you would throw the cut while passing back with the left foot. Conversely, if I'm a righty and want to throw a *roverso*, I would want to step forward with my left foot. Then, if you wanted to throw a concordant *roverso* while retreating, you would perform it with a pass back of the right foot. We can also use this to describe how we form our guards. In any of the *coda lunga* guards, in order for them to be concordant, we would want to have our non-dominant foot in front as that way our hips and our true edge are both point in the same direction. Relatedly, all of the *porta di ferro* guards would need to be formed with the dominant foot in front in order to be done concordantly.

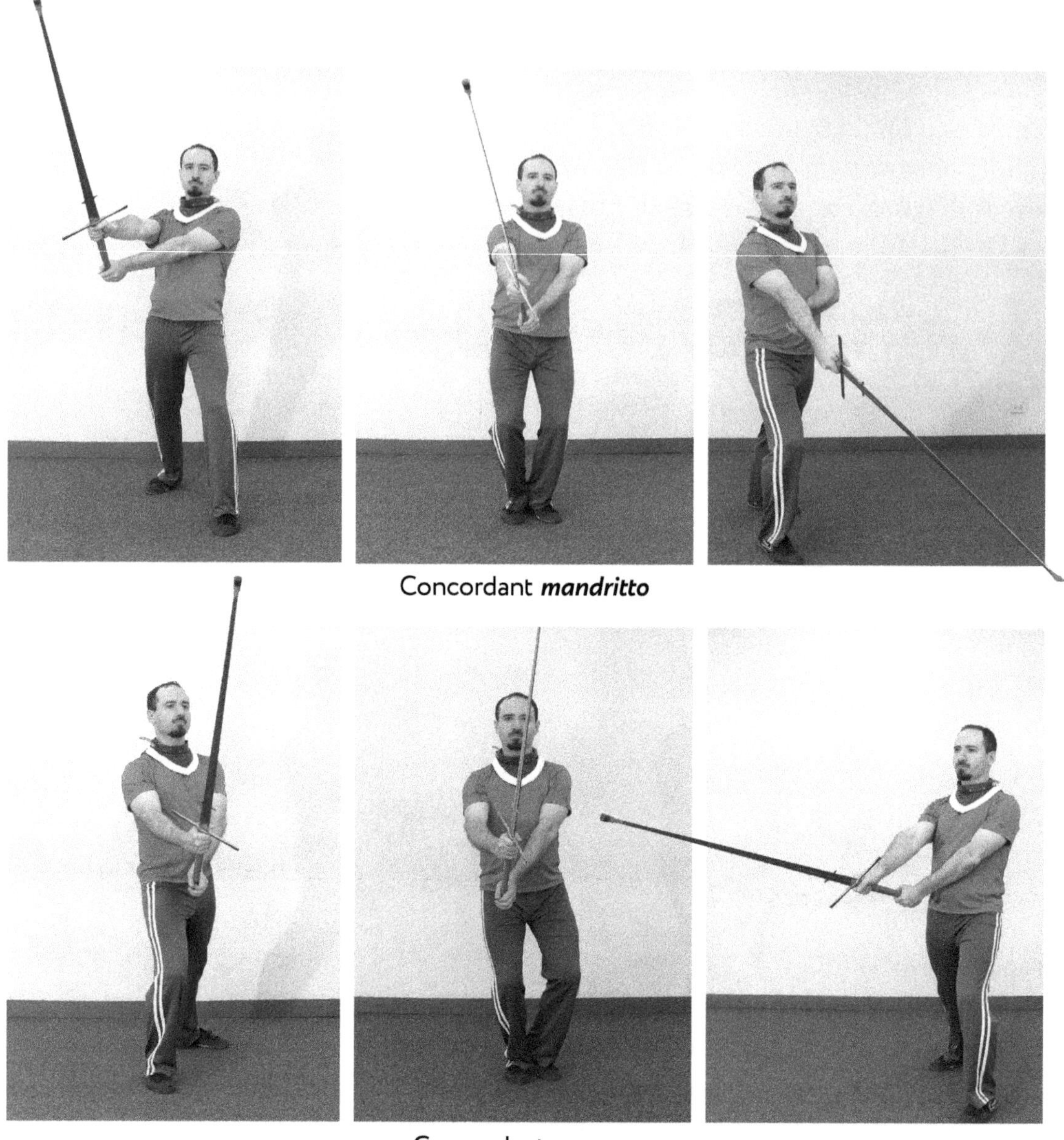

Concordant *mandritto*

Concordant *roverso*

Discordant Action/Guard

Now do it all, but funny footed. So, if you're a righty and want to throw a discordant *mandritto* you would step forward with your left foot or do it by stepping back with your right foot. Alternatively, if you're a lefty, you would perform a discordant mandritto by stepping forward with your right foot or backward with your left foot. If you're a righty and want to throw a discordant *roverso*, you would throw it by stepping forward with your right foot or by stepping back with your left foot and if you're a lefty, you would throw a discordant *roverso* by stepping forward with your left foot or backward with your right foot. If you remember the *cinghare* guards from earlier, these are all done discordantly. Same goes for any of the *coda lunga* guards with the dominant foot in front.

Discordant *mandritto*

Discordant *roverso*

These discordant actions are a hallmark of the Bolognese style. You see them pop up occasionally with other authors, but if you see a random fencer pulling them out a lot, there's a good chance you're both reading from the same book. Now, these actions are of course less structurally sound than concordant ones. That said, being able to step with either foot in order to support whatever bladework action you've got set up has its advantages. Sometimes you're going to have the opening to throw a *mandritto* while your right foot is stuck with all your weight on it. You could let the opportunity pass you by, or you could come in with something unexpected. Your choice.

One thing you'll often notice with discordant stepping is that it often ends up with the front foot turned out along with the step tending to be at more of an angle than with a concordant step. The reason for this is that if your knee points straight forward and your cut is aimed in a way that crosses the line of the knee, the two are now at odds. By turning your foot out, and keeping your knee and toe pointing the same direction, your knee is now pointing the same direction as the action you're making with the sword. This is a really powerful tool and can help to keep your knees healthy, but it definitely comes with a smaller margin for error than concordant stepping, so just be careful. If things start to hurt, take a break and try to figure out what it is you might be doing wrong.

The Glove Game

This is a drill I took from modern fencing, but it applies just as well to what we're doing here. For this game you need two people and each one needs to be holding a glove (not a gauntlet).

STEP 1 -Fencer A gets to advance forward once and then lunge.

STEP 2 -At the same time, Fencer B gets to retreat backward twice.

STEP 3 -The very instant Fencer A has finished their lunge, the roles reverse and now Fencer B gets to attack.

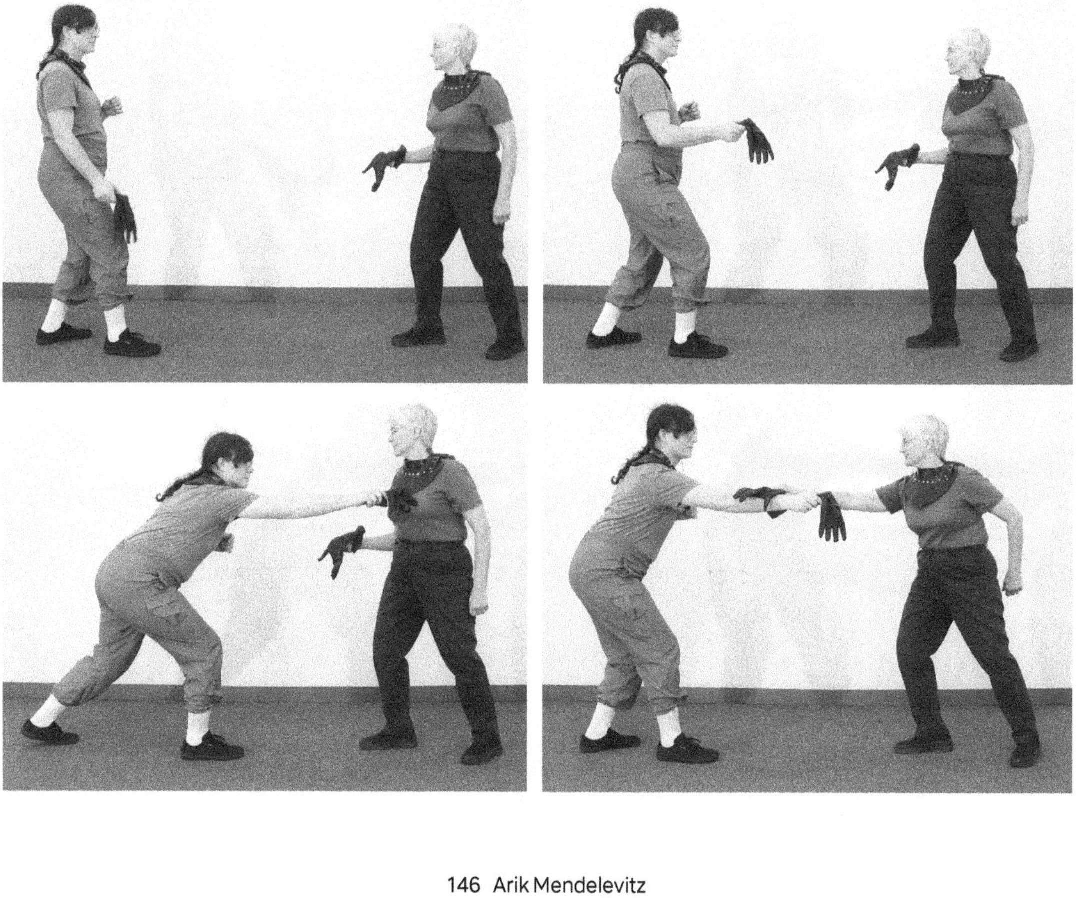

Each fencer's goal is to use their glove to hit the other fencer while also trying not get hit, despite the fact that they aren't allowed to parry.

There's a few different things this drill teaches really well. First and foremost it teaches that fencing is fun. It's hard not to laugh when you and your friends are trying to slap each other with a glove. The next thing it does is that it teaches you that as long as you are in a consensual setting, it is okay to hit someone else. Lots of folks come into this without a martial background or having been raised with the notion that any sort of roughhousing would never be allowed. Going from that to full on sparring can be a huge jump for people, and this drill in particular can help ease that transition. After that, this drill teaches **measure** really really well. You are in a low risk scenario where you constantly get to experiment with whether or not you can reach a moving target. Also, after you run this a few times, you'll likely start to notice that it also teaches you the importance of **balance**. If you launch your attack, but go so far out you can't recover easily, you're going to get bopped on the back.

If you've got that down and your quads don't burn too much, there are a few variations I like to throw in. First is to unlock other footwork options. Now instead of it just being an advance, a lunge, and two retreats, you can try it with a passing step, or a gather. After that, I'll take away the two step limit. Now Fencer A gets to step forward as many times as they want before firing. This way, Fencer B has to react in the moment as opposed to knowing when it is that Fencer A has to go. Relatedly, you can also mess with the rhythm of this. Fencer A can take one fast step and then pause. If Fencer B is suddenly asked to stop on a dime but can't do so without losing their **balance**, Fencer A is suddenly presented with a new opportunity to strike. Another way I like to add a little bit of flavor into this drill is to give people specific targets to hit. Going for a shoulder is pretty attainable, but being asked to hit your opponent in the ankle takes a little more thought. Finally, I'll have folks gear up and try this with swords. You can limit it to just thrusts, just cuts, or leave both choices open. It's all up to you.

11: Provocations

Sometimes, you just gotta make your opponent move. Sure, if they stand there perfectly still the whole time you can just walk up and stab them. Generally, though, they'll have at least some sense of self-preservation and will try and do something to stop you. If they feel really brave, they might even try to hit you with their sword. Thankfully you can use this instinct of theirs to your advantage.

Giovanni dall'Agocchie teaches us that provocations are performed for one of two reasons.[59] The first is that you can perform a **defensive provocation**, causing your opponent to stir from their guard so that they try to hit you. The way you do this is by providing them with what we like to call an **invitation**. Now, an invitation is nothing more than a hole in your defenses that you put there on purpose and are planning on acting on. This differs from an **opening**, which is one that's there without you wanting it to be.

There are two kinds of invitations you can provide: **static** and **dynamic**. A **static** invitation is just whatever line your guard doesn't cover. So, if you've formed a proper *porta di ferro stretta* and know how to use it, you are inherently providing an invitation to your outside line. Alternatively, if you picked *coda lunga e larga*, you know your opponent isn't going to go for your legs, at least with their first strike. You don't have to exaggerate the guard or leave anything more open than you normally do. Just think about each and every guard and where it both does and doesn't cover.

The opening we see used more often is a **dynamic** invitation. All this means is that while you're moving, there is a place for your opponent to go. So if you go from *guardia di croce* and try to crash down on your opponent's sword by cutting down into *cinghare porta di ferro stretta*, you are opening yourself up for your opponent to disengage over your sword. This might sound like a lot, but it's really the same as a static invitation, except instead of it being a single snapshot, you let the video keep going. Conversely, if you paused the video of your dynamic invitation, you would be able to point out a static one. The other thing to keep in mind here is that static invitations occur when your opponent is standing there with all their faculties

59 Dall'Agocchie, 30.

available to figure out whether or not it's a trap. In a dynamic invitation, people are already using a good bit of their concentration to try and move around and are less likely going to be able to get a good read on whether what you presented is an opening or an invitation.

The other one dall'Agocchie gives us is what I like to call an **offensive provocation**. The difference here is that with a defensive provocation/invitation, we are waiting for our opponent to do something so that we can take advantage of it and punish them for their mistakes. With an offensive provocation, it's us who's taking the initiative. Again, this breaks down into two different possibilities. The first are provocations **against the sword**. This might entail your finding their sword, threatening to strike them with a *stocatta* if they don't disengage. Alternatively, it might mean beating their blade away with a *falso dritto*, clearing the way for you to step in and threaten them even further.

The other kind of offensive provocation is one done **against the body**. These generally involve starting a bit closer than provocations against the sword, as you need to start your motion at a distance from which you could reasonably hit your opponent. From there, throw a cut or a thrust aimed at whatever body part is open, forcing your opponent to either react how you're predicting they will or get hit. Alternatively, if you're even closer to them, you could perform a provocation against the body with a *presa*, threatening to throw them to the ground, or with a pommel strike, offering to speed up their next dental appointment.

12: Tempo, The Best-O?

Out of the three main building blocks of Italian swordsmanship (structure, measure, and tempo), tempo is by far the most elusive of the bunch. Both structure (how well your bones are lined up) and measure (how far apart things are) are things I, as an instructor, can just point to in space. We can freeze time, either on a video or by having students stay in place, and examine these two aspects of the fight with relative ease. This does not mean that these are concepts without depth, just that they are often easier to grasp at the beginning stages. Tempo, however, is something we experience more than something we can just point to. As a teaching aid, I put together the following as a handy guide for students to better grasp how tempo was understood by the fencing masters of old. This is in no way meant as an exhaustive dive into how 16th- century Italians conceived of time, nor is it meant as a definitive statement of what each kind of tempo is singularly defined to be.[60] Instead, think of this as a handy guide to be used as you see fit.

To start with, we first must define what exactly a "tempo" is. To answer that, we must circle back in time. The way the Bolognese authors understood time was due to two main factors: a classical education and an absence of clocks. Now clocks definitely existed by this time (the first mechanical clocks came about in the thirteenth century). However, they were hardly as big of a factor in people's lives as they are now. Back then people were mostly concerned with sunrise, mid-day, and sunset. Before factories or pocket watches came around, people in the West didn't spend all that much time counting each and every moment by the second. Instead, they understood a tempo according to how Aristotle described it, a moment between two stillnesses. So if you make an action going from guard to another, that would be a tempo, regardless of how long it would be on the clock. There are of course shorter and longer tempi, but the important thing to think about here is that you want your action to take less time than your opponent's. However, that doesn't necessarily mean setting a world record in regard to how we perceive time now. All you need to do is have an action that's relatively smaller within the same moment than what your opponent's.

---

[60] For a more complete history of the early modern conception of time, check out Ken Mondschein's book *On Time: A History of Western Timekeeping.*

Giovani dall'Aggochie, the last of the Bolognese masters we have writings from, lays out five different tempi in a fight you can safely strike in.[61]

1 After parrying.

2 After a blow passes your body.

3 While they raise their sword to strike.

4 Injudiciously changing guards.

5 When they lift their foot to advance.

Let's take a look at what each of these teach us. **OPTION 1** is fairly straightforward. They throw a blow at you and you move to parry it in one tempo. After that, you use a second tempo to move to strike them. Nice and simple. One example of this would be that they throw a *mandritto fendente* toward your head. In response you move to collect in *guardia di testa* as you gather your back foot forward to meet your front foot.[62] From there you turn your sword into *guardia d'intrare* and hit them on top of the head with a descending *falso* while stepping forward with either one of your feet.

Parry-riposte

Alternatively, they could throw a *roverso tondo* at your head. You then respond by parrying in *coda lunga e alta* while gathering your feet together and then thrust an *imbrocatta* in *guardia di croce* while stepping forward.

[61] Dall'Agocchie, 36.
[62] Dall'Agocchie, 16.

OPTION 2, my personal favorite, requires even less work on your end. They throw a blow and miss. They could, for instance, throw a *mandritto sgualimbratto* at your head, but in that same tempo you triangle step to the side and hit them with a *roverso sgualimbratto*.

After their blow passes your body

While dall'Agocchie lists this as only applying when they try and hit your body, we can extrapolate it to also include when they try and act against your blade, but in that very same tempo your sword ceases to be where they expected and instead moves to strike them. For instance, and this is one of my go-to actions, they could throw a *mandritto fendente* in order to try and either bind your blade or beat it out of the way. In response, you could perform a *sfalsare* over the top and strike them with a *roverso* to their hands.

Manciolino also points out this tempo specifically. He tells us, "as the opponent's attack has passed outside your presence, this is the correct tempo in which to follow with the riposte you deem most appropriate."[63] As he says, the extra fun part of striking in this tempo is that now you get to strike your opponent however you want. If you have the only sword in a swordfight, the world is your oyster.

OPTION 3 is generally a very small window, but an incredibly powerful tool if you can master it. Here you don't even have to wait for them to actually begin their blow, you just strike them during the preparation. A really easy example could be that they try and raise up from *cinghare porta di ferro larga* into *guardia alta* in order to come down on you with a particularly powerful *fendente*. While their sword is still going up, but before they begin the actual strike, you seize the tempo and strike them with a thrust in *guardia di faccia*.

63 Manciolino, 74.

While they raise their sword to strike

More often though, your window is going to be a bit smaller than that. For instance, from porta di ferro stretta they could use a *falso manco* in order to prep a *mezzo mandritto* to your hands. To counter this, you could get under their sword and strike them with a thrust.

We can also extrapolate this to cover striking whenever they are preparing any sort of offensive preparation with the sword. So, if we find their sword in *porta di ferro stretta* and they disengage with a *sfalsare* underneath our sword in order to find us on the outside line, we could perform a *volta stabile* and then thrust into them from *coda lunga e stretta*. The trick here is to fire while their disengage is still in progress. If you wait until they get all the way around, then you're attacking into their attack as opposed to striking while they are still performing their preparation.

As you may have noticed, we talked about this same action earlier in the chapter on blade actions. This time, though, we've shifted our focus from mechanics to tempo. A lot of drills can be reused to focus on other aspects of your game. So, if you're wondering how to solve a specific problem, you might already have the tool in front of you.

OPTION 4 can be a bit of a tricky one, but is really fun when you can get it. This pops up more often with sword and secondary (dagger, buckler, cloak, etc.), than it does with longsword, but doesn't mean you won't see it at all with two-handers. It often pops up with fencers who tend to get really antsy. They'll sit there waiting for you to do something and then, possibly out of boredom, will shift to a different guard without stepping, hoping that either you'll attack them down this new line or that it'll let them more easily find your sword. For instance, they might be sitting in *coda lunga e stretta* and then, without moving their feet, shift to *cinghare porta di ferro stretta*.

The other place we see it is when someone makes a bad choice and goes to a guard that doesn't cover their opponent's sword, aka acting in the right time but with the wrong move. As an important note, option #4 only works when they're in measure. If they're changing guards so far out you can't hit them, then they're just showing off for the crowd.

Now if you wait for them to finish changing guards, it'll be too late to act. But, if you fire while they're still going from one to the other, then you might be able to get something. Now be warned, they could also be doing this as an intentional, dynamic invitation. That said, if you were already sitting still when the move to do this, it won't be that good of an invitation as your brain won't be busy worrying about anything else at that moment.

The other time this shows up is when both of you are already moving and one of you goes to take the wrong guard for the job. If Fencer A feints a *mandritto sgualimbratto* at Fencer B's face, then Fencer B might move to parry it in *porta di ferro alta*.

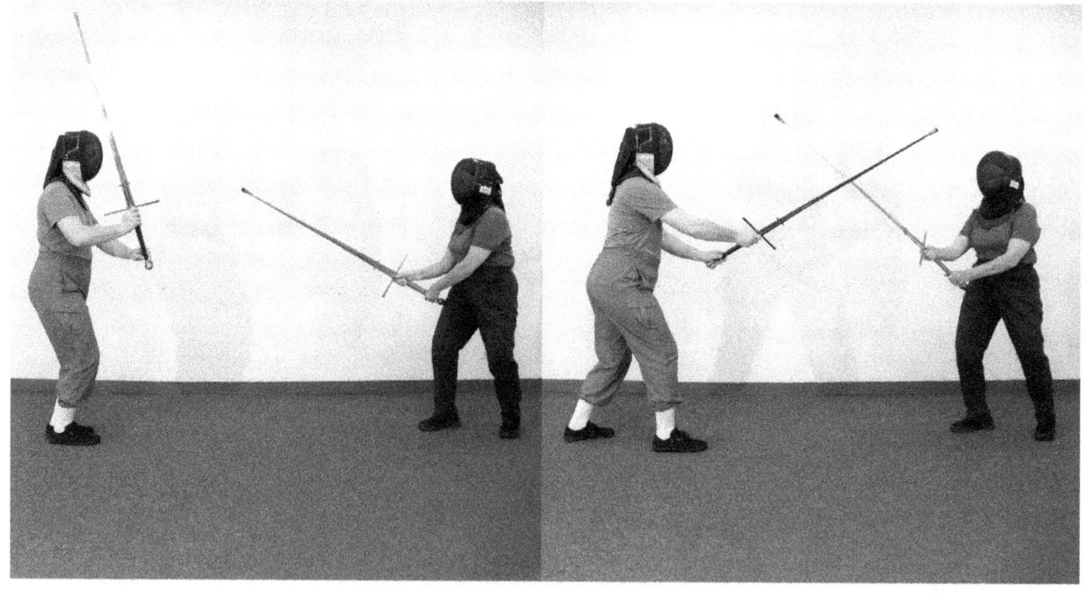

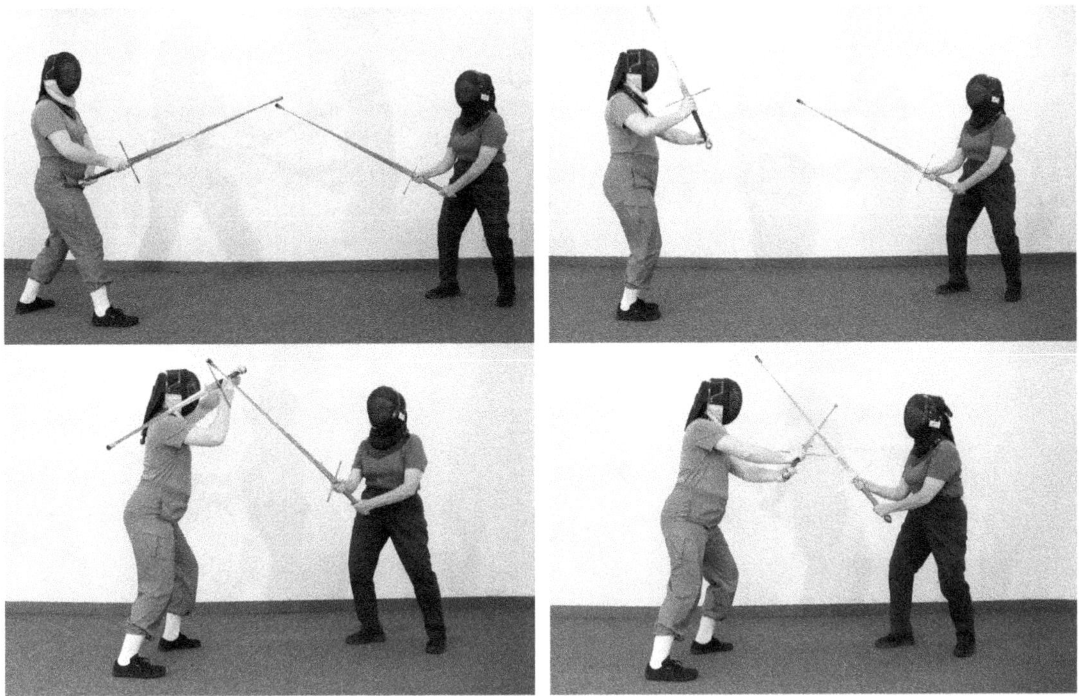

If fencer A then performs a *molinetto* and comes around to strike the other side of Fencer B's head, Fencer B would be wise to cover that line in *coda lunga e alta*.

Sometimes, though, the brain short circuits and instead they drop down into *porta di ferro larga* thinking you were going low. Hitting them at this moment would also be considered acting in the tempo of the injudicious guard change.

OPTION 5 is essentially the footwork version of **OPTION 3**. The difference here, as we talked about earlier, is that the foot functions as a binary whereas the sword works along a spectrum. If they begin to prep a blade action, they can always bail if things change. If they begin to step forward though, once that foot leaves the ground they've committed themselves to that action.

Here's an exercise I like to use to try and train this specific tempo.

Step one: Both fencers start the drill out of measure.

Step two: Fencer A's initial plan is to do a full gather forward, prepping their attack by going up into *guardia alta* and then delivering a *mandritto fendente* to Fencer B's head.

It's vitally important here that Fencer A fully intends their strike to land. If they throw short or don't step in far enough, it trains their opponent to respond to something besides a real and viable threat, thereby giving them bad defenses and making them even more susceptible to feints. In order to make sure my partner is fully committing in a drill, I'll oftentimes just not move to parry and see if their blow lands.

Step three: Fencer B's job is to wait for Fencer A to fully bring their back foot up. When Fencer A's front foot leaves the ground, Fencer B then comes in with a thrust in *guardia di faccia*.

As something to be aware of, as both of you are moving toward each other at the same time, there's a higher probability of it turning into a total train wreck. I haven't had that issue whenever I've led this drill, but just be careful.

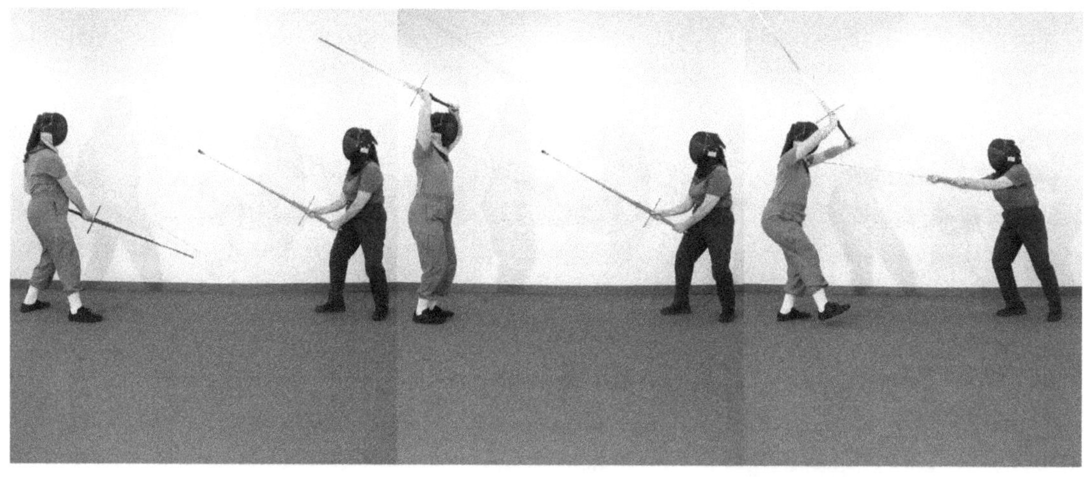

Striking when their foot comes up into the air

If you wanted to take this drill and shrink it down to a smaller, more realistic scale, there's only a couple things you might need to change. Now instead of Fencer A going all the way up into *guardia alta*, just have them perform a *falso manco* and then throw a *mezzo mandritto*. In response, Fencer B should come in with a *stocatta* in *porta di ferro alta*. You could also have this where Fencer A's *mezzo mandritto* is aimed at Fencer B's hands instead of their head.

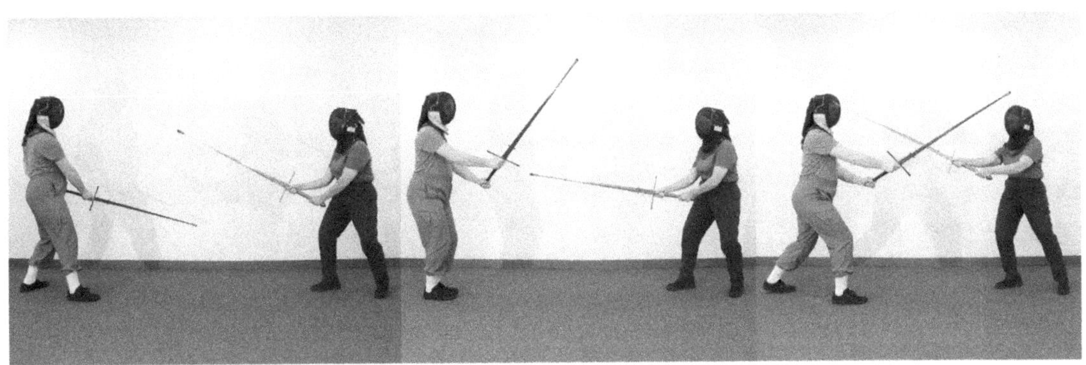

Counting Tempi

Dall'Agocchie goes on to answer the question, "How many tempi should any one action take?".[64] The first answer would be to have a response in two tempi (*dui tempi*). This describes option #1 as it takes one tempo to perform the parry and then a second tempo to strike. Depending on whether you take a full tempo in order to perform a void of the body, it could also cover option #2 as you're using one tempo to have them miss and then striking them in the tempo after that. Next, he tells us that you can perform an action in a single tempo (*stesso tempo*). This covers option #4 as you went from standing still and then used a single action in order to strike them. It also covers option #2 if you get them to miss inside the same tempo as your strike. Finally, he tells us that you can perform an action in half a tempo (*mezzo tempo*). This covers options #3 and #5 as you are attacking inside of their attack. As you might have guessed, actions that only require half a tempo are often performed only using half cuts.

[64] Dall'Agocchie, 30.

	Dui Tempi	Stesso Tempo	Mezzo Tempo
After parrying	X		
After a blow passes your body	X	X	
While they raise their sword to strike			X
Injudiciously changing guards		X	
When they lift their foot to advance			X

To add a little bit of granularity to our understanding, we can also tease out the concept of **mezzo tempo** from that of **contra tempo**. All the Bolognese authors use the term *mezzo tempo* to describe when you make short actions that don't end with your point leaving your opponent's presence. On top of that, dall'Agocchie, like Ridolfo Capoferro after him, also explains it as acting while your opponent is still preparing their attack. This might mean thrusting while they're pulling back to prepare a cut, or it could mean striking while they're disengaging as opposed to waiting for them to get all the way to the other side. In addition, the Anonimo gives us the concept of *contra tempo* (counter time). This is just striking during their strike or as he says, "Contratempo happens when the enemy wishes to strike, and you interrupt his attack, rendering it useless, while you simultaneously make one that strikes him."[65] So while *dui tempi* is waiting from them to throw their attack, parrying/voiding, and then performing an attack of your own, *contra tempo* is you firing at the same time they do, ideally pushing through their sword in order to hit them. If you have the choice, *mezzo tempo* is generally going to be your strongest option as it takes place a hair before the other two. That said, if there's an open moment for you to move, don't worry as much about all the specifics.

65 Anonimo Bolognese, 64.

Three Micro Tempi

In addition to viewing a tempo as one singular action, there's another more granular view that can be helpful to take. Let's say someone is trying to stick you with a *stocatta* and you've chosen to parry them as opposed to watching your organs spill out onto the floor. You have the option to perform your parry during the find, the gain, or during the strike.

Option one: Fencer B can move to parry the instant their sword is covered.

Parry during the find

Parry during the gain

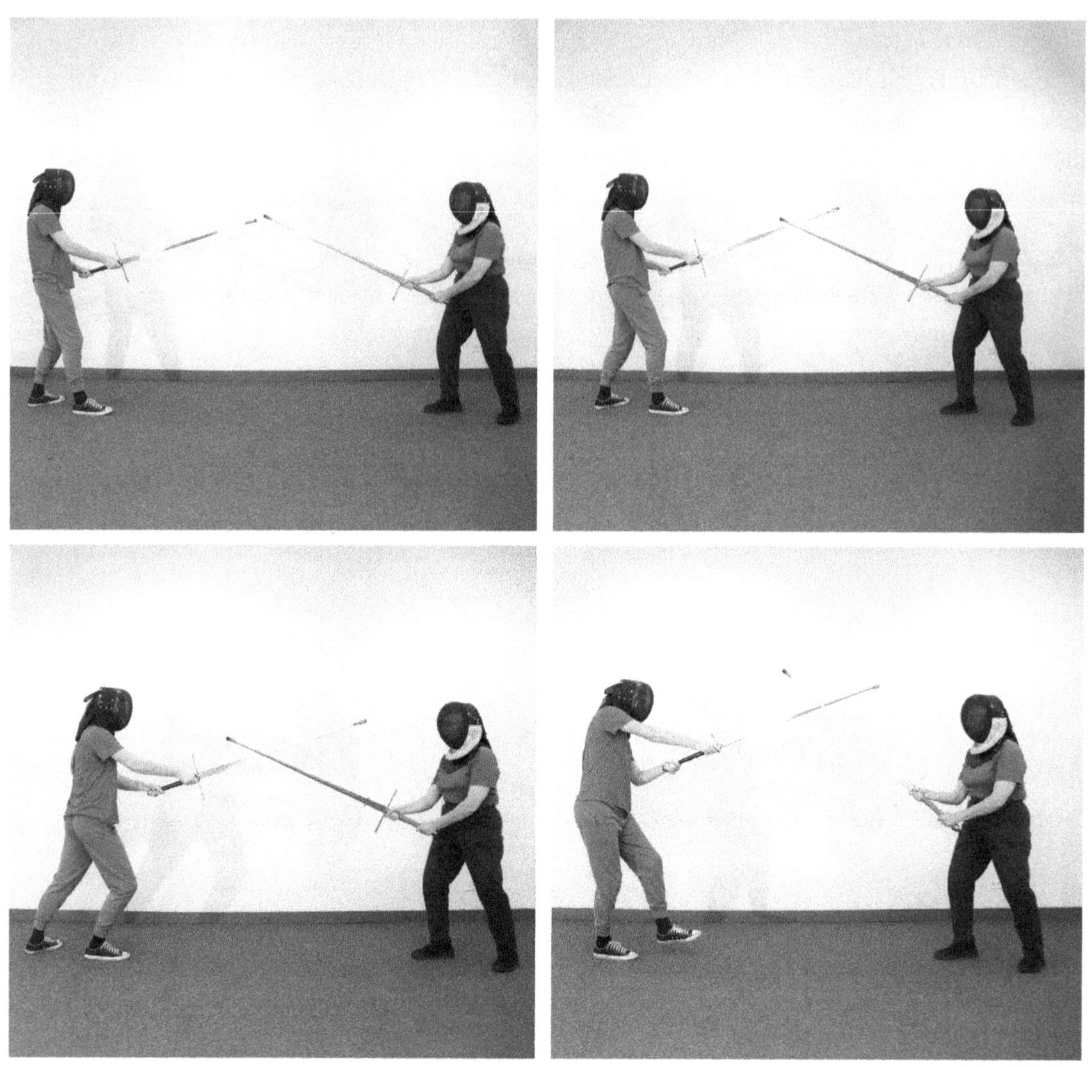

Parry during the strike

Something you can do to really mess with people is to get them really used to you parrying during one specific part and then suddenly switching it up on them partway through the fight. Lots of people will have it programmed in them that you either parry only during the find or during the gain. If they're used to you moving during the gain and you suddenly react one step before they were expecting, now it's their turn to play catch-up. Alternatively, if you wait until they move to strike, there's a good chance they'll have come off your sword and ceased to worry about mechanical advantage as they thought they had everything locked in. A fun bit of spice to add in to most any drill is to change which part you have someone react during. This way you now have up to three versions of any given drill, letting you take the same concepts you've been working with and tune them a little bit more finely. Just remember, most of the time the smaller the motion, the quicker you'll get to where you want to go.

Acting In/Out Of Tempo

Sometimes you'll hear instructors tell you that the reason your plan didn't succeed was that you executed it "out of" tempo. This can be really vague and unhelpful phrasing if people just assume you know what they mean. Here's a little secret: lots of people throw the phrase around without fully understanding what it means.

One way of viewing it is by looking at tempo as a rhythm, just like how we see in music. If you were supposed to move during this beat but instead acted during the next one, you've missed your opportunity and if you do it enough times your opponent is going to wise up and seize on your mistake. Alternatively, if you had fired during the correct beat, then you would have acted "in" tempo. This way of looking at acting in or out of tempo has its uses, but I generally don't find it to be the most helpful way of looking at things. That said, I never got particularly far in my music education, so if you or your student have then your results may end up differently from mine.

The way I find to be more helpful is looking at **proportion**, which I talked about a bit in chapter 8. In fencing it is always our goal to get to where we want to go before our opponent can get to where they're aiming. This is partly due to the velocity at which each of you move. That said, there's not a ton you can really do to improve your hand speed after a certain point. Where you do have a lot more room to grow, though, is in making your motions more efficient. In that light we can see acting "in" tempo as having an action that's proportionally smaller than your opponent's. Remember, you don't have to get your sword to land faster than anyone has before in the history of fencing, you just need it to move into place faster than your opponent's sword can. So if you take a path that's proportionally smaller to your opponent's, you're now in the advantageous position. On the other side of the coin, acting "out of" tempo is just taking a path that was proportionally larger in comparison to what your opponent did.

13: Gioco

Gioco (play) is a concept fairly unique to the Bolognese system. We see Fiore use a similar concept (spelled *zhogo*) a century beforehand, but otherwise it's not a concept that other systems of fence really have a term for. The important thing here is not to confuse *gioco* with the later idea of *misura* (measure). *Gioco* is all about what actions you're free to do at any given time, which does have some relation to distance, but the two aren't quite one to one.

Gioco Largo (unconstrained play)

Gioco largo is big, it's sexy, and is a great way to cleave straight through an opponent. The question to ask to figure out whether or not you're currently in *gioco largo* at any point in the fight is just, "Is my sword free to leave presence?" If moving your sword out of the way means your opponent's point is free to strike you in a single tempo, that means you shouldn't have left. Sure, sweeping back to *coda lunga e distesa* and up to *guardia alta* in order to deliver a false-edged *fendente* is a great way to show off and has its tactical uses, but if that means they get a chance to poke you in the face while your sword is nowhere to be seen, you made the wrong choice.

None of this means that playing in *gioco largo* is inherently bad for you. It's a great place to knock your opponent's sword out of the way and deliver devastating blows. You just have to remember when's the right time for any given tool.

Gioco Stretto (constrained play)

Gioco stretto is small, it's subtle, and it's sharp. This happens when your opponent's blade is in presence and if you pull your blade away, you get hit. *Gioco stretto* is the land of half cuts and thrusts. Lots of *gioco stretto* techniques won't necessarily kill an opponent, but sometimes a good cut to the forehead is all you need for someone to reconsider why they entered a duel in the first place. If you aren't sure which of the two modes to be in, *gioco stretto* is generally the safer bet. That said, a *stretto* cut won't always have the oomph to answer a *largo* one.

The Anonimo teaches us that, "if you were fighting against one that understands the narrow play, should you try to fight against him from the wide play, then your talent will be confounded."[66] So if one of you only knows how to fight in *gioco stretto* and one of you only knows how to fight in *gioco largo*, money is on the *stretto* fighter. That said, just knowing how to fight in *gioco stretto* is not a magic bullet that will solve all of your problems. He also warns us that we have to really know what we're doing in *gioco stretto* in order to ensure that we won't let our opponent find our sword.[67] That is, unless we really want them to.

Putting Them Into Context
You might have noticed that we've seen these terms *stretto* and *largo*, or conjugations thereof, before. Several of the guard names include these descriptors in their titles, indicating how they should be used. While a large cut might go through a *stretta* guard, it'll rarely begin or end there. Similarly, a *stretta* action probably isn't going to finish in a *larga* guard.

If you're a bit more academically inclined, you'll also notice that many of the Bolognese authors split their chapters up into sequences purely comprised of *larga* or *stretta* actions. This doesn't mean that in a fight you'll never move from one to the other, but the division makes the study of the art a little bit easier to digest. As well, for anyone coming to this book with a later period background (rapier, smallsword, etc.), you might have noticed that as things slowly became more thrust-oriented that *gioco largo* starts to fade away. Even by the time of dall'Agocchie, we see that he's almost entirely eliminated *larga* plays from his repertoire.

Another thing to think about is which mode of play suits you best. I know fencers who really excel when they constantly move throughout a fight, often going through larger actions and slowly reeling their opponent in with a consistent rhythm that they can break from at a moment's notice. Other fencers want to keep their point online and will sit perfectly still until it's time to move. If you aren't sure which one you are, play around a bit with it next time you're at your local practice. You might be surprised to find out that something you never considered before works beautifully with how you approach the fight.

As the Anonimo teaches us, "when you run across a fencer that fights in the narrow play, then you will act as though you plan to fence in the wide play, and then astutely strike him from the narrow play; and so too, if you find a fencer that fences from the wide play, you should act as though you intend to fence in the narrow play, but actually strike him with an attack from the wide play."[68] Essentially, refuse to play whatever game your opponent wants you to and then, once they finally start to play by your rules, beat them under theirs.

[66] Anonimo Bolognese, 69.
[67] Anonimo Bolognese, 71.
[68] Anonimo Bolognese, 69-70.

14: Feints

Feints are one of those things that can seem really intimidating to try and grasp at first, but once you understand them, they are pretty straightforward. In the simplest terms, a feint is just an attack that you lie about in order to do something else. The key here is intention. If I'm in *guardia alta* and my opponent is in *coda lunga e distesa*, I could feint a *mandritto fendente* to their head, knowing that they're going to try and respond in *guardia di faccia*. From there, without having committed fully to my *mandritto*, I can perform a *sfalsare* over their sword, hit them with a *roverso sgualimbratto* and compass out.

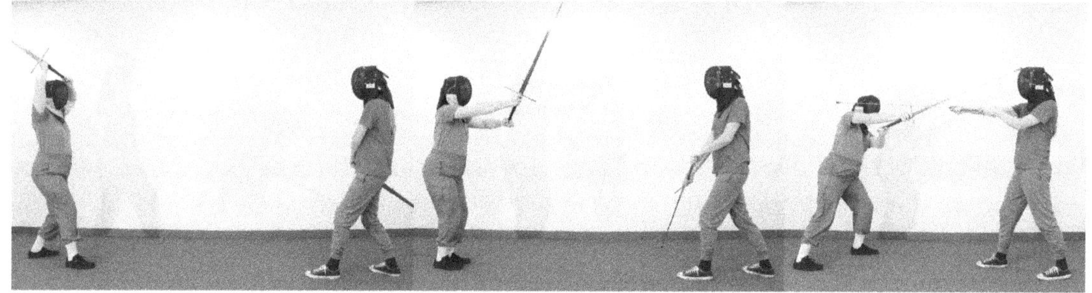

Feints

The difference here is that the plan from the beginning is for your *mandritto* not to hit. Now, if your opponent doesn't do anything you should just continue forward and hit them on my original line. This is a thing that intermediate fencers often trip over, expecting their opponent to react with the intelligent play and then getting in trouble when they move to disengage around a blade that wasn't there and end up getting skewered. Alternatively, you could intend for my *mandritto* to hit and adapt when they end up responding. It's the same physical set of actions, but the intent is different. That intent is key not just because we like being precise in our terminology, but because it affects how quickly we can react. If your plan is to feint from the get-go, your second move is going to come out way faster than if you had to problem-solve in the moment. That said, if they don't move and we intended to feint, it might take you a moment to realize that we should keep going forward with our initial plan.

We can contrast feints with what we call **mutations**. A mutation is just going through the fight step by step, trying to make your first intention succeed and then

pivoting if it doesn't. The difference between mutations and feints is intention.
If I throw a *mandritto* as a feint, I am planning on it not landing. If my opponent
doesn't move to stop it I can continue on, but it might take me a moment to figure
out that's what's going on. With a mutation I expect that *mandritto* to land and then
have to figure out what my second intention is once my opponent moves to parry.
The two are mechanically the same, but function differently in a psychological
sense. Whichever plan I'm preparing for I'm going to be able to execute faster. So if
I expect that I can just win via mechanical advantage, I'm going to want to put my
chips on that and bail myself out with a mutation. If I know that my opponent is
going to be able to blast right through my blade, it might be wiser to place my bet on
a feint knowing things are about to change.

Feint-Direct

A feint-direct is when you lie about throwing an attack on the line you're already
on.[69] So if you have their sword found to the inside, you would perform a feint-direct
just by extending your point down that line. Alternatively, if you've chambered a cut,
a feint-direct would be to just begin to throw that cut into the opening that's already
there. Something to remember is that if you already have control of a line, there's
no reason to give it up. I wouldn't want to give up a line I already have control of by
going around and feinting to a different line that my opponent likely has closed off.

For example, if I am in *porta di ferro stretta* and my opponent is in *coda lunga
e stretta* with their false edge facing my sword, I could perform a feint-direct by
pushing a *stocatta* toward their face. Assuming they move to parry it, I could then
perform a *sfalsare* over the top of their sword and hit them on the other side.

Feint-direct

[69] Gaugler, "The Science of Fencing", 39.

Alternatively, if we are both in *guardia di croce*, I could feint a *molinetto* as if I was going to hit their face with it. When they go to parry, I could then just perform a *sfalsare* and strike them in the hands on their outside line.

Feint by Disengagement

A feint by disengagement is just feinting with a disengage (*sfalsare*). In other terms, it's going from the line you're currently on, going around their sword, and throwing a feint to a different line.[70] This doesn't necessarily mean that the final strike is delivered with a disengage, just that the initial lie is given in the form of a disengage. Eventually you'll get to adding in a second disengage or even a half disengage after the feint, but that comes later. This kind of feint is performed when you don't currently have control of the line you're set up on at that moment. This might mean that your opponent has found your sword, or it could mean that they've set up in a counter guard to where you are. So, if you're up in *guardia di croce* and they're in *cinghare porta di ferro alta*, the path for you to unwind and throw the big *mandritto* you have set up isn't open to you. Thus, it's now time for you to go around, perhaps with a *punta roversa* to the other side in order to get them to open up their guard for you to come back around with a *sfalsare* under their blade and throw that *mandritto* you initially wanted to perform.

70 Gaugler, 41.

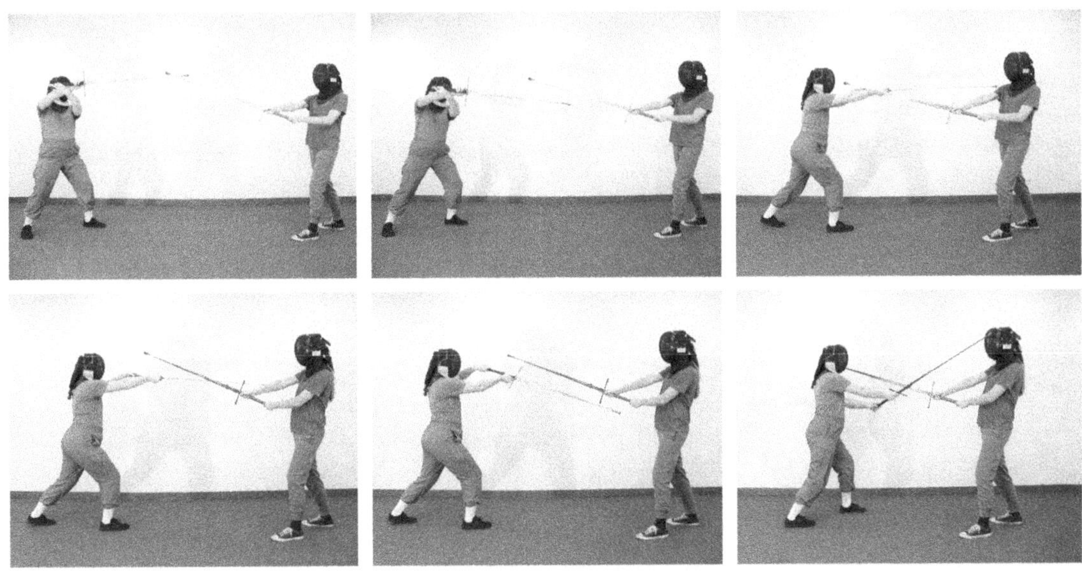

Feint by disengagement

Alternatively, if you are in *coda lunga e stretta* and they come to find your sword in *cinghare porta di ferro stretta*, you could perform a feint by disengagement by performing a *sfalsare* under their sword in order to threaten their outside line. When they go to parry you could come back around and thrust in *guardia di faccia*.

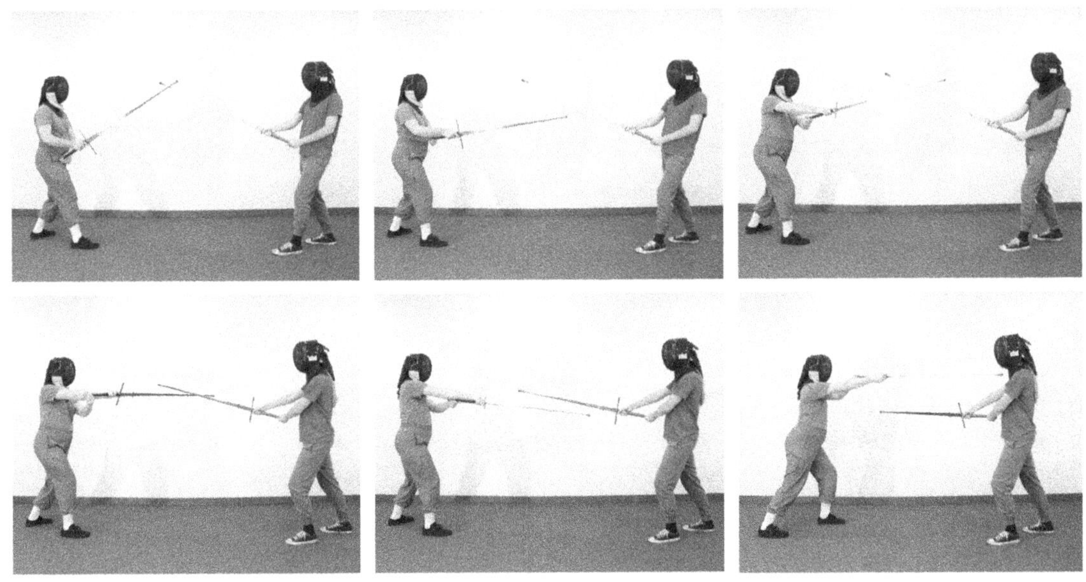

As a note, I'm using "feint by disengagement" to denote any feint that's performed by changing lines and going around your opponent's sword. This doesn't necessarily mean that you have to perform a *sfalsare*. You could feint by beginning to throw a *stramazonne* a *molinetto*, or any other action that gets you from one side of their sword to the other. As well, this doesn't mean you're restricted to going right to left or left to right. You could also throw a feint that changes the line from high to low or low to high. Some instructors will break all of these out into their own categories, but I personally find that in the heat of a fight, it helps to boil things down to either going through or going around.

Now that we have the ideas of feint-direct and feint by disengagement down, we can also apply those concepts to regular, committed attacks. Any attack on its own could be considered an **attack-direct**, where you attack straight into an open line, or and **attack by disengagement** where you have to go around your opponent's blade in order to strike.

Attack to Hit

The other way we can divide feints up is by saying that that specific feint is either an attack to hit or an attack to miss. An attack to hit is generally the default kind of feint where you're throwing your shot at a viable target. So, if you're in *guardia alta* and throw a *mandritto fendente* aimed straight at their head, if they don't move to parry it or void out of the way and it connects, that's an attack to hit.

Attack to hit

While plan A will be to disengage after your opponent goes to parry, if they freeze then you have the option to just continue through on that initial line. You'd be surprised how often this second scenario pops up. Fighters at all levels freeze all the time. It might not be for a long time, but sometimes our brains think, "If I don't move the bear won't see me" at the most inopportune times. Inversely, what I see happen more often is fighters throwing their feint as an attack to hit and then abandoning the line before their opponent has had the chance to commit to their next move. Sometimes you can in fact move too fast for your own good.

Attacks to Miss

Most of the time when we throw a feint, the intention should be to hit our opponent if they don't move. However, there are times when it's to our advantage to throw what's called an "attack to miss," where we throw a blow without ever intending for it to hit. For instance, I'll often start in *guardia alta* and then throw a *mandritto fendente* to miss in order to provoke my opponent to bring their blade out, so that I can disengage around it and strike them with a *stocatta* on their outside line.

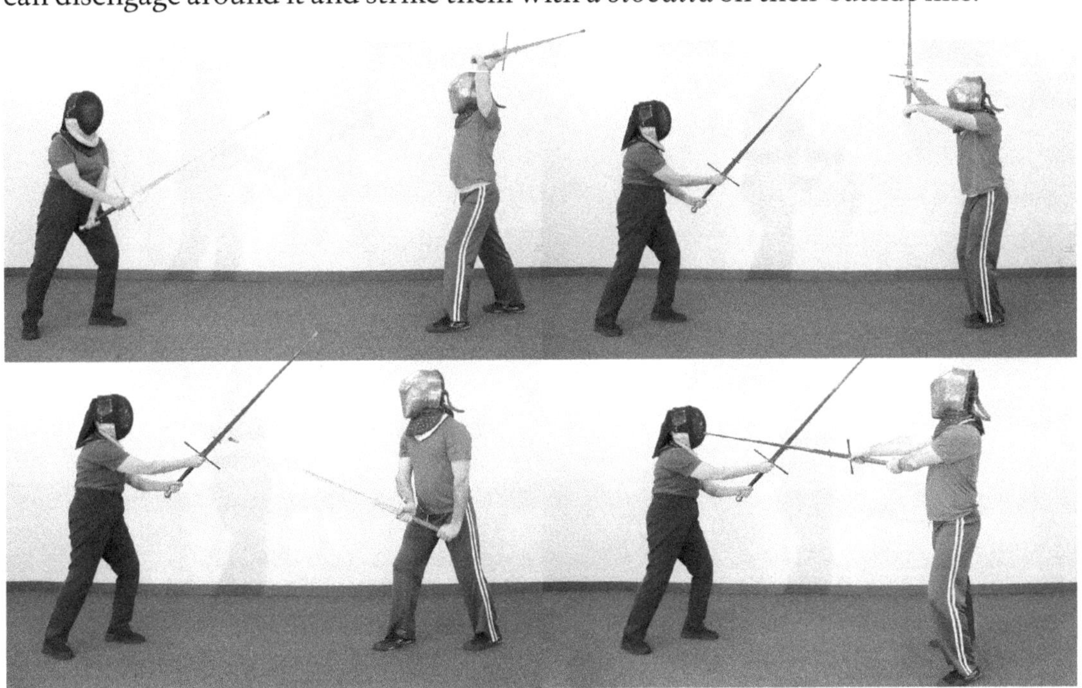

Attack to miss

Attacks to miss can either be thrown **shallow**, or they can be thrown **wide**. Throwing it shallow means not going far enough on the z-axis and having your blow not come out as far as you could reach. This is a great way to lie about what your measure is to your opponent as well as a way to get them to react while you still have reach to spare. Throwing them wide means having them aimed outside of your opponent's silhouette. These work really well as a second intention as once your opponent reacts to an initial threat, they're going to have less faculties available to get a good read on that second feint of yours. Now they're chasing after your sword, but meanwhile you know that they're being forced to reach wide, giving you some extra time to bring your sword back online and strike.

For example, starting in *porta di ferro stretta* I could throw a *stocatta* as a feint-direct. When they move to parry it, I could intentionally make my *sfalsare* wide, pulling their sword out of the picture allowing me to come back in line without having to face any opposition.

Attack to miss

Move Continuously

Here's an important note about feints that will not only help you win more fights, but will also keep your joints nice and happy. Have your feints keep moving. This doesn't mean you should disengage to the other side before your opponent bites, but it does mean that you should use the conservation of angular momentum to your advantage. If you do what's often referred to as a "pump fake" you'll be throwing an attack on a given line, halt it abruptly, pull back, and then try and strike somewhere else. Not only is this slow, but the added mass of your sword makes this a great way to mess up your shoulders and elbows. Instead, try and have the blade continuously move forward as you move from the feint to the actual strike.

How To Teach Feints

In order to teach feints, you break it down into a decision tree where there's only two available paths (with only one being the smart choice) at any point. Eventually you can add more, but getting rid of that white noise early on will make the whole process easier.

The first step is to build good striking mechanics. Feints aren't going to work if they're going foot, body, sword. A good feint is going to be sword, then body, then wait to see what your opponent does, all without having stepped yet. Only then do you get to strike. That said, if you tend to pass more than lunge, you can definitely load your weight on to your front foot during the feint, moving yourself even closer to your opponent and thus selling your feint all the more.

After that, if you haven't already, you need to build strong finding and gaining mechanics. Just like with any fundamental technique, you need a solid foundation before you can start adding on all the bells and whistles. From the other side a feint should look just like any other strike coming in, otherwise people aren't going to bite on them. Your opponent needs to feel threatened in order to stir up a reaction. If they don't feel threatened, they'll either ignore you or seize your tempo and punish you for your mistake.

The next step is to figure out which line is open. Never feint into a closed line, that's how your end up running your face into their point. It may sound obvious, but you'd be surprised how many people I've seen just throw committed attacks straight into a closed line and then get punished for it. Encourage your students to learn from other people making those mistakes for them. Anyhow, have them approach the edge of measure, then have them feint to either the inside or the outside line. whichever is already open. From there one of two things will happen.

Feint by *stocatta*, and then hit down the same line

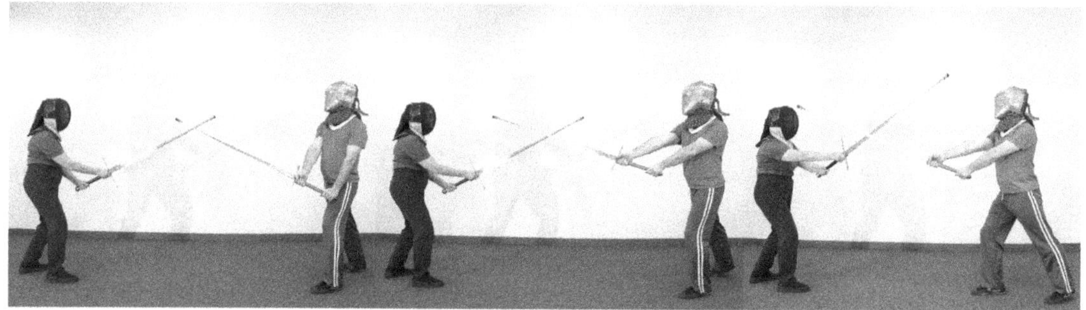

Feint by *stocatta*, parry

For **OPTION 1**, if your opponent doesn't move the answer is to just continue forwards and hit them on that same line. For option #2 the response is to disengage, use the sword to close the line on the other side, and strike.

There should be the slightest of pauses to see what their opponent is going to do. If they just go through the whole series of actions without waiting for a response, they are going to run their face straight on to their opponent's sword. Far too many folks, especially on the younger end (ask me how I know), have a tendency to be too fast for their own good. Speed is a helpful tool to have, but if it means they're always jumping the gun, it's going to start being a hindrance. The other common mistake here is not properly closing the new line with the sword. Just because you've moved your point from one side to the other doesn't mean you've finished the job.

Next, have them do this whole sequence on both the inside and outside lines. Lots of folks, especially right-handed fencers, only train for how to fight on the inside line. If your students or drill partners are comfortable on both the inside and the outside, they're instantly going to have a huge leg up on a large amount of the competition. After the student gets that down, change who's approaching.

So now instead of them coming forward, it's you who steps in to find their sword in wide measure. Once you've committed to that action, they feint.

Do this on both sides.

After that, work on feint-direct vs. feint by disengage. As a note, the feint by disengage is going to pop up more frequently, but I have personally found the feint-direct is easier for students to initially approach. This can vary student to student, though. My recommendation is to start with whichever one is easier for that student to comprehend. All that matters is getting the material through in a way that will click with the other party.

Next, have them deliver a feint by disengage by going from inside to outside as well as outside to inside.

With that done, now cross apply the previous part as to who is approaching and who is receiving. Once you've done that with the feint by disengage, you essentially build a matrix of feint-direct/feint by disengage, approaching/receiving, inside/outside.

Now that you have that part under control, start adding more and more actions to the front end. It's important to remember that the plays in the books shouldn't be read as purely opening actions. Oftentimes they're showing us a clip having started partway through the video. So, feel free to take any of the fundamental techniques we've gone over and then tack on a feint to the end. By burying the lead and having them throw the feint in as a later part of a sequence, it will create a safe environment to stress test their technique and force their brain to recall the technique in the midst of a mildly stressful situation as opposed to in during the quiet tranquility of feinting from stillness. Doing this will help to bridge that gap between tightly prescribed drills of one to two actions and the chaos that is the fight itself. I have seen too many schools only drill short, scripted sequences and then when their students go out into the larger world, they wonder why it is they're getting smoked by people who seemingly have worse mechanics than they do.

It's this last part of the progression, adding things in before the feint itself, that tends to trip people up. Often-times folks will try and feint from stillness during a fight, because that's what they were taught to do during drills, and then get frustrated that none of their feints are working (the other reason is bad mechanics, but we already covered that). Approaching any technique in a vacuum is a helpful way of refining the mechanics needed, but it's important to remember that mechanics alone are not the whole picture. A feint, unlike finding and gaining, is at its core a psychological trick. The dumber we can make our opponent be, the easier it becomes to pull the wool over their eyes. The way we do this isn't by putting something in their drink, but is instead by overloading their brain. The further down the decision tree we get, the more fatigued our minds become.

The more fatigued our minds become, the less intelligent they become. So that means that the best time to throw a feint isn't at the outset when your opponent is standing there at full capacity. Instead, it's a couple moves in when folks are ready to jump at anything that moves.

The important themes here are:

1 Proper striking order and mechanics.

2 Having to pick from only two options at any time, which are dictated by what our opponent does or doesn't do.

3 Understanding that people get dumber the further down the decision tree they get and using that to our advantage.

It all boils down to, "Did they stand still? Stab them right there." "Did they move? Stab them somewhere else."

Bonus Lesson!
Did you both make it through that whole progression and are hungry for more? Wonderful, I now have a justification for all the sword books I keep getting for Hannukah.

The short version is that now you're going to start tacking things on to the end instead of the beginning. So, if you open with a feint-direct, have the other side move to parry both the initial feint as well as the strike coming off the disengage on the new line. Then, as they go to parry your second motion, just disengage back and strike them on the original line. This is also known as a **double feint** or more broadly speaking a **compound feint**.

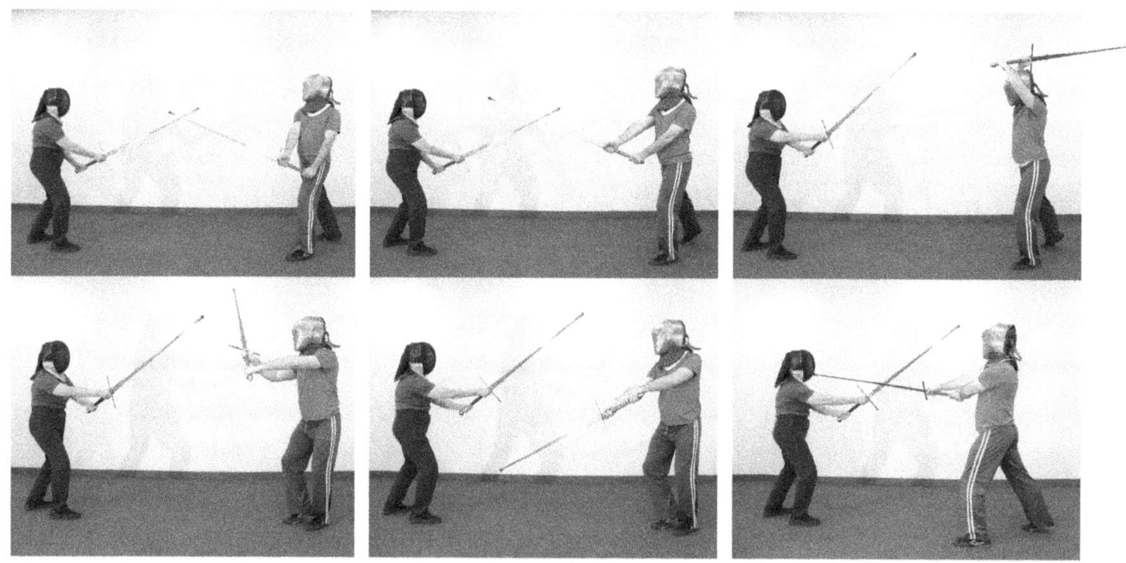

Double feint

On this one, as well as on the standard feint by disengage, it will help to make that first disengage a bit wide with your tip pointing outside of their silhouette. Especially if they're already relying on their lizard brain to react at this point, going wide will cause them to parry wider than normal, leaving a nice open window for you to enter through. The only reason this works is because you're getting them to make a mistake in a way in which you can predict from the get-go. If you just start throwing attacks wide, they're not going to work.

If your opponent is especially fast though, and you can't seem to find the time to get through the entirety of that second disengage, there is another option. After your first disengage, instead of drawing a half circle on the way back, just draw a quarter circle and slip your blade underneath your partner's hilt. This last move is also known as a **half disengage**.

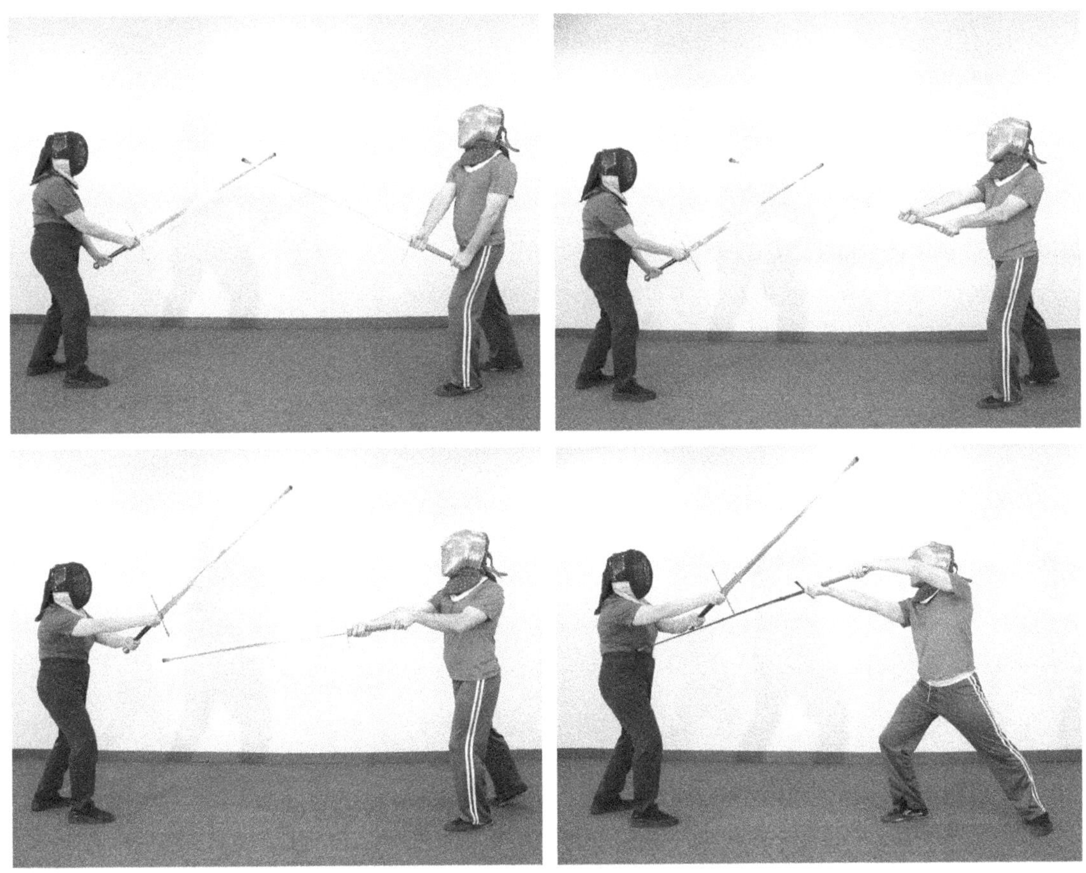

Feint, half disengage

Unless you feel like dropping your body really far down for something like a double leg takedown, my suggestion would be to bring in your off hand and place it on either their hilt or their forte. This one also tends to work better with a pass than with a lunge.

Solo Feinting Patterns

Here are a few patterns you can do on your own to help train your feints. Again, this is not an exhaustive list of the possible feints out there. Instead this is merely a jumping off point to get you started. Play around with these, see how they feel, and see which you can pull off in sparring. After that come back and figure out what other feinting patterns might work well for you.

1. Feints (thrust to thrust, thrust to cut)
   - Feint *punta roversa, sfalsare* underneath, *punta dritta*
   - Feint *punta dritta, sfalsare* underneath, *punta roversa*
   - Thrust to the face, *mezzo mandritto* to the hands
   - Thrust to the face, *mezzo roverso* to the hands
   - Thrust to the face, *sfalsare* over their sword, *mezzo mandritto* to the hands
   - Thrust to the face, *sfalsare* over their sword, *mezzo roverso* to the hands
   - Feint to the center, *punta infalsata*
   - Feint *imbrocatta* to the face, lower point to strike the hands

As you might have noticed, the Bolognese authors really like opening by attacking to the face. Even with a fencing mask on, evolution really doesn't want anything to come at our eyes. If I feint a thrust to your chest it might hit or it might not, but it isn't immediately going to hit the off switch on your computer. A thrust to the face, though, not only is hard for people to judge as the human eye isn't great at dealing with the z-axis (hence the need for brake lights), but our body also knows that there aren't any spare organs rattling inside your brain cage. Once you've gotten your opponent to instinctually recoil, go ahead and hit them in the hands they so generously just served up to you. Conversely, you'll also see a lot of plays that feint to the hands and then once those are pulled back and out of the way, they then instruct you to strike to the face. You succeed in hitting either one of those and the fight is over and done.

2. Feints (cut to thrust)
  - *Mandritto sgualimbratto* to miss, *punta roversa*
  - *Roverso sgualimbratto* to miss, *punta dritta*
  - *Mandritto fendente* to miss, *stocatta*
  - *Roverso fendente* to miss, *stocatta*
  - *Mandritto ridoppio* to miss, *roverso imbrocatta* into *coda lunga e stretta*
  - *Roverso ridoppio* to miss, *mandritto imbrocatta* into *porta di ferro stretta*
  - *Falso dritto* to miss, *punta dritta*
  - *Falso manco* to miss, *punta roversa*
  - *Falso dritto* to miss, yield into *punta roversa*
  - *Falso manco* to miss, yield into *punta dritta*

15: Grappling

I want to preface this with the fact that I am in no way a grappling expert. I've been spending more time with it lately, but if you want to actually get good at grappling I cannot recommend signing up for classes with your local judo dojo highly enough. There are a whole bunch of other grappling options out there these days such as Brazilian jiu-jitsu or collegiate wrestling that can also help give you a great foundation. I've personally found the stand-up work in judo to have the most cross over with what the Bolognese masters show us in their texts, but I'm sure that other options can work great as well. There's not really much ground work when swords come into play, so we mostly see the plays end either with a throw or a standing joint lock. That said, there's only so many ways to turn someone into a pretzel so the more grappling training you can get, the better.

As well, if you're looking to add some grappling into your fencing I'd recommend checking what grappling your fencing group does and does not allow. Seeing which grappling rule sets most align with what you're trying to do can be a big help when deciding what other arts to pursue. If you're doing full-on throws on top of mats layered over a sprung floor on Monday and then show up Tuesday sword in hand on a hardwood floor, you're going to have to do some serious code switching to make sure you're using the proper techniques for their respective environments.

Falling

Knowing how to fall properly is the single most useful skill you can learn in a martial arts class. Realistically, no one is going to call on you to fight a duel to the death with swords in hand. Marginally more likely you'll have to use your fists to get out of a bad situation in a bar, but even still the number of times that's going to happen to you is going to be pretty low.[71] However, you are going to fall. Falling makes up the highest number of non-life-threatening ER visits because gravity affects us all, rich or poor. Working on your balance can definitely help you fall less, but even still, it's going to happen. If you're in any sort of martial arts class where there's a chance of two bodies running into each other, the chances skyrocket. Same

---

[71] As of writing this, I have been in a grand total of zero bar fights.

thing even if you're just fencing at a distance and the floor just got waxed or you're on wet grass. One of my teachers just fell the other day while trying to sit down on a stool that happened to not be on level ground. Falling happens and practicing how to do it safely is going to come in handy, especially as you get older.

Now, the two biggest things to remember about falling is to tuck your chin and not to land on your hands. If you're falling back and you tuck your chin there's a chance that you'll hit the back of your head on the ground (albeit a lot lower chance than if you don't tuck your chin) and your chin ends up getting pushed into your chest. This isn't a particularly fun feeling, but you'll recover. Now, and do not actually go out and physically do this, imagine if you fell but this time your head got pushed forward. While right now you could probably touch your chin to your chest without much effort, your head is not built to come into contact with your back. So by tucking your chin in, you're not only making it harder for your head to slam into anything, but you also keep the nerves in your spine intact, making sure you can keep fencing for many years to come.

The other big hazard when falling is landing on your hands. The issue is that this is a really built-in response that you're going to have to train out. While landing on your hand is better than having your head hit the ground, it comes with one major issue. Your wrist is not built to absorb the impact of your entire body. At one of my classes recently someone got pushed back hard, started to fall, and then put out their hand to catch them. They broke their wrist and are going to be out of the game for the next eight to nine months. You don't have to have a black belt in some sort of grappling art in order to be a top-level longsword fighter, but getting some training in how to fall properly will definitely help extend your career.

Here's what I like to call the four **cardinal falls**. Again, if at all possible please try and go over these with someone in person. I'm including them here because I think that they're important info to have, but falling especially is something that's especially difficult to teach through a book.

With that said, the first option I want to show you is what's called a **back fall**. For this you want to tuck your chin, round your back, and pull your arms in. Then, when your belt line hits the ground, slap out to the sides with both of your hands. You're not trying to catch yourself with your hands here, but you are trying to distribute the force a bit more so that it doesn't all go into your head. The trick here is that you want to roll through as opposed to landing flat on your back and having the wind knocked out of you.

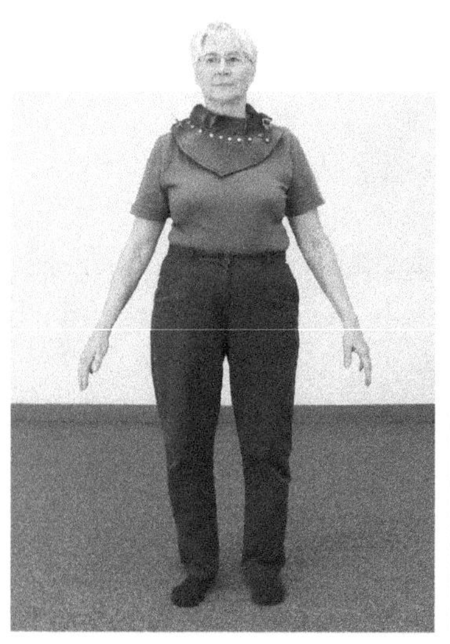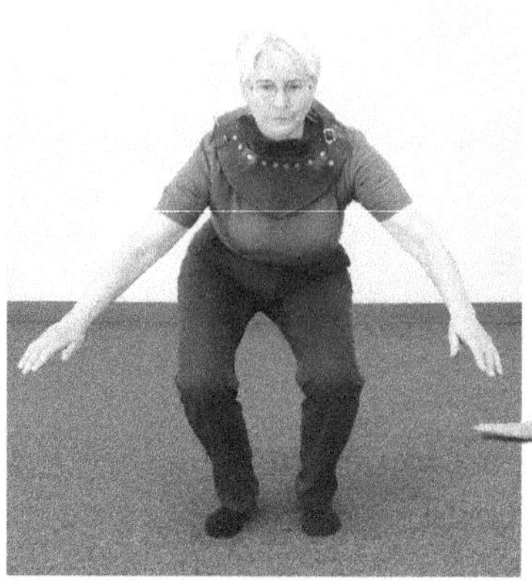

Back fall

Another option, particularly if there's a lot of momentum leading up to your fall, is to do a **backwards shoulder roll**. This is going to be similar to the back fall, except this time you want your momentum to keep going as you roll over one of your shoulders, pulling your head as far out of the way as possible. Bonus points on this one if you can end standing back up.

Backwards shoulder roll

Next let's look at **side falls**. To practice these you're going to want to start by tucking your chin again. Now, whichever way you're being pushed, take that leg and swing it across your body. So, if you're being pushed toward your right shoulder use your right leg and swing it to the left. If you're being pushed to the left, take your left leg and swing it out to the right. From there you're going to want to bend your knee and roll from your hip to your shoulder as you slap out with your hand. Please do not try and body-check the earth. You will not win. The younger you are the less of a big deal it will seem if your hip or your shoulder slams into the ground. The older you get, the more you'll appreciate having done it the right way from the get go.

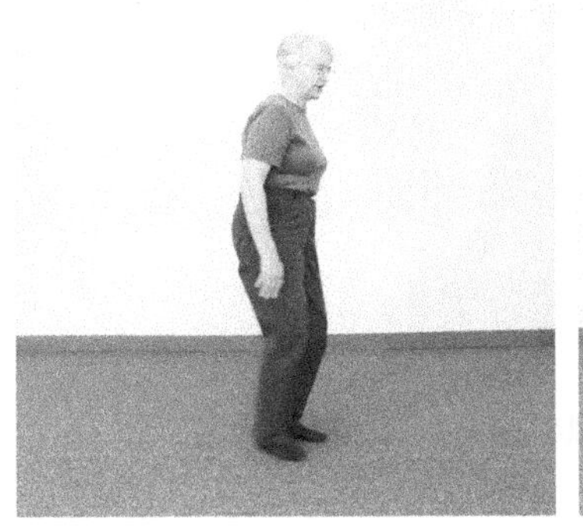  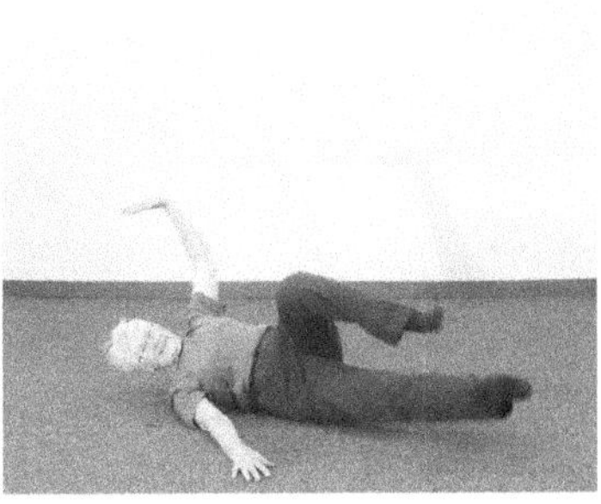

Side fall

Finally, let's look at the **forward shoulder roll**. You'll find that you likely have one side that works way better than the other, but it's vitally important to train both as you don't get to be the one who chooses which way you're thrown in a live situation. For this one you're going to want to tuck your chin again and then reach out with one hand as you step forward with the same foot. From there you're going to touch the back of your hand to the ground and then roll down your arm, over your shoulder, and across to your opposite hip. One of the things to watch out for here is landing with your legs crossed. Not only is this a great way for you to slam your bony joints into each other, but it'll get exponentially worse if your partner ends up falling on top of you. Also, depending on how you're built, it can also result in you squeezing your own junk between your legs.

Forward shoulder roll

Just A Gentle Push

One of the nice things about grappling with swords is just that, SWORDS! Most of the time I get close enough in to grapple, it largely becomes a contest of which one of us remembers they have a sword first. Someone can get you to the ground, but if you cut them in the head it's not going to do them much good. Almost all of the *prese* (grapples) we see in the Bolognese manuals for the sword in hand chapters are really just pushing your opponent's arms out of the way, or wrapping your arm around theirs, in order to clear a path for your sword. This is also likely why we don't see a lot of ground work in the medieval and renaissance European martial traditions. If you've got a sword, or even a knife, trying to choke someone out on the ground suddenly becomes a much riskier strategy.

Let's look at a couple of the most common entries to the grapple. The first
is from what we call an **outside yield**. For this, both fencers are going to cut
a *mandritto* (assuming they're both right handed or both left handed). From
there, take your hand off your pommel and, while maintaining blade contact
with your opponent, roll your guard up and to the outside. From there, take
what was your pommel hand and use it to push their arms out of the way. At that
point, depending on how close you are, throw a *roverso* to their head or, as the
Anonimo says, "Feed them the apple."[72]

Outside yield

The other common option would be to perform an **inside yield**. For this, both
you and your opponent need to throw a *roverso* at each other (assuming you're
same handed). The very instant the two swords meet, let go with your pommel
hand and use your dominant hand to push their blade across your body, with
your tip now pointed at the ground.[73] From there, you can either use your free
hand to push their arms out of the way or, if you're a bit closer in, wrap it over
their arms and then pull up, bringing your elbow in to your ribs. At this point
you can either throw a *mandritto*, strike them with the pommel, or just give
them the opportunity to peacefully surrender.

Inside yield

[72] Anonimo, 124.
[73] This, incidentally, is also dall'Agochhie's ***guardia di testa.***

One of the other main places we see the pommel hand coming off your own sword is to squeeze the two blades together. This one works a lot better on the inside as you don't have to reach as far, but if you step in far enough you could get away with it on either side. Now the thing to remember here is that these are swords, and not lightsabers. You can touch the blade of a sword and it won't instantly go through your hand. You can even place your hand on a sharp blade and as long as that blade doesn't move, you'll be just fine. This is doubly true if you're wearing a nice pair of leather gloves. While it's not ideal, sometimes you just have to risk your hand getting cut in order to prevent getting absolutely skewered.

For this technique, you both need to throw the same blow (*mandritto* vs *mandritto* or *roverso* vs *roverso*), but this time from further out as opposed to the previous two plays. Then, assuming they don't immediately move to disengage their blade, reach out with your hand and sandwich the two blades together. The key here is to press your fingers against the flats of both of the blades as opposed to trying to wrap your hand around the edges. After that just turn your hand and then step in to either strike them with your pommel or come in and continue grappling further.[74]

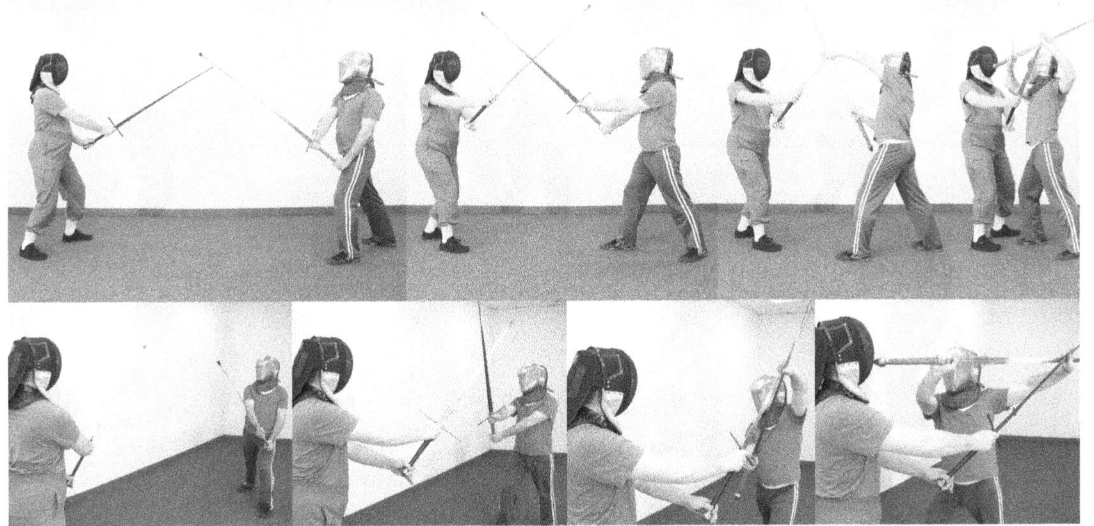

Pommel strike

As an important note, please be extra nice if you're going to pommel strike someone in the face. Unlike your sword, your pommel doesn't bend, so all of that force is going to be absorbed directly by your friend's skull. You can tap them lightly on the mask, or gesture threateningly showing off what you could have done, but for the love of daddy Manciolino, please do not blast people with your pommel.

[74] Not all clubs allow pommel strikes. If yours doesn't, please don't attempt one and then try and get away with it by saying I told you to do it. There's a lot of things you can blame me for, but please don't make this one of them.

16: Drills

There's this idea out there that drills are just you doing a single action a thousand times off to the side, all on your own. While that definitely is an option, I think we'll both agree that there are generally better things for you to do with your time. The simplest way of looking at drills is seeing them as an interaction that is more limited in scope than full freeplay. This could range all the way from lunging against a target to full-on fighting but only using thrusts. If you have any one thing you're trying to work on, it's only going to show up so many times during freeplay. What a drill helps you do is cut out some of that white noise in order to narrow your scope and increase the frequency you're able to train any one aspect of your fight.

Blocked vs Variable Drilling

When most people think of a drill, what they're imagining is **blocked drilling**. This is doing any one action a bunch of times in a row and then possibly doing another action for the same number of times afterward. For instance, throwing a *mandritto fendente* ten times and then following it up with ten *roverso fendenti* would be a blocked drill. Alternatively, you could work on a specific variation of find, gain, strike and work that against an opponent however many times in a row. Blocked drills are helpful for getting an initial understanding of a motion. So if you've never had to find someone's sword while they're in a high guard, slowing things down and working that a few times is going to help you a lot more than just being told to do it in the middle of a high stress fight. While blocked drilling is good at helping you get an initial understanding of an action or principle, it's really bad at helping you to pull that out when you randomly have to pull it out during a fight.[75]

Variable drilling is what you do when you need to really get something into your bones. Instead of going AAAABBBBCCCDDD, a variable drill might have you go ADCBBDCABDDADCB. The randomness of it teaches your brain to be able to pull out a given technique at any given moment. If at all possible, try and spend most of your practice time doing variable as opposed to blocked drilling. Sometimes you will see this instead referred to "interleaving."

[75] Franklin, "Block vs Random".

Cooperative vs Non-Cooperative Drills

Here's another axis we can add in to how we build out drills. Like with blocked drilling, **cooperative drills** are what most people are expecting when they're told it's time for drills. These are drills where you know when exactly everything that is going to happen. For instance, fencer A might have a choice to either throw a *stocatta* to fencer B's inside line (to be parried in *porta di ferro stretta*), eliciting a disengage to the outside followed by a strike by fencer A. Alternatively, fencer A could thrust to fencer B's outside line (to be parried in *coda lunga e stretta*) eliciting a disengage back to fencer B's inside line followed by a thrust from fencer A. Alternating between the two options might be done in either a blocked or a variable setting, but the intensity and commitment will be fairly set.

Once you have that down, though, it's time to move to what are called **non-cooperative drills**. As we saw in chapter 9 "The Shitty Parry Drill," our opponents aren't going to always react to the same degree every time. Sometimes they might throw a bad parry, in which case you get to blow straight through. Other times they might try and shove your sword into the ground if you aren't fast enough on your disengage. Not knowing how much intensity your partner is going to commit with during any given pass of a drill makes it non-cooperative.

Alternatively, fencer A in this scenario could decide to make the drill non-cooperative by randomizing when they fire their initial attack. One of the really big traps I see people getting sucked into during drills is to always fire on the beat as if there's a metronome dictating when people should initiate. During a fight people tend to fire when they want to as opposed to following any particular rhythm. So, you could go from both of you standing there and having fencer A fire their shot off in a cooperative context, to both of you moving around and having fencer A initiate the play randomly in order to make it non-cooperative and better help you create a bridge from structured drilling to being able to perform under pressure.

Complexity vs Intensity

There are two other main dials you can play with in order to help someone take an idea taught in a drill and help them create a bridge to being able to pull it off during a fight. The first of these is **complexity**. If I'm teaching someone how to do a feint by disengage, it will only help so much if I start us both out standing still and have them throw the feint from there. Both my and my student's brains are at full capacity and neither one of us should be distracted or mentally exhausted. A fight isn't going to be so forgiving. To help with this, I'll often have the student throw a few techniques in front of the one we're working on. Now I'm not just having them swing their sword around in the air all by themselves before coming into feint. Instead, I might try having them come in to find my sword, step back, maybe throw a cut, step back again, and only then throw the feint we're working on. If you have a student who seems to be able to pull off a technique inside a fairly structured drill but can't get it to work while they're fighting, upping the complexity can help get them there.

The other option is changing the **intensity**. This might mean having the whole drill move faster or slower than they're used to.[76] Alternatively, you can deliver the same parry, but stronger. If their mechanics are in the right place, changing how strong you parry shouldn't affect anything. However, it's often at this stage that things begin to fall apart. I've seen a lot of fighters drill with overly compliant partners who then don't know what to do when someone pulls out a counter find during a fight. This is a solvable problem: all you need to do is add in a bit of pressure testing to the drills you run.

[76] You'd be surprised how often things fall apart at slower speeds.

Building an On-Ramp

Perhaps the biggest issue people have with drills is that they often feel too far removed from an actual match. Some teachers will tell you that all you need to do is practice a set of highly structured drills enough times and suddenly all of the proper responses will fall into place, and you'll be able to use it all in an actual fight. Those teachers are full of shit.

Highly structured drills where each person is limited to a small set of actions and only get to use them when it's their turn is indeed a helpful place to start. It's not a great place to stop. You as a coach need to build an on-ramp from that highly structured place to the actual fight. Here's a drill I often use when working with someone on their calibration.

STEP 1: I start by having them strike a stationary target until they can do it with proper control.

STEP 2: From there I'll have them go to a moving target.

STEP 3: After that I'll have them start to try and strike a moving person.

STEP 4: Then I have them try and strike a moving person who's allowed to parry.

STEP 5: Then I have them try and strike a moving person who can both parry and find but not yet strike.

STEP 6: Eventually I'll move both the student and their partner to just sparring, but with a focus on controlling calibration.

STEP 7: Finally I'll just have the two of them fight without consciously focusing on calibration.

If I just have you hit a wall until you stop feeling when you've hit it too hard you might be able to control yourself in a fight, but it probably won't work as well as if we slowly built you an on ramp to your final destination.

Alternatively we could look at the "Hunt the Debole" drill from chapter 6. We started with a fairly loose drill with both people acting at the same time, but with feet planted and without any strikes. Then we let our two fencers start moving their feet and only after we'd done that for a while did we allow them to eventually gain and then strike. While what we started with didn't look much like an actual fight, the end result did.

Common Mistakes

For any drill, regardless of the type, make sure your partner is actually trying to hit you. Oftentimes I'll check this by just not parrying an incoming blow. It's incredibly easy to get caught in the trap of throwing short or only aiming for their blade instead of their body. This is a disservice to both you and your partner. Not only are you training yourself to miss, but you're also training your partner to parry something that isn't a real and viable threat. This is a really easy mistake to make at any level, so try and keep an eye out for it and keep both you and your partner honest.

Next, make sure you aren't trying to "win" the drill. If the drill itself comes with a specific victory condition, such as hitting the other person with a loud thwap in the "Glove Game" from chapter 10, it's fine to strategize in order to work toward that goal. What I'm talking about here is treating a drill like a fight and setting your personal win conditions as such. So, if your role is to give only slight pressure when your opponent comes in to find your sword, don't push their sword into the ground in order to prevent them from hitting you at all. Alternatively, if the drill limits you to only a specific set of actions, don't repeatedly use an action outside of what you've been told you can use as if your partner actually followed the instructions, there's no way for them to succeed. Yes, what you're doing could definitely work in an actual fight, but that's not the point of a drill. Drills are there to help you narrow your focus so you're not just dealing with the whole art at once.

A similar mistake is what I like to call "right answer, wrong time." This one happens particularly at higher speeds when your hands just go ahead and do what you've trained them to do as opposed to what the drill is asking of you. Lots of times they'll make what could be a correct answer given the situation, except that what you just did isn't within the bounds of the drill. This is similar to what we were just talking about with the difference here being intention. With this mistake, just laugh it off, slow things down a bit, and try to stay within the bounds of the drill. Alternatively, if you and your partner both agree, feel free to loosen things up a bit and explore what might happen if either one of you takes a slightly different path.

Another common mistake while drilling is to get into too much of a rhythm. If you're working the four-corners drill and you're just throwing one cut after another, it can be all too easy for your partner to be parrying your rhythm instead of your technique. To combat this, try pausing every once in a while or change the rhythm you're throwing things. We're here training swordplay, not DDR.

Finally, and this is by and far the biggest mistake people make in drilling, is giving unwanted advice. This is something we are all guilty of, so don't feel bad if you do it every once in a while. Now if you and your drill partner have a previously established relationship where they've made it clear they're open to your advice, you're then free to give it. If you're brand new to working with each other you can always ask if they'd like to hear a suggestion, just be ready for them to say "no" and accept that answer without any arguing whatsoever. However, there are few worse turnoffs in a class than when somebody assumes they have the answer to all your problems and proceeds to hand it to you whether you want it or not. If you're just walking into that situation, you have no idea what aspect the other person might be focusing on. You might be getting one thing out of a drill whereas they might be getting something completely different. It's one thing if you say something like, "I think we're supposed to do this from the right side instead of the left," but that's different than telling someone, "Oh, I think it would help if you did it this way." Particularly if you're in a more formal classroom setting, don't try and take over the class if you're not the teacher. That said, if they ask you for your advice, feel free to give it.

Three to One

Some of the best advice I ever received on how to coach came from Guy Windsor in his online course, "How to Teach Historical Martial Arts (or anything else)". What he suggested is simple and incredibly effective. It encapsulated so much of what I see being done right by the top-level coaches and what I see being done wrong by some of the others. It's an easy rule that makes a huge impact in how well a student can take information in. The rule on its own won't guarantee success, but it'll sure make it more likely.

Fencing is ultimately a physical art. We can write about it, give speeches, and draw diagrams. However, at the end of the day, fencing is about two people moving around with swords in their hands. This part seems pretty obvious, but so much of fencing instruction ignores this essential feature. We as teachers and coaches have so much that we've learned and often try and pass all of it along at once. A phrase I've heard more times than I can count is folks telling students to "drink from the firehose". This implies that your teacher is going to throw everything that have at you and it's your job to try and drink up as much as you can. While there are definitely people who have succeeded with this approach, it's not a particularly effective one. It also makes the mistake of centering the lesson on the coach instead of the student. When running a class or working with someone one on one, the purpose of that session isn't to demonstrate how knowledgeable you, as the authority figure, are on a subject. It's to help the student or students progress along their journey.

There are times that you might give them a little bit more than they can handle or a little bit less than they have bandwidth for, but ultimately you want them to walk away with something they can digest. Sometimes that means they'll walk away with something immediately actionable and other times it'll be something that they'll sit and ponder on for months. Either way, though, if you're giving them something to chew on, first make sure they have room to fit it in their mouth.

Okay, so back to that rule I mentioned. The rule is just:

"For every minute of explanation there has to be at least three minutes of implementation."

What that means is that it's fine if you take some time to verbally explain what's going on or what you're about to do, but you should spend at least three times that amount on actually doing the thing. It doesn't matter if that's highly structured drills or more loosely coached sparring. In a physical art people learn best by *physically* doing it.

I've seen so many teachers try and fill space during the lesson by talking the whole way through and students who try and connect to it by bringing up a story that only vaguely relates and then spending the majority of the lesson on that instead of the task at hand. I understand those urges, I really do, but it's important to save those for later and to spend the lesson working through the actions themselves. It's imperative that you give clear instructions and helpful feedback, don't just hit your student a bunch and hope they figure it out. That said, the only way to really get better at doing swords is by actually *doing* it and getting it all in your bones.

17: Fencer Alignment Chart

I realize that personality tests are a dime a dozen. We even see these in some of the period authors basing different types of fencers' personality types off of Galen's humors (sanguine, choleric, melancholic, & phlegmatic). While those have their uses, I find them far enough removed from how we as twenty-first-century people describe things that relying on classical-age medical diagnoses to explain fighting so overly cumbersome that I don't really bother. Instead, I'd like to offer the following. Now, be aware that this is just how I think of things in my own head. If you describe how different fencers line up in a completely unrelated way, keep doing that.

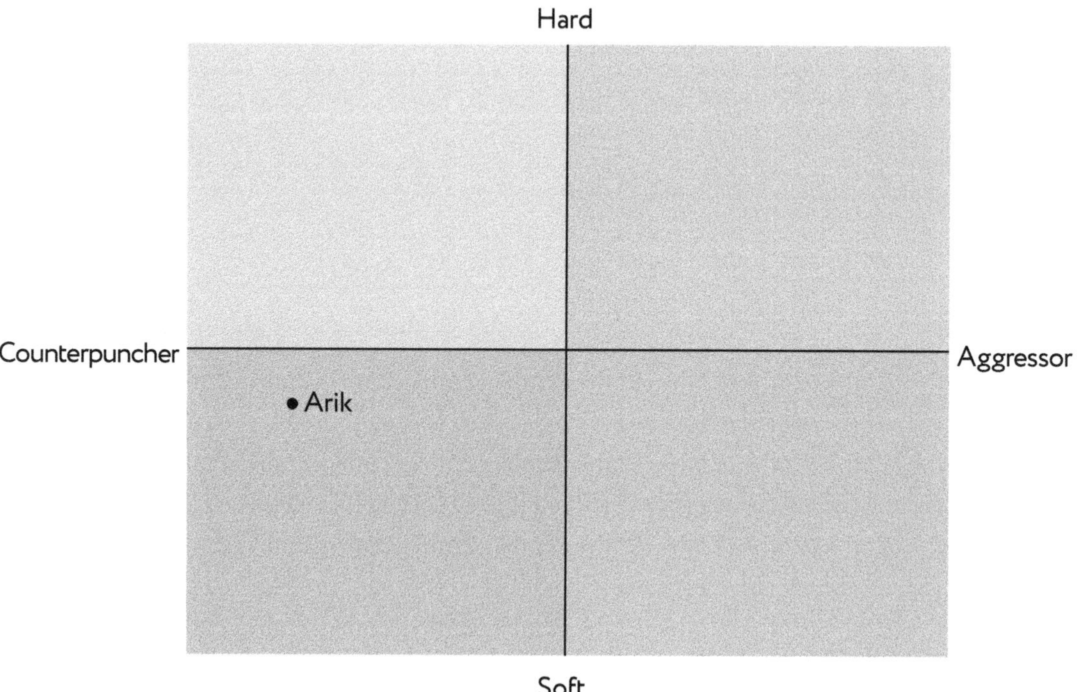

Aggressor vs. Counterpuncher

Like with anything, these are generalizations about someone's fight. No one is any one thing all the time. This is just to help you identify what someone generally defaults to. With that in mind, let's dive in.

One of the biggest differences between how we fight with swords now and how it was done back in the day are the roles. In the 16th century, were you to get into a formal upper-class duel, there were rules as to which party was supposed to do what. If Marozzo called Manciolino a cheat and Manciolino called him a liar, each would then have a specific role to play. Marozzo would be responsible for choosing the exact time and place the duel would take place. Manciolino, as the defendant, would get to choose the weapons and what armor may or may not be involved.[77] As you might have guessed, you really want to do everything you can to be the defendant here.[78]

Without getting too far into it, there's another piece to these roles, one that may seem even more foreign to our modern sensibilities. As a part of the duel, the accuser would be tasked with throwing the first committed blow of the fight. Generally, when we think of a fight, whether it be two people "taking it outside" or a regulated sporting match, neither side is specifically instructed with having to try and throw the first hit. Particularly if it's not just any blow, but a committed one, being forced to do so puts the accuser in a much riskier position. This was created intentionally as a cultural norm back in the day in order to dissuade people from just openly trash-talking each other. Particularly when you live in an honor-based society where if people think you're a cheat, no one will do business with you and your family will end up on the street, it was important to put barricades up to prevent real life from turning into an internet comment section. That said, the popularity of duels shows us that this was hardly a fully successful tool in dissuading real-life trolls.

How does this affect us now? Well, in pretty much any modern sparring session or tournament, we don't have these specifically assigned roles. As such, people tend to find themselves drifting toward one of two roles, **aggressor** or **counterpuncher**.[79] Being an aggressor is exactly what it sounds like. You like to make the first move. Instead of waiting around, you get in there and force your opponent to make a mistake that you can then exploit. Not only do you tend to move first, but you're constantly trying to constrain your opponent's blade or throw feints at their face as you move in.

---

[77] In his book, Manciolino tells us that if you're the shorter of the two combatants and you have the choice, you should make it such that both parties are only allowed to wear armor on their top halves. If you're the taller fighter, he suggests making it such that you are both only allowed leg armor.

[78] Tom Leoni, *In The Service of Mars: Volume I*, 245.

[79] Anonimo Bolognese, 72.

The counterpuncher, on the other hand, tends to take the opposite approach. They like to hang around and wait to see what their opponent does before committing to any one choice. Instead of attacking in the tempo of their opponent's preparation or step like the aggressor might, the counterpuncher instead tends to favor the tempo after their opponent's blow passes by. Particularly if there's no timer, the counterpuncher will try and win with patience, using conservative movements and not committing until they absolutely know they have the opening to do so safely. I'd also note that between the two Manciolino specifically says, "he who strikes with the riposte is more praiseworthy than he who strikes in first intention,"[80] but I'm also a tad bit biased.

Hard vs. Soft

This mostly has to do with blade contact, but I figured that saying "really loves to fight inside the bind" and "flighty" would be a little more clunky. Essentially, if someone likes to fight **hard**, that means they want to press through your blade. They might be bigger than you, rely on their strength, or (and most frighteningly) know they have better mechanics than you do. Particularly if they're in that last category, it's going to be to their advantage to try and physically push through your blade, forcing you to constantly play catch up. If someone is fighting hard and they're only getting there through strength, you can overcome them by just having better mechanics. Particularly if they're used to being to just blow through people, they're not going to know what to do against someone who can just cross over their blade and shut them down. If they have the better mechanical understanding, though, you're going to want to try and invite them to overcommit and then punish them accordingly. If you can, winning through mechanical advantage alone is a hell of a power move.

Manciolino also gives us some advice for how to deal with someone who likes to power through with strength. He tells us that there are two things we should do as a response: "The first is to let his blow pass and feint a parry and carefully push your own attack; the second is to rush forward and parry before his attack gains momentum."[81] He then goes on to tell us that the other option is to just hit them in the hand. Turns out, it's a lot harder to recklessly swing a sword around without hands.

Alternatively, they might be someone who likes to fight **soft**. This is someone who might bait you by leaving their sword out for you to try and dominate, but the moment you come in they're already out of there. They're going to have tight

[80] Manciolino, 77.
[81] Manciolino, 73.

disengages and likely have a couple really solid feints. Another way of thinking about this kind of fighter would be to call them "slippery." No matter what plan you try and throw out there, if they're at a high level they'll know how to weasel out of it and suddenly appear somewhere else. When fighting against someone who's soft, it's best to give them a singular and clear option at any given time. They'll still slip out from your initial move, but at least now you know where they are going and can plan accordingly.

Which One Am I?

At the end of the day, look at aggressor vs. counterpuncher as one axis and hard vs. soft as another. You can be an aggressor who fights hard, pushing people's blades into the ground and running them down. You could also be an aggressor who relies on feints and doesn't make blade contact until the very last moment, or you could just play measure games, lunging in and out whenever you force an opening. As well you could be a counterpuncher who relies on mechanical advantage and forces people into having to take oblique lines in order to get all the way around your well-formed guards. Alternatively, you could counterpunch with as little blade contact as possible, relying on your superior grasp of tempo. It's also important to remember that no one is any one of these things all the time. I know that personally I have two different modes I switch between depending on what problem I'm trying to solve, with one of those being the default and the other requiring me to actively turn it on. Play with it a bit and see where you land, then circle back in a few years and see how much your game has changed. You also don't have to be just one or the other and can incorporate elements of both as you slide back and forth across the spectrum as you fight.

There's a fairly simple workshop I've run on this multiple times. Get everyone paired up and then assign each person one of the four fencer types. You can assign both sides to different types, or you can occasionally make both fighters try and approach the other in the exact same way. By the end of it, everyone should have tried each of the four out. This will give people who otherwise couldn't have told you where they want to be in a fight language to describe what they do, and perhaps more importantly, don't like.

If you want to add an extra layer to this, after you go through the four fencer types I've laid out you can run the whole thing again with dall'Aggochie's five tempi as described in chapter 12. Some folks will click better with the four fencer types, while for some it'll make more sense to describe their fight in regards to tempo. One of the marks of a great teacher is the ability to explain something to a student in a multitude of different ways as opposed to being stuck using the same old metaphor regardless of how much sense it makes to the next generation.

Area of Excellence

Ultimately the goal here is to figure out your own personal **area of excellence**.[82]
What is the space that if you can get your opponent into it you'll have the fight
locked down? For me that's inviting in *porta di ferro stretta* and then throwing a
roverso sgualimbratto to their right hand/forearm when then come in to take the
line. For someone else it could be striking during the tempo where your opponent
raises their foot while trying to enter measure. Another option is that it might be
that you just love being in the bind and striking from *guardia di intrare*. If you're
just starting out, then don't worry about this, right now you just need to focus on
getting your sea legs, nailing down those fundamentals, and exploring what's out
there. Once you've been at it for a few years and are starting to be at least in the
middle of the pack, only then is it time to start figuring out where in the fight you
want to be. Otherwise, you'll end up pigeonholing yourself and hitting a plateau
when you find that everyone around you has figured out how to deal with your one
and only trick.

The Funnel

Once you've figured out what your area of excellence is, it's time to figure out how
to funnel your opponents into it. On its own, your area of excellence is a place
you end up in right before you strike, but isn't necessarily a jumping off point. To
start off, ask yourself who in the fight you ideally want to move first. One of my
main teachers wants to run you down with a lot of blade contact, but will sit there
patiently until you make the first move so that he can punish you for your mistakes.
I really want people to overcommit so that I can dip around their sword and strike
them on a different line than where they started. To do this, I generally set up in a
stretta guard in order to entice my opponent into trying to forcefully bind with me.

One of the big things here, especially with the *stretta* guards, is to make sure you
are only inviting to one line at a time. If you're trying to set up in *coda lona e stretta*
and your point starts to drift inwards you are forming what Alfieri (one of the rapier
masters) calls *guardia mista* where you're leaving yourself open to both the inside
and outside lines. If you don't know where your opponent is going to go, then you
get to play a very dangerous game of catch up. Your goal here should be to limit your
opponent's options as much as possible in order to force them into highly predictable
responses that you can then easily deal with.

82 Harmenberg, "Epee 2.6", 10.

Denial

This is one of the hardest parts of overall strategy, but will pay dividends if you start reaching that upper end of the competition circuit. The idea here is that you figure out what your opponent's area of excellence is and then refuse to let them play their favorite game entirely. So, if they love to work in the bind, you refuse blade contact either by sticking to *gioco largo* or by sticking to stretta constantly keeping your blade just out of reach. If your opponent is a judo black belt and sees their sword just as a grappling lever, you're going to want to keep on your feet and strike from the edge of measure instead of ever trying to play the close game against them. Your opponent could also be someone who has really strong guards on the inside line but gets queasy when they're forced to properly gain on the outside. The answer to that one I'm going to let you figure out on your own. Overall, this piece of the puzzle is going to require you watching video, spending your time in between rounds carefully watching everyone else's fights, and overall getting really good at pattern recognition.

18: Strategy

So now that you have the building blocks in place, let's take a look at some more overarching strategies. Some of these are for training, some are for a long day of tournaments, and some are for fighting more broadly. Here's hoping you find something in here that resonates and helps you along your journey.

Hand Hits

Hand hits are a big topic of conversation these days. Some people find them cheap and don't like to focus on them, whereas others make it their entire game. Thankfully, Manciolino himself waded into this topic himself in order to tell us exactly what a good Bolognese practitioner should do about hand hits. He says that, "The part of the opponent's body you should attack the most is that with which he performs the most attacks on you — namely, the hand." [83] Hard to be more direct than that.

If you still had any doubts, the Anonimo comes in to agree with what Manciolino says. He tells us, "blows to the hand are the most profitable attacks that you can make," he continues, "because the hand guards the body, but the body does not protect the hand." [84] Turns out, if you're the only one who can protect themselves, the fight is yours.

Now, while hitting someone in the hand isn't going to kill them, running the sharp end of a three to four-pound piece of steel through their metacarpals is going to cause them to drop their sword and cease being a threat. Poking someone in the forearm might not stop them, but a nice *mezzo mandritto* to the hand will. Remember, duels at this time weren't necessarily to the death, they were to incapacitation. If the other person can't hold a sword in a swordfight, then that means the fight is over. The things to be careful of are first and foremost the fact that hands are made up of lots of little tiny bones and no one should have to go and get an x-ray after a fencing match, so make sure to play nice. Hitting someone in the hand can make it incredibly difficult to close out the line in the same tempo, so you

[83] Manciolino, 73.
[84] Anonimo Bolognese, 65.

leave yourself open to being on the worse end of a double with their sword possibly having a clear and open lane straight to your head.

Attack Where They Will Be

If your opponent has any idea of what they're doing, they probably won't just sit still once the fight has started. Now they may not move to react if you throw a shitty feint or they might just freeze up—things that occur with upper-level fighters all of the time—but when presented with a credible threat they are more than likely going to try and counter it. A trap I find a lot of mid-level fighters finding themselves in is getting stuck trying to plan out their first intention, without giving enough thought as to what happens next. You need that threat your first intention provides in order to get things going, but it's important to realize that that move is almost never going to end the fight. Don't skip over it, because otherwise you're just going to fling your face into a sword tip that hasn't yet moved, but don't get hung up on trying to land that first blow. Instead, try and figure out where their hands are about to be and then hit them before they've settled into their new guard.

High vs Low Guards

One of the things Manciolino explicitly teaches us is that whenever possible, we should try and avoid being in a low guard when our opponent is in a high guard. It can seem like the natural rhythm of things to go low when they go high, but by doing so you give your opponent not only a structural advantage over you, but they also get to move faster because gravity is on their side. Remember, it is our job to make our opponent's life as inconvenient as possible. Hence all the hand hits.

Good Over Pretty

A lot of martial arts spend a good deal of their time on aesthetics. Kata contests, clanging your pommel against your buckler, using the fanciest moves possible, you get the point. What's important to remember here is that this was an art intended to take people in life-or-death situations and give them a way to come out of it alive. Aesthetics are great, but they aren't what will keep you safe. As the Anonimo teaches us, "so often it happens that a fighter who will play politely and gallantly, others will say he fights well even though his play is not useful."[85] Sure, being flashy will get you noticed, but it's not necessarily the martially sound choice.

Every once in a while I'll be working with a student and they'll tell me that this or that technique works on lots of folk, but they'd never try it against people who are at a high level. Sometimes this comes down to them not knowing how to properly

[85] Anonimo Bolognese, 68.

execute the technique and the folks at the lower levels just haven't picked up on the flaw yet. Whenever their self-assessment is right, though, my answer is always the same, "Only use techniques that work on the best fighters." The nice thing is that those same techniques will also work on the people at the lower end. Maybe you won't have to go as many steps down the decision tree and instead of that cool triple feint you have planned, you just end up hitting them on the first move, but that's fine. If your goal is to win fights, practice what works against the people at the very top and you'll be set regardless of who your opponent that day happens to be.

As the Anonimo says, "the graceful fighter upon coming to grips with one that fights brutishly does not perceive that the brutish fighter will come out on top, because the brute cares only for utility and does not give a damn for beautiful play as his mind focuses upon only what will work and dispenses with all pompous displays."[86] Essentially, just be a thug and hit them. Don't worry about being fancy, worry about not getting hit. Hone your fundamentals and use them to encourage your opponent to make better life choices.

Three Kinds of Problems

Say that there's just one fighter at your practice that you just can't figure out how to beat. Alternatively, maybe you're performing great at practice, but just can't make it work in tournaments. While I don't have the power to give you an exact answer sitting here in my chair, I can help you break things down a bit in a fashion that I've seen make a real difference in people's progressions.

In fencing, if you can't get something to work it's going to be due to one of three reasons. The first category are **mechanical** problems. This is what most of the book so far has focused on. You might be trying to gain your opponent's blade in order to hit them, but you haven't crossed their sword enough or your blade isn't turned far enough in. Alternatively it could be that you're relying on the muscles in your arms when you should really be activating the muscles in your back to do most of the work for you. Focusing on mechanics, whether it's blade mechanics or body mechanics, is incredibly important and improving your mechanics will make a huge difference not only in how many fights you win, but also how many years you can keep fighting for. That said, too many instructors stop after trying to address problems at this stage, only teaching specific techniques without putting them into a larger context.

The next category of issues are **tactical**. You can have all the right moves, but if you fire them at the wrong time they won't do you much good. Not only does this encompass a good understanding of tempo, but it's also about how to beat your

[86] Anonimo Bolognese, 68.

opponent's mind and not just their hands. If you know they love to work in the bind and then try and beat them at their own game you might find yourself suddenly outgunned against someone you thought wasn't even in your weight class. It also means knowing when to feint, when to yield, and when to counter-find. Not just performing them within *mezzo tempo* or *contra tempo*, but more broadly knowing when to use any given technique during the fight.

Finally we have **psychological** issues. Sometimes this can be being able to convince yourself to get up from the couch and head out to practice. Other times it's performing perfectly at practice, but not being able to turn it on when you show up to a tournament. It can also be something such as avoiding working on feints because the concept as a whole seems overwhelming and you just need someone to break it down for you into digestible chunks. Relatedly it could also be trying to take in too much too fast instead of trying to take things in at a more reasonable pace.

Overall, knowing what kind of issue you're faced with won't in itself solve the problem. It will, however, make it easier to try and figure out what tools you might reach for in order to get yourself to that next step.

Getting Over Roadblocks

Sometimes though, you will end up faced with an issue that you just can't find a clear answer to. You might be able to identify what kind of issue it is and have tried using every tool in your toolbox to try and solve it, but with no luck whatsoever. My suggestion? Go around it.

Sometimes the best answer is not to focus on the issue whatsoever. There are times that it might just be a technique that's too difficult for where you're at and you just need to wait until your overall game improves. Other times it's just the right move to focus on something less frustrating instead of burning out by hitting your head against the wall. In times like these, my suggestion is to go and find something else to focus on. If you're studying Bolognese, this might mean putting the longsword down and focusing on how to use a partisan or sword and buckler. Other times, it might be more beneficial to switch which topic you spend your time focusing on. You might be someone who wins most of their fights with tempo, but maybe it's time to focus on your mechanics instead. Alternatively, you could be someone who likes to win through mechanical advantage, but instead you end up taking a break by focusing on feints for a while. Either way, you are still engaging with the art and progressing down the overall path even if it means veering this way or that.

Playing With Your Opponent's Head

No, I don't mean that you should close in to grapple in order to play their head like a bongo drum. Instead I'm talking about playing mental games with your opponent before the fight even starts. The Anonimo tells us that you should walk in acting like the scariest motherfucker you can in order to get your opponent to reassess their life choices there and then. As the Anonimo tells us, "The true virtue of this art consists in being intimidating, and in possessing such ferocity as to appear to be on fire." He continues, "Every slightest motion you make must exude a craving for delivering cruel blows."[87] Scary stuff. He then finishes it out by telling us, "It wouldn't be a bad thing if you could make yourself look like a great devil and act like you wanted to whisk away his soul."[88] Next time you have a big match, see what you can do best emulate the spirit of what he's taught us.

Looking at the other side of the coin, Manciolino tells us to "never let the opponent win by overwhelming you with his blows or with his audacity."[89] I've definitely seen people show up to a tournament and heard other people say, "Well, hopefully I'll get second." While I don't recommend giving up before the fighting has started, making your opponent resign themselves to being second best before the fight has even started is a time tested strategy. I also did once have a match with a friend where I repeatedly said, while we were fighting, "I'm in your head. I'm in your head." I don't recommend trying that particular trick unless the other person likes you, but it is fun if you can pull it off.

The other angle is to get people to underestimate you. This might mean not dressing as well and not having as nicely polished equipment. It could also mean not talking up your accomplishments or throwing your mask down and screaming when you win the match. If you just don't make a big deal of how much you've trained and just calmly shake hands with folk at the beginning and end of every match, people might not expect what comes out. If you have award or accolades in one organization and then go to play somewhere else where those don't immediately translate, people are likely to underestimate you without you wearing that group's usual rank insignias. This is also a great incentive for you to travel and fight folks from all over, something that every single period fencing master encourages you to do. If you want to be a top-level fighter, you're going to have to figure out how to use your tools to solve all sorts of problems. This also means that if you find a teacher who tells you to never train anywhere else and that you shouldn't bother crossing swords with people from other groups because they have everything you'd ever need right there, run.

[87] Anonimo Bolognese, 66.
[88] Anonimo Bolognese, 66.
[89] Manciolino, 76.

Energy Expenditure

It's of vital importance that you pace yourself. If what you have to do that day is fight one big prize fight against someone else, you're going to spread your energy out differently as opposed to if you have three different tournaments that day. Fencing is also a weird sport in that there's both a low-level energy required for the whole fight, but then that spikes dramatically for very short moments throughout. It's not a marathon, but it's also not a sprint.

One answer to this problem is to go and get your fight over with fast. Things change if you're in a tournament with specific time-based rules, but if it's just "until X number of victories," running straight through people the instant "lay on" is called is definitely a viable strategy for not burning yourself out. The other end of the spectrum is to beat people with patience. Just stand there at the edge of measure and wait for them to overcommit. If you have the stamina to hold your arms out there, you can just wait until their patience runs out and they go for it when they really shouldn't have. Both of these strategies rely on using as little energy as possible for any given fight, allowing you to keep performing well at the end of that day.

I'm also going to give you a cheat for lasting longer in your fights. If nothing is happening but the fight is still on, take a step so that you're just outside of your opponent's offensive measure and rest your arms in any of the *larga* guards. The important thing to remember is that you aren't just resting your arms, you're just taking up a less strenuous guard. Lots of people think that you need to hold your arms up or out for you to really be "fighting," but that couldn't be further from the truth. I know lots of top-level fighters whose bread and butter is fighting from low guards. You just have to make sure that the ref knows you're on guard when they call "lay on," even if you haven't moved your arms to indicate anything. The other position you can take up that's more restive than you might think is *guardia alta*. This doesn't work with single handed swords, but with a longsword everything just stacks up in *alta*. You're still up in a guard, but your bones are lined up the same direction as gravity.

Win Conditions

I cannot emphasize enough how important that day's win conditions are. Sometimes only certain blows are allowed or they might require different gear than you're used to. As well, throwing in something like an afterblow can really change things if you're only used to fighting until the first hit and aren't used to putting your guard up on your way out. Some organizations have fairly standardized rulesets, but if you're playing with a group you're not used to, make sure you double check what the rules are that day. This in part will help your victory record, but more importantly it means you should be aware of how one group operates as opposed to another. If your group allows for hilt strikes and you go somewhere that doesn't, they're not going to be prepared when you come in and quillon punch them in the face. Women's hockey has a higher concussion rate than men's hockey, because in the rules the women aren't allowed to physically check each other.[90] Checking still happens and penalties are called, but because the players aren't prepared for them, things end up going a lot worse. On top of the physical rules, it's also important to be wary of the social conventions. Some groups expect fighters to have corner coaches and for people to cheer loudly when they win. Other places don't have either of those and will look at you askance if you have either one. Now, there is of course a time and a place for social conventions to be broken. I'm just saying that if you're going to break those rules, it should be intentional, not accidental. It's also important to remember that on any given day there's the tournament winner and there's the best fighter. Those two are often the same, but that's not always the case. Between the two, I'd rather be remembered as the best fighter than just have gotten another medal to hang on my wall.

Play Your Game

Years ago, when I was first starting out, one of my friends was running an informal class where folks could just ask him any fencing related question that came to mind. My question that day was, "There's so many different kinds of fighters out there who do so many different things. How am I supposed to have a different answer for each and every one of them?" His loving response? "You're an idiot." He then went on, "You're never going to be able to have a different answer for each and every person. Don't even try. Just figure out your game and do it as best as you can and then make them deal with YOU." That advice has kept me going to this day.

Now some people love doing lots of opposition research. They'll hunt people down at events and ask about their upcoming opponent or they'll go online and watch as many videos of that person fighting as possible. This strategy definitely has merit and I know people who it's worked well for. As I run into the same people over and over again, I definitely start to make small changes here and there depending on who I'm fighting. Overall though, my focus is being the best version of me I can be. If I can be the problem my opponent has to solve instead of the other way around, then I'm already one step ahead of the game.

90 Brainard et al. 2012

Fight Like an Old Person

I've primarily learned how to fight from old people and I think it's served me pretty well. Fighting is inherently a young person's game. So if you can find someone twice your age who can still go toe to toe with you, then they've probably got something to teach you. My ultimate goal isn't to win any one specific event any one time. My goal is to keep winning them, time after time, for as long as I can. Have you ever seen someone in their sixties or seventies mop up a whole field of twenty-somethings? Fear them.

The trick here is learning to do things the right way as early as possible. This doesn't mean you have to get it right on the first try. The world's greatest fencers are constantly working on making their fundamentals just a little bit better. What I mean is that you should try and learn how to win via proper technique from the get go as opposed to relying on natural attributes (height, speed, strength) to get you through until you inevitably plateau.

There's an old tale of the short and long path and the long and short path that I think helps illustrate this point.[91] The story goes that one time a man was traveling to the big city for the very first time and was unsure how to enter. He sees a local kid playing by the road and asks the child how best to get to where he's going. The child responds, "Do you want the short and long path or the long and short path?" The man thinks for a moment and responds with, "The short and long path, please," knowing that it will be the more direct route. The child then gives him directions and the man goes on his way. The man sees the towers of the city off in the distance, but as he gets closer he discovers the path he's been sent down is packed tight with gardens and orchards without a clear way through. Annoyed, he returns back to the child and asks, "Didn't you tell me this way was short?" To which the child responds, "Didn't I also tell you it was long?" After that, the man having learned his lesson, goes off along the long and short path, eventually reaching his destination.

If you walk in the door with a few natural attributes helping you out, learning to do things the right way might feel like a slog and you're more than likely going to see other people who started at the same time as you find success a lot faster. That success is fleeting, though. While yes, everything else equal those attributes will still make a hell of a difference. Relying on those attributes alone though, will only get you so far. You might have fast hands, but physics tells us that the tip of my sword can go way faster. If you're stuck taking giant disengages at really high speeds, your opponent who's only making small motions is going to get where they're going much faster. You should strength train and work on your fast twitch muscles, but overall try and work on technique.

[91] ben Hananya, "Eruvin", 53b.

That person in their seventies sure isn't beating you on speed or endurance. They're beating you because they spent time reading the book and figuring out how to beat you with mechanics and strategy.

Also, training is not only focused on success down the road but that more importantly allows you to keep playing for decades to come. If your goal is to go win gold in the Olympics, you're going to push through the pain and then retire in your early thirties. This might mean you had to tear your meniscus or messed up your ankle along the way, but you made it to your goal and no one can take that away from you. That's fine and I don't really have any problems with it as long as the things you want are aligned with the actions you take. In what we do though, there is no gold medal at the Olympics.[92] There might be tournaments big and small, but nothing that pushes us to grind ourselves down for just a single event. Keep training and keep competing, but do so in a way that leaves you healthier than when you started.

Always Work To Better Your Situation

Here's an overarching concept that applies regardless of what technique is being applied. Every move you make should put you in a better position than where you were before it. Lots of times when people parry the result is just to end up in parity with their opponent. Sure, if someone is swinging for your head your priority should be to keep your head attached to your neck. That said, if at all possible, try and also get something out of that tempo instead of just canceling out their attack. To further illustrate this point, Manciolino tells us, "Correct parries, in fact, are preformed going forward and not backward". Now, I'm not saying that you will never win a fight after parrying while stepping back. No, what I'm pointing out is that even in a parry you have the opportunity to provide a greater threat to your opponent than you did the tempo before.

The other thing that helps me with this personally is to think of it as a counter-find as opposed to just a parry. Whenever I play video games that have separate attack vs block buttons, I end up having a hard time and generally just choose to hit the dodge button instead. In my head I am almost never just purely blocking my opponent's sword. Instead, I'm trying to retake the line from them. This doesn't always work and I'll often end up having to disengage in order to get out, but my first move wasn't to tell my opponent "no". It was to tell them, "That's my line now."

Programming Your Opponent

This is a trick as old as time. Remember that you don't need to win the fight with any one specific blow. Oftentimes it's more beneficial to slowly lull your opponent

---

[92] Please let this still be the case whenever you happen to find this book.

into a feeling of safety and then hit them with a surprise. For instance, Manciolino instructs us to "deliver the same attack three or four times in a row, almost as an invitation."[93] The human brain loves to look for patterns in things in order to help us make sense of things. Once is chance, twice is coincidence, three times is a pattern. If you do the same thing three times and your opponent has survived, they're going to start making plans around it now that they know it's coming. Use this to your advantage.

On the flip side, you can poke and prod your opponent to figure out their built in patterns and then save that information for later on. Even if you throw a shitty, undercommitted attack, your opponent is likely to still twitch this or that way. If you can figure out what those specific twitches look like, you can save that information in your brain. The issue is if you try and seize on that info immediately, they'll likely have figured out that you're doing the same thing a few times in a row in order to provoke a response. However, if you wait a couple minutes they won't be as honed in on it and now you can use their built in reactions to create an opening.

It's really easy to fall into predictable patterns, particularly when someone is trying their best to hit you with a sword. One really common example of this is constantly switching from right to left or from the inside line to the outside line. You might be used to feinting a *mandritto* and then as they go to parry, striking with a *roverso*. To be clear, there's absolutely nothing wrong with this plan. We see it pop up all the time across every single fencing tradition. Every once in a while, though, it can be helpful to change things up. One way we can do this is to repeatedly strike to the same side. We see this pop up a few times across the various authors where they'll have us feint a *mandritto*, proceed to feint a second *mandritto* all without moving your feet, and then finally strike your opponent as you step in with a third *mandritto*.[94] If you can pull this off in two moves instead of three, all the better.

The larger picture here is that people get really used to fights playing out a certain way. Fighters trade off which side things are happening on and at the end of the day, whoever threw the better feint or had the better mechanics comes out on top. Every once in a while, you can get your opponent to short circuit and leave themselves wide open. They might start to parry that first attack, but under commit knowing they'll have to turn their sword in just a moment to deal with the other side. All you have to do is let their hand go where it's used to and then strike them where it isn't. In fact the Anonimo specifically tells us that the spot they were just guarding is inherently the spot that will open up when they move to guard anywhere else.[95]

[93] Manciolino, 75.
[94] Manciolino, 75.
[95] Anonimo Bolognese, 73.

Which of These Techniques Should I Actually Use?

Glad you asked. The amount of techniques throughout the Bolognese system can definitely feel overwhelming at times. Now there is definitely a time and a place for all of them. That said, the ones you spend your time on are going to be dependent on what your goals are. If your goal is to focus on the academic side of things, then by all means find the most unique techniques passed down by the masters and explore each and every one of them. If your goal is to win the most fights, you're going to want to narrow things down a bit. In period, combat was split between *spada da gioco* (sword of play) and *spada da filo* (sharp swords). If you were fighting as a part of a display of arms, your goal wasn't necessarily to win the most matches. Instead, if you could prove your bravery and show off a bit for that cutie standing there in the crowd, whether you won or lost wouldn't matter as much. When the blunt training swords got put away and the sharp pointy ones got brought out, things changed a bit.

Manciolino specifically tells us that, "In the Art of the *spada da filo*, you should not depart from the low guards."[96] I know for me, whenever I'm fighting specifically to win, I hardly ever depart from *porta di ferro stretta* and *coda lunga e stretta*. I might go down to *porta di ferro larga* if my arms get tired. If I'm feeling a bit more adventurous I might come up into *guardia di intrare*, but that's about it. Now there's definitely a time and a place for all the other guards. For me, at least, those tend to be edge cases. I might have to void this particular *tondo* by going up into *guardia alta*, or I'll have to pull all the way back to *coda lunga e distesa* in order to create a specific invitation, but those incidents are fairly rare. More importantly, though, figure out what your personal goals are and train accordingly.

Fighting From Principle

I realize that I just said that if you want to win more fights you should focus on a narrower set of techniques, but I'm going to go against that a bit for a moment. I had some conversation with a good friend years ago driving to and from practice over a few years and we developed a way of looking at the progression of any given fighter that I've found to be really helpful. I found out a few years after that that what we had created was essentially just a simplified version of Bloom's Taxonomy, so if you want to dive deeper into this topic, I'd highly recommend giving that a read. In the meantime, though, here's the version I helped put together.

To start with, you have **technique** fencers. These are folks generally starting out earlier in their careers whose focus is trying to land a specific technique. They

---

[96] Manciolino, 76.

might be trying to execute a good lunge, or have one really powerful *fendente*. This is a stage you have to pass through when trying to add most anything new to your fencing vocabulary. So while it is both a phase for fighters overall, on a smaller scale it's also something to go through whenever you're trying to learn something new with your sword.

The second set of fighters are what I like to call **script kitties**. This is a term I stole from the programming world. All it means is that they have a specific script they can execute really well, but that's it. That might mean they're really good at feinting a *stocatta* and then disengaging around, or that they wait for you to strike and respond with a *falso* followed up by a half cut. Their whole game is built around either throwing one attack at you really well or getting you to attack into one specific opening. This stage is where a lot of fencers stop. Now, you can definitely win tournaments being at this stage. The issue is that if someone does something you've never seen before, you won't have an answer to it. This is also a problem I see a lot at more formal martial arts schools where everyone fights like the one teacher and then they only ever fight against each other. If you're having trouble getting past this stage in your journey, the easy answer is to try and get out of the house and fight more kinds of people. If you're studying Bolognee, go fight people doing Fiore, or Lew, or Meyer. Fight people who tend to use different rulesets than you. Fight people who use different equipment than you do. Just go out there and fight everyone you can.

What I see as the ultimate stage is what I like to refer to as **principled** fighters.[97] These are people who, instead of relying on any given set of techniques, concentrate their fight on overarching principles. This might mean that they win all their fights by rolling out there and using proper mechanics to bully their opponent's sword, no matter where it goes. Alternatively they might win most of their fights by looking for the right tempo and using whatever strike happens to work in the moment. While principled fighters are of course going to use certain techniques more than others, the singular technique itself isn't what matters most. They aren't worrying about only beating their opponent's blade with a *falso manco* and then striking with a *mandritto sgualimbratto*. Instead, they're just going to remove their opponent's sword as a threat and then proceed from there.

[97] For a further breakdown of how people progress through various stages of learning, I recommend looking up "Bloom's Taxonomy".

Summarizing The Entire Art

Sometimes you just need a nice way to wrap everything together, something you can think of in the middle of a fight that doesn't involve climbing over mounds of vocab. Thankfully the Anonimo provides us with just that. He teaches us, "if you find your enemy in a wide guard, then you will use your art to bring his sword into presence. If he has his sword in presence, then you must, by means of feinting, make him put his sword into a wide guard."[98] Essentially, is your opponent presenting you with an immediate threat? Get them to pull that threat away. Do you know where their sword is? Get them to bring it up to you so that you can control it and step in. That's it, that's all of Bolognese fencing.

[98] Anonimo Bolognese, 75.

19: Tournaments

Fencing tournaments are one of my favorite things on earth. While I have no particular desire to ever get into a duel or any other kind of fight where serious injury is more than likely, I do appreciate the pressure testing that a tournament environment provides. For most every top-level fighter I know, tournaments are the only time you get to see what their game looks like turned all the way up to eleven. Part of that is the fact that they use their practice time to focus on this or that aspect of their game as opposed to trying to "win" practice. The larger piece, though, is that most top performers need that extra pressure in order to bring out their best. Also, while drills are great and I get a lot out of them, I do really like winning, and practice on its own just doesn't do it for me.

The first thing to acknowledge is that while all social violence has rules, martial arts in a competitive setting inherently have a larger dollop of bullshit that comes along with them. Not only are the swords blunt, but people also have to go to work the next day. Add to that the fact that we aren't fighting to incapacitation, so we have to artificially decide what counts and what doesn't. In a fight with sharps, a thrust to my face might only pierce my cheek but would otherwise leave me able to continue fighting on. With fencing masks, there's no great way to tell how much of your brain cage would have been affected by this or that blow. Sometimes when you get hit in a fight you have enough adrenaline pumping that you don't notice your left hand is only hanging on by a thread, and you continue on fighting only to collapse after the fact. Other times you stub your toe and shut down completely. Wearing safety gear and requiring proper calibration cuts most of that out. That's not a bad thing, it's just something to be aware of.

Another thing is that different tournament formats will reward different kinds of fencers. Without even getting into different ways a bout could be scored, a "bear pit" or "king of the hill" tournament, where the winner stays in and keeps fighting until someone defeats them, inherently reward fighters who have a lot of stamina. A single-elimination tournament, on the other hand, doesn't require much stamina, but instead shifts the focus to breadth over depth as any one fight could knock you out, so you're incentivized not to try anything too complex. Having each fight be best of fifteen lets you experiment a bit more.

The biggest thing is that in order to perform well at tournaments, you're likely going to have to spend some time doing tournament-specific training. If you're coming in to competitive fencing already having a one-on-one competitive background (tae kwon do, debate, wrestling, etc.) this will likely be a whole lot easier, but that's not universally true. Here's something I've been doing at one of my local practices in order to help people mentally prepare for tournaments. Most weeks we'll spend the last twenty minutes or so of practice having people do tournament fights. This means each person stands on one side, we have a marshal adjudicating the bout, each fencer does a formal salute before beginning their fight, and everyone else stands there and watches. That last part is really key. If you haven't performed in front of a crowd, it's a whole separate experience from just doing something on your own or with a partner. Another way to artificially recreate this is by having a camera set up for your fights. Not only does this give you something to go back and look at later, but it also comes with the added bonus of making you feel like you're being watched even if there aren't too many people there.

Once a month I've also been running an in-house tournament for the second half of practice. This way people get a chance to warm up first and work on whatever they on their own want to focus on, and then we all come together for the second half. At the end of the day, you get good at tournaments by doing them, the more the better. Getting everyone, particularly your newer fighters, out to a tournament once every month or two can be logistically complicated to say the least. By having a space at your local practice though where people get to practice fighting in a tournament, folks not only get more reps in but you've also now shortened the feedback loop from one tournament to the next. If you only pressure-test things every few months, that's a long time to see if that new idea is going to work this next time or not.

Each month I also try and rotate tournament formats. At a certain point the various formats will inevitably come back around. The important thing here is that I'm training folks to perform under pressure in a variety of environments. If you only ever practice fighting in pooled round robin tournaments, you might feel uncomfortable entering a double elimination tourney. As well, this way I'm helping to train folks to fence under pressure more broadly as opposed to just training for a specific ruleset.

One last thing about tournaments is that they are hardly the only reason people come to study this art. Some folks are looking for something that will keep them fit that's more engaging than running circles around a track. Other people are primarily interested in the history side and see this as a hands-on way to engage with it. Lots of people use fencing as an excuse to be social and hang out with other fencers without really caring whether or not they're a more dangerous fighter than they were yesterday. Others might just think that swords are cool and haven't thought much past that. Most people are some combination of all of these. There isn't any one of these options that's inherently more legitimate than the others. However, if for instance your goal is to do well in tournaments and you spend most of your time just hanging by the sidelines chit-chatting with people, you're likely going to come away frustrated. That said, as long as you're a generally good person and are interested in learning what I have to teach, you're more than welcome to attend any workshop I might be teaching regardless of which of the above goals you most align yourself with.

20: Equipment

I'm going to refrain from listing any particular manufacturers here, as my aim is for this book to be able to stand the test of time. Instead, my goal for this chapter will be to look at different kinds of equipment that can help you in your Bolognese journey, regardless of who the top manufacturers of the day happen to be. Additionally, my intention isn't to cover every single piece of equipment you might use. My plan is just to cover the ones I have specific suggestions on. So please don't take this as a complete list of things you would need in order to fence safely.

Swords

I mean, this is why we all came here, right? To play with swords. So let's take a look at a few different options that can help us best practice the art. To start with, any sword is better than none. I'm sure every last person reading this book swung a stick around when they were a kid pretending it was a real sword. If that's all you have, keep on swinging. If instead what you have looks just a bit more sword-like, even better. It can be really easy to get wrapped up in what the perfect sword might be, but especially for folks just starting out almost anything (that isn't sharp) can work.[99]

That said, let's take a look at what characteristics of a sword can help you better engage with this beautiful art. First, the blade. A lot of schools start people out with synthetics or wooden swords, and that's a totally understandable move when you're trying to get folks started out, especially if you don't know who all is going to be sticking around. That said, if you can get one made out of steel, that's always ideal. Compared to other longswords used across the continent, the Bolognese (as well as the 16th-century masters more broadly) liked them a bit longer, largely because they weren't also trying to use them in one hand while on horseback. As such, I tend to recommend roughly a 40-45" blade for what we do. If you can get other people to invest in the larger two-handers go for it, but if you're generally going to be fighting against folks with slightly shorter swords then a 40" will do you just fine.

---

[99] Training with sharps definitely has its place. I just try not to hand them over to beginners for obvious reasons.

As a note, while the two-handers used by the Bolognese were on the larger side, they weren't quite the massive *spadone* we see a little later on. Throughout this book I've been using the term "longsword" as it's become a modern catch-all for all European two-handed swords. That said, the actual term used at the time would have been *spada a due mani* (sword in two hands). Overall these swords would come up somewhere between your armpit and your chin, as opposed to the fully person-sized *spadone* we see later on.

Working our way down, let's look at the guard next. The only pictures of two-handers we get from the tradition are from the two different publishings of Marozzo's work, showing us a blade with lugs sticking out from the side in front of a guard with straight quillons and no side rings. If you're trying to stay as close to the text as possible, then make sure to put all of those features on your shopping list whenever you're looking for your next sword. That said, you can get by just fine without the lugs, and while side rings make a couple of the *prese* a little bit awkward, I'm of the mind that they're perfectly fine to use.

Next let's look at the handle. Compared to earlier Italians like Fiore, the Bolognese went for much longer handles on their longswords. If I'm borrowing someone else's sword, I find that the blade length doesn't really matter, but if my hands are constantly running in to each other then I'm not going to have a great time. In general, my advice would be to have a handle that has space for at least three of your own hands on it, not including the pommel. Everyone's hands are different so I'm not going to bother with an exact measurement here.

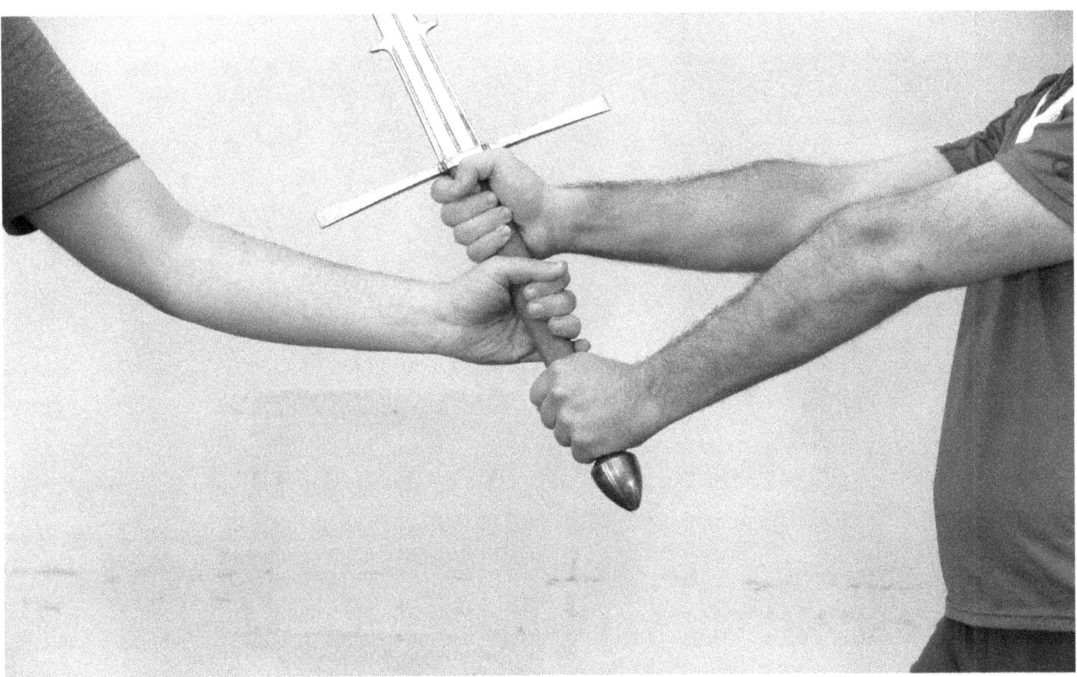

I don't have any huge preference on pommels. We see a pretty wide variety of options made in period, so go with whatever you think feels best. That said, I generally prefer a pommel that's screwed on as opposed to peened on with a hammer. I realize that peening it creates a stronger connection, but if anything breaks, a peened pommel makes things incredibly difficult to get in and try to fix. I've also definitely swapped in different blades, handles, and pommels on to several of my hilts so I particularly look for swords that leave that option open to me.

Circling back to the very top of the sword, I'm a big advocate of putting some sort of tip on any blade you're going to be poking people with. I've seen blades with spatulated, swelled, and rolled tips to try and address this issue. While those can help a bit, I find that having a piece of leather taped over the top, or a rubber blunt attached instead, really helps to soften the impact of any incoming thrusts. Relatedly, try and get a blade that has a decent amount of flex if you're going to be hitting anyone else with it. It shouldn't be a wet noodle, but if you're poking people with something that's as stiff as a board, you're going to hurt someone with it.

Gorgets

Unlike modern Olympic fencing, what we do really requires a gorget (neck protector) in order to be safe. Our blades just pack too much of an oomph for the bib of a modern fencing mask to take. There are several options these days for different kinds of gorgets. My recommendation is to get one that lays flat and that covers your collarbone. The reason for this is twofold. First, if people are throwing lots of *fendenti*, you're really going to want something in between your clavicle and their sword.

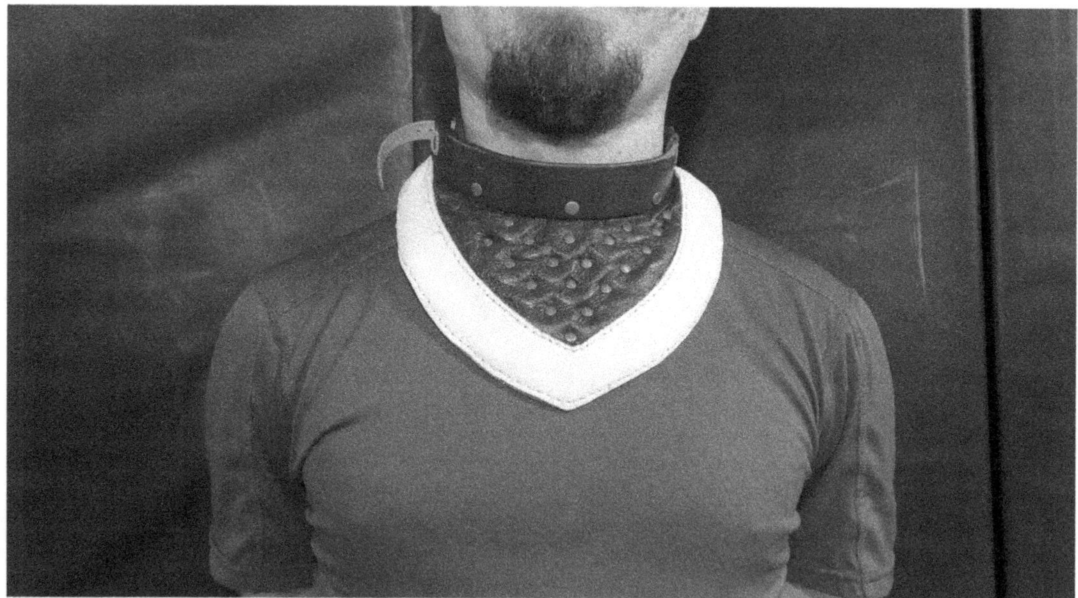

Safe gorget for falling in

A lot of gorgets just protect the throat and while that's fine for protecting you against thrusts, it doesn't help much against cuts. The other piece is that this style makes it a lot safer to fall, something that comes up a lot if you do any amount of grappling.

I know someone who took a fall once in what's often referred to as a "dog collar" style gorget where the metal points directly down into the bone. When they went to take a fall they'd done plenty of times without their gear on, they found that having that particular style of gorget directed all of the energy straight down and ended up fracturing their collar bone. I realize this is just one data point, but it's a really easy problem to solve with just a simple change in your gear.

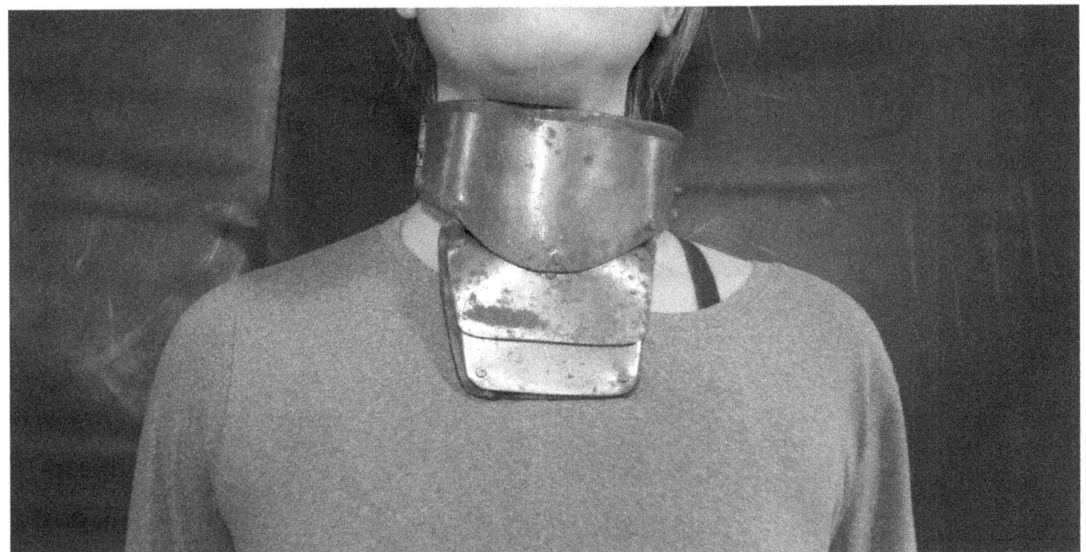

Dog collar gorget

Gauntlets

One of the things about our art is that outside of one chapter on polearms in the Anonimo, the entire art is done as what the Germans would call "blossfechten," or in English, unarmored fighting.[100] In order to recreate this safely I'm all for wearing protective equipment and fully believe that every period fencing master would have gladly thrown on a modern fencing mask if they'd had one. That said, whenever possible it's best for our protective gear to allow us to move as naturally as possible. As a result, I generally recommend that people go with finger gauntlets as opposed to "clamshells.". You can do some light drilling with just leather gloves, but for any full-speed sparring, I definitely recommend getting an actual set of gauntlets to keep all the little bones in your fingers safe. If at all possible I would also recommend getting ones made out of steel as opposed to plastic, but that's more an issue of aesthetics than it is practicality.

[100] Or in British English, "unarmoured" fighting.

Shoes

Footwear is a surprisingly deep topic where people have very firmly held beliefs pointing all such ways. Without wading too deep into those waters, my recommendation is to go with a low-profile shoe that doesn't have a raised heel. Raised heels weren't something we saw much of in this period in history and the shoes you wear will definitely affect the way you fight. I'm not going to take a side as to whether you need to ditch rubber soles entirely for treadless period leather ones, but modern gym shoes raise the back of your foot up more than I like for when I'm trying to fence. I know some people who will even go so far as to wear knee-high boots to fence in. Generally, I like to have as little between my feet and the floor as possible when I fight, even though in my day-to-day life I tend to walk around in hiking boots. That said, if you find something that works for you, then go with it.

Passing the Knowledge On

It is my sincerely held belief that in return for receiving all of these lessons from our teachers, it is our responsibility to pass it along to the next generation of fencers. As Manciolino says, "Nobody can be deemed perfect in this art (as well as in others) unless he can impart his knowledge to others. As the Philosopher said in *Ethics*, the mark of the expert is the ability to teach."[101] Being a top-level competitor is great and all, but I think that along with acting as an example of what a fighter should be like on the field, it is also your responsibility as a student of this art, to pass the knowledge along.

This is exactly how the masters themselves saw it. Marozzo teaches us that "it is a fine skill to know well how to teach others, more so than it is to know well oneself how to fence."[102] He goes on to say that being good at fighting helps you, but being an even better teacher helps everyone around you as well. Now this doesn't mean that you need to go up to everyone around you and start forcing them to listen to your lectures on how Manciolino likes to step back and forth with the same foot repeatedly whereas Marozzo tends to switch his feet more. It does mean, though, that once you know what you're doing, there is an obligation for you to teach it to those around you looking to learn. This doesn't necessarily mean teaching large formal classes or workshops. Some people work best teaching one on one, some folks write articles, others work on translations. Regardless of which of these suits you best, it's important that you find some way to give back and help the art flourish once more.

[101] Manciolino, 76.
[102] Marozzo, 82.

Appendix I: 101 Curriculum

So, this is a big honking book and sometimes instead of reading pages upon pages of theory, all you really want is a jumping off point. For any coaches looking at how to start off their students' journeys, here's an intro curriculum to get them through the first few weeks.

LESSON 1 : How to Stand with the Sword

This part may seem obvious to anyone who's been doing this for awhile, but how you stand is vital to how well you fight and more importantly, how happy your joints are. The stance for longsword isn't anything special, you've got your feet shoulder-width apart, one foot in front, and knees bent. The two things to home in on here are making sure that the front knee and toe are both pointing in the direction you want the student to step. If people lunge with their foot turned in, that's a recipe for knee problems. Fencing is a fun hobby and we are no longer training people to fight for their lives in 40 days. Winning the tournament at the end of the month matters a whole lot less than making sure your students' joints keep working decades down the line.

The upper body tends to be a bit less straightforward than the lower body here. To ensure students are engaging their lats instead of relying on their rotator cuffs, I have them grab the sword with one hand on the handle and another hand on the blade. From there I have them rest the sword on the back of their neck, which results in them pulling their shoulder blades back and engaging their lats. From there I direct them to keep that engagement as they let go of the blade and move the sword in front of them. Along with knees, shoulders are by and far the most common injury in what we do. This is almost never from people getting hit in the shoulder excessively hard, but is instead because of the person using the sword relying on smaller muscles (i.e. the four rotator cuff muscles) to do the job intended for larger muscle groups.

The next spot I have them focus on is how their hands interact with the sword itself. I know a lot of more old-school places have people focus just on footwork for the first year or so. While I definitely see the upside of that, my thought is that people walking in the door came here to swordfight. So, if I want them to stick around, I'm going to put a sword in their hands on day one. There are multiple valid ways to grip a longsword, so without getting too far into that here's just the fundamental bits I have people focus on to keep their wrists happy. First, I have them line up the bottom corner of their top hand (find your pinkie, go down until you reach the bottom of your hand) with the handle of the sword. This way the bones in their arm line up with the sword itself as opposed to running beside it, meaning they're relying more on structure than on hand strength. To note, most people will put their dominant hand on top when using a longsword. However, I do know of a few lefties who prefer to put their right hand on top. Whatever works for them.

After that I have them form a ring with the index finger and thumb of their bottom hand and place it around the pommel. Some people like to hold a little higher on the handle and that's okay. I just use this as a default as it makes your handle into a longer lever, meaning you have more leverage and can move the blade around more quickly. The more important thing with both hands is that you want the wrists to bend up toward the thumb instead of down toward the pinkie. There are definitely positions that will end up with the wrists being held out straight, but as a general rule of thumb your wrists will get angry if they're exerting/receiving force while bent down toward the pinkie.

LESSON 2: Footwork

Footwork makes the dream work. You've got your students to hold a sword for a little bit, but now it's time to start building the foundation. To start with, I'll demonstrate **gathering forward** and **gathering backward**, having them bring the back foot up in order to drive the front foot forward or having the front foot come back in order to drive the back foot backward. Once I've shown those first two steps, I'll have folks gather forward all the way across the hall one direction and then gather backward all the way the other way. Then I'll have them switch which leg is in front and do it all over again. For footwork drills in particular, I highly recommend you do them alongside your students instead of just walking around handing out corrections. It can often be difficult to immediately see the value of footwork, but if you do it with them there will instantaneously be way more buy-in.

Next, it's on to **passing steps**. You can pass forward with your back foot coming to be in front of what was just your front foot. As well, you can pass backward by taking your front foot and pulling it behind what was just your rear foot. I tend not to have students do this one all that much on its own as it can easily feel like they're all walking around like cowboys. Instead, I add this in to the gathering forward/backward I just had them do in order to allow them to change up which foot is in front.

Finally, I show them a **compass step**, where you pivot on one foot and have the other foot trace what'll essentially be a quarter circle (plus or minus) on the floor. This is mostly something that's added on to the end of another action in order to make sure you're sufficiently out of the way. For putting it into play, try this:

STEP 1: Pair students together

STEP 2: Have fencer A advance toward fencer B with gathering steps.

STEP 3: Have fencer B pass back in order to stay out of the way.

STEP 4: Next allow fencer A to use either gathering or passing steps when moving forward.

STEP 5: Have fencer B pass back and then compass out of the way.

LESSON 3 : Mandritto Fendente

Once a student has learned how to stand and hold their sword, I go and teach them their very first cut. Again, footwork is likely more important here, but people who show up to fencing practices tend to want to learn how to swing a sword before they want to relearn how to walk. Even if what you're teaching is more "correct" it doesn't much matter if the student doesn't come back the next week.

Mandritto fendente might seem like a big scary Italian phrase, but all it means is a descending cut that goes from the opponent's left eye to their right knee, assuming the person throwing the cut is right-handed. If they're a lefty, it goes the other way. As an instructor, you can feel free to disregard the technical terminology (or use a phrase from a different system). I find it helpful as it's concise and is used by pretty much everywhere else working out of any of the Italian traditions.

To start with this cut, I tend to start students in *guardia alta* as it's a neutral guard that makes it easy to start any descending blows from.

Guardia alta

Once I've gotten the student in guard and explained what line they're supposed to be cutting down, I let them go through and throw a dozen or so cuts before I step in with any more details. If they naturally do the right thing, there's no reason at this stage to explain what all they need to keep their eyes out for when performing this technique. If, however, they don't magically get it right on the first try, the main thing I focus on in this lesson is the order of operations.

The most important part here is when moving forward to go **sword and then foot**. Outside of "be nice to your opponent" this is likely the most fundamental lesson in swordplay. Not only is **sword and then foot** faster as it better breaks the inertia of a static guard, but it's also safer for both you and your opponent. Firstly, it keeps your opponent safe by reducing how hard they're being hit. As it turns out, swords are sharp and pointy. Next time you're eating a steak (or a Beyond Burger) try poking it with the tip of your knife. It takes incredibly little pressure for that tip to sink right in. Next, try throwing a really hard cut at it. As you've probably already guessed, hitting it harder doesn't make the cut go deeper in. Swords are not hammers, please don't use them as such. By having the sword move before the foot, you prevent the possibility of winding up before you release your shots. If you look at baseball players, you'll notice that their foot moves before their bat swings. This is to maximize the amount of force being transferred into the ball. Please, for the love of whatever deity you do or do not pray to, do not swing your longsword like a baseball bat.

In addition to keeping your opponent safe, moving **sword and then foot** keeps you safer as well. Not only will your opponent be less inclined to hit you like a baseball, but your sword is also clearing the line for you to more safely step in. If you step in and then move your sword, you're throwing your body closer to your opponent's without doing anything to prevent them from hitting you.

The last part of this lesson is how to not get hit in the hands when trying to perform the *mandritto fendente*. The trick here is from the shouldered position to pull your hands in to your chest before pushing the blade out. Not only does this come with the added benefit of hitting with less force, but it also means there isn't a tempo with your hands being significantly closer to your opponent than your body. If you try and throw this cut like you're fishing, you are asking your opponent to hit you before you can do anything about it.

After the student starts to get this down, I have them switch which shoulder their sword starts on and then throw a *roverso fendente*, cutting down toward my right eye toward my left knee. This will almost inevitably seem alien to the student as it's being thrown from their non-dominant side, but starts readying them to deal with different kinds of blows and also makes it easier for right handed students to drill with left handed ones and vice versa.

LESSON 4 : **How to Win Against a Cut**

Now that your student has a basic understanding of how to deliver a cut, it's time to learn how to counter one. The first response I like to teach is a simple **parry**. You throw a *mandritto fendente* against them and they respond by doing the same ending with the tip of their sword pointing across the line of yours. The larger lesson here is to solve problems via geometry instead of strength. If they line up their sword correctly, your cut will automatically be diverted away from them, leaving them an open line to attack on.

There are three advantages which determine who wins when two cuts meet. The first is **true edge**. For those who haven't heard the phrase before, the true edge is the edge of your sword pointing the same direction as your knuckles. So if you punched someone with your blade, that's the edge that would be making contact. For anyone who's ever done test cutting with sharps, you'll have noticed that lining the edge up just right makes a world of difference, whereas hitting the target harder didn't really do much to make your cut go any deeper. In addition to the geometry of the blade itself, your hand really wants to use tools along one axis and not the other. You aren't meant to backhand something with a hammer. If the head of the hammer is pointed correctly, that nail is not going to go in the way you want it to. Same goes for swords, except this time the nail is hitting back. If I can get more of my true edge to line up with more of your flat, I suddenly have a huge mechanical advantage.

The second most important factor is **leverage**. As it turns out, swords don't have muscles. Thus, they aren't able to generate any force on their own. As a result, the closer the crossing of the blades is to your hands/hilt the stronger it is. At the same time, the closer to the tip the crossing is the weaker you become and the longer a lever you hand your opponent. I like to demonstrate this by having the student have the sword straight out and pulling up first with me having one finger on the tip and then again with my finger closer to the hilt.

Lastly, we come to **crossing**. If I can cross the line of my blade over my opponent's I've aimed the point of my triangle through the flat side of my opponent's. I'll often do this by either stepping in or stepping out at an angle. Not only does this gain me the advantage of crossing, but it's also a nice way to start introducing a little bit of footwork to the student. It's important to remember here to do this by pointing the tip of your sword across as opposed to trying to push your hilt through. If you go with option B you might think you're gaining leverage, but you're effectively collapsing the angle of your sword and handing over the advantage of crossing to your opponent. I often describe this as "punch blocking" as you're essentially trying to punch your forte into your opponent's. Learning to point across instead of punch through is right beneath **sword and then foot** in things that will seem like you suddenly have superpowers when you add them in to your game.

After the student figures out the fundamental parry, I introduce a couple of other options for how to respond to a cut. One of these is what we call a **collection**. There are a couple ways of doing this, but the main one is by stepping in and striking your opponent's blade with your quillons by pushing up into *guardia di testa.*

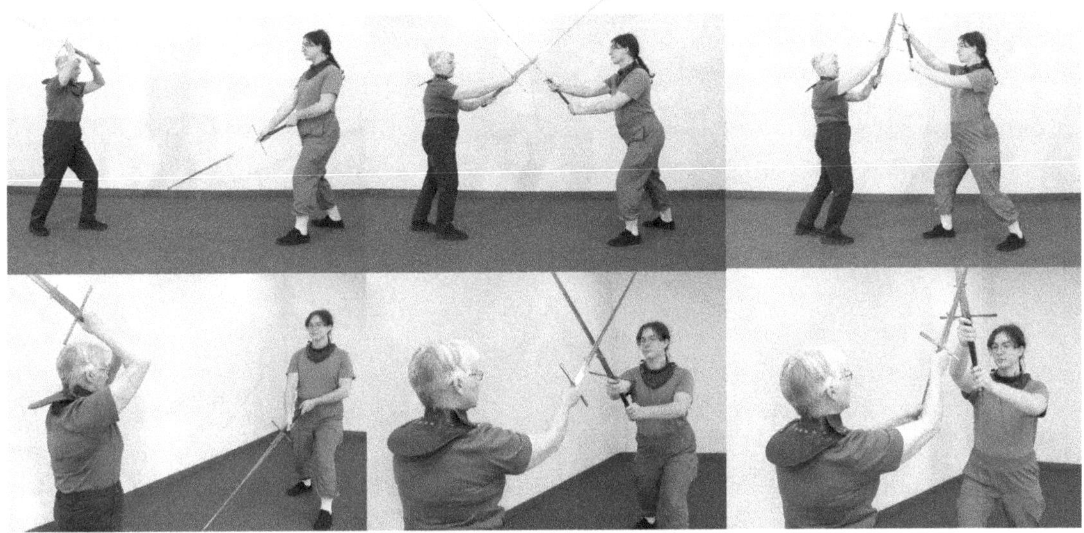

Collecting into *guardia di testa*

This move ignores the advantages of both true edge and crossing by dumping 100% of your stats into leverage. It's an especially fun technique for people who are more inclined to fight aggressively (as opposed to natural counter punchers) and is also a great opening for a whole lot of grapples, if that's something that either you or your student is interested in.

The last option for dealing with a cut is a **deflection**. This is done by cutting either with the true or false edge into the opponent's flat, sending their tip flying away from where it can immediately threaten you. There are a few options for how to do this, but I tend to start students off by having them stand in *porto di ferro larga* and have them throw a *falso manco* (a rising false edge cut that aims up into the opponent's right cheek assuming you have your right hand on top in your grip). I have at least one friend who calls this move the "shoveler" at his school.

This not only shows the student a new way to deal with cuts but is also a great way to start introducing different kinds of cuts and guards. You'll notice how I've waited until now to start mentioning anything other than variations on one cut and one guard. A lot of places start by having students memorize all of the guards, all of the cuts, and all of the thrusts. While this is helpful later down the line, I find that this can often be more than a bit overwhelming for people just starting out. Plus, if they don't have any context for how these might be used, the names for everything just won't stick as well.

The next lesson I tend to teach is the fundamentals of thrusting. For this I start students off in *porto di ferro stretta*, with both of us having our true edges pointed slightly toward to inside line.

Porta di ferro stretta

I start by throwing a simple *stocatta* (rising thrust), just extending my tip forward, pointed at their centerline, and proceed to step forward. To counter this I have the student perform a smaller version of the same parry we went over for cuts. The one thing to note here is that the order of importance reverses from being true edge, leverage, crossing; to crossing, then leverage, then true edge.

I then repeat the lesson starting in coda lunga e stretta doing all the same stuff on the outside line. Some students (particularly left-handed ones) might find the outside line to be easier, but most will take a few minutes to adjust to it.

Once they've learned that simple parry, I teach them how to find, gain, and then attack with a thrust of their own. After that we work on responding to one of my thrusts with one of their own. Just because your opponent is throwing an attack at you, doesn't necessarily mean that it's a well-formed one. If the student is using proper structure and you as the instructor throw a less than ideal thrust at them, they should be able to counter-find into it and proceed to stab you in the chest.

When they just start to learn how to thrust, they're likely to be pushing with the hilt of their sword instead of pointing their tip across, so keep an eye out for it. The earlier you can correct this, the better.

LESSON 6: Disengages

Now that the student has a decent understanding of how to meet a blade head on, I move them to how to go around their opponent's blade. The first bit here is how to disengage an opponent's blade. I go back first to how to deal with a cut. I have them hold their blade out in front of them as I come in cutting a *mandritto fendente*. Their goal is to make a *mezza volta* with their blade by cutting over mine and either gaining my blade or immediately striking. If they seem to have decent control of their sword, I'll have them just hit me with a cut to my mask. If they look like they're still swinging a bit hard, I'll just have them cut over to regain my blade and then focus on calibration separately. Ideally in this drill, they should move to disengage their sword before mine makes contact. We then repeat the exercise with me cutting a *roverso fendente* from the other side.

Next, we move on to thrusts. We both start with our swords extended and I move in to strike the same *stocatta* we learned earlier. Here I'll try and end with my sword not too terribly angled up and have the student disengage their tip underneath mine. The thing to remember is that the disengage should be accompanied with a step (either forward or backward), be as tight to the opponent's sword as possible, and should leave you in a position of strength over your opponent's sword as opposed to just being on the other side of it.

From here we go to building the student's very first decision tree. I start by stepping in with an attack (either a cut or a thrust). The student then has to decide whether they can counter it by pushing through it, or whether they are forced to go around it. Play around with different levels of intensity here as well as how well structured your attack is. As a note, this bit is perhaps the most fundamental of decision trees in fencing. To a certain degree, every point in a fight comes down to whether it's safe for you to proceed forward or if you have to go around.

Once we get that covered, we move to how to counter an opponent's disengage and make and force it to be as large as possible. There are three ways of doing this. First is through **penetration**. The closer my point gets to my opponent, the more sword they have to go around, and the larger their disengages become. Next is what we call **angulation**. If I raise my tip as I lower my hilt, my opponent now has to go around a significantly larger hypotenuse, slowing down their response. Something to note is that the more angled your blade becomes, the shorter the disengage over the top becomes. At the same time, the more you straighten out, the more the disengage underneath becomes the better option. Finally, we take a look at **breadth**. If I cross over my opponent's blade instead of remaining straight on, my opponent's sword now has a longer path to go along the x axis.

I spend some time walking through all of these with the student, letting them test out scenarios incorporating all three to see how they play out in front of them.

Once we've covered the more conceptual side of things, I walk them through one of their second tactical decision tree: ***volta stable* vs *contrasfalsare*** (stable turn vs counter-disengage). I have the student come in to find my sword and respond with a disengage. If I come in and our blades cross past the first *palmo* (one palm's width from the tip of their sword), the correct response is to perform a volta stable. All this entails is having them switch from pointing on one line (inside or outside) to having them point their tip the other way and engage their true edge. Once they start to get this on one side, I then switch to the other side and then proceed to alternate between the two.

The other option occurs when I disengage from farther out. At this point, because I have less penetration, the contracavazione becomes the faster option. All this entails is after I disengage, the student performs a disengage of their own.

LESSON 7: Measure.

With most of the fundamental blade mechanics down, I then tend to move students on to a couple fundamental ideas about fencing more generally. The first of these is **measure**. All measure is, is the distance it takes to strike your opponent. So, if you're 6'5" and your opponent is 5'4", your opponent is going to be inside of your measure far sooner than you are going to be inside of theirs. To give the idea a little bit more granularity, I give students five different measures at which actions might occur.

- Out of measure – Within a single action you cannot hit your opponent
- *Misura largissima* (widest measure) – You require a passing step (stepping forward with your back foot) to hit your opponent.
- *Misura larga* (wide measure) – You require a step of the front foot in order to hit your opponent with your sword.
- *Misura stretta* (narrow measure) – You can hit your opponent just by leaning forward, but without having to pick up either of your feet.
- *Misura strettissima* (narrowest measure) – You are so close that you can hit your opponent without even leaning forward/you can hit them while stepping back.

This is a great place to start introducing more footwork options as well as to create games for your students that let them explore the idea of measure in a fun way that isn't just 100% unrestricted sparring.

LESSON 8 : Tempo

- *Primo tempo* – You strike as your opponent enters measure.
- *Dui tempi* – You require two tempi to respond to their attack and then return with one of your own (think parry-riposte).
- *Contra tempo* – You strike as your opponent moves to strike.
- *Mezzo tempo* – You strike as your opponent prepares to strike/disengages.

At this point I like to have students think of scenarios where each of these might be the case and then drill that specific scenario correcting mechanical issues along the way. If they can't think of any instances on their own feel free to provide some for them, but if at all possible it'll generally click easier if the student is the one thinking of examples.

LESSON 8 : Cuts & Thrusts

It's only at this point that I walk students through all primary cuts and thrusts. We've covered a few of these already, but now it's time to see how they all fit into the larger schema. I tend to leave things like throwing a *montante* for a later lesson instead of trying to cram everything in all at once

- *Fendente* – Cut from temple to foot
- *Sgualimbratto* – Cut from shoulder to hip
- *Tondo* – Cut straight across, sideways
- *Ridoppio* – Rising cut
- *Falso manco* – Rising false-edge cut from your non-dominant side
- *Falso dritto* – Rising false-edge cut from your dominant side
- *Stocatta* – Rising thrust
- *Imbrocatta* – Descending thrust
- *Punta dritta* – Thrust with the true edge turned to your outside line
- *Punta roversa* – Thrust with the true edge turned to your inside line

LESSON 9 : Guards

This is the last major step on what I like to refer to as Mt. Vocab. While I have used a few technical terms here and there, this is generally the part where you find the most amount of specific vocab words. I know of some schools that try and make this easier by just referring to all the guards by their translated English names. I personally prefer to stick to the original language, but will generally teach them by referring to them first in Italian and then in English for the first while until the student gets familiar with them.

Appendix II: Guards

Guardia Alta (high guard

Guardia d'Intrare (guard of entering)

Guardia di Croce (guard of the cross)

Becca Cesa

Becca Possa

Guardia di Testa (head guard)

Guardia di Faccia (face guard)

Coda Lunga e Alta (high long tail)

Coda Lunga e Stretta (narrow long tail)

Coda Lunga e Larga (the wide and narrow tail)

Coda Lunga e Distesa (extended long tail)

Porta di Ferro Alta (high iron gate)

Porta di Ferro Stretta (narrow iron gate)

Porta di Ferro Larga (wide iron gate)

Cinghare Porta di Ferro Alta (boar's high iron gate)

Cinghare Porta di Ferro Stretta (boar's narrow iron gate)

Cinghare Porta di Ferro Larga (boar's wide iron gate)

Guardia di Fianche (guard of the hips)

Guardia di Piede (guard of the foot)

Appendix III:
Rank Examinations

Below I've included a list of possible questions I ask of anyone testing for rank in the Bolognese track of the group I cofounded, The Carbonari, with my good friend Tony Francis. These ranks aren't intended to serve as an end all be all, but instead work more as a way to help structure a student's learning journey and to help them provide clear benchmarks along the way. Everyone in the group has access to the full list of questions regardless of what rank they hold. The point here isn't to surprise people, but instead to help guide them. If you want to test your own knowledge after reading this book, see which of these questions you can answer off the top of your head.

Rank 1: Foundations
- Explain structure and how it's used in fencing.
- How do you properly hold a sword?
- What does it mean to find your opponent's sword? Please demonstrate.
- What does it mean to gain your opponent's sword? Please demonstrate.
- Demonstrate how to gather forward and backward.
- Demonstrate how to advance.
- Demonstrate how to retreat.
- Demonstrate a proper passing step.
- Demonstrate how to maintain measure.
- How do you properly execute a *mandritto fendente*?
- How do you properly execute a *stocatta*?
- How do you properly recover after attempting to deliver a strike?
- How might you control your calibration?
- Demonstrate a proper *sfalsare*.
- Explain the different parts of the blade.
- Explain what a line is.
- What are the four quadrants you can attack into?

Rank 2: True Fight [103]

- What are all of the Bolognese guards and how would you properly form them?
- What is the difference between *gioco stretto* and *gioco largo*?
- What are the pillars of Bolognese fencing?
- In what order should an offensive action be performed?
- In what order should a defensive action be performed?
- What are all the different thrusts and how are they properly executed?
- What are the three advantages when thrusting?
- Demonstrate a proper *contrasfalsare*.
- What are all the different cuts, both true and false edge?
- What is the difference between a full and a half cut?
- What are the three advantages when cutting?
- Demonstrate how to respond to a cut to the leg.
- How do you properly stand when in guard?
- How do you stand in a *coda lunga* guard as opposed to a *porta di ferro* guard?
- What does it mean to present a strong vs a weak angle?
- Demonstrate the three ways to regain a blade without losing blade contact.
- Explain the difference between offensive and defensive measure.
- What is a tempo?
- What are the four categories of tempo?
- What are some examples of instances of tempo?
- What are the three aspects of proportion and how do they affect the *sfalsare*?
- Describe the three factors of *stringere*: proportion, invitation, and constraint.
- Demonstrate how and when to counterfind.
- What are the three turns of the sword?

[103] Boorman, 152.

Rank 3: Deceptive Fight[104]

- Demonstrate how to do a proper fall in each of the cardinal directions.
- Demonstrate how to do a proper fall, with weapons in hand, in each of the cardinal directions.
- Demonstrate how to do a proper fall, with weapons in hand, while entangled with an opponent, in each of the cardinal directions.
- How is a feint properly performed?
- What is the difference between a feint and a mutation?
- Demonstrate an example of a double feint.
- Explain what defines a feint-direct.
- Explain what defines a feint by disengagement.
- What is the difference between an invitation and an opening?
- What is the difference between a static and a dynamic invitation?
- What are the three major sword and dagger invitations?
- What does it mean to act in tempo?
- What does it mean to act out of tempo?
- Demonstrate the two named *falsi*.
- How do you perform a beat against someone's blade.
- Demonstrate how and when to properly half sword.
- Demonstrate how to perform a *stramazonne*.
- Demonstrate how to perform a *molinetto*.
- Demonstrate an inside yield.
- Demonstrate an outside yield.
- Demonstrate a *punta roversa*.
- Demonstrate a *punta dritta*.

104 Boorman, 206.

Rank 4: Adaptive Fight[105] & Single-Lesson Coaching

- Demonstrate how to form a counterguard (*contrapostura*).
- What does it mean to proceed with resolution?
- What factors do you consider when giving feedback to a student?
- When two blades meet in the bind, what are the four possibilities each side could do?
- Explain blocked vs variable drilling. Demonstrate examples for a given topic.
- Explain cooperative vs noncooperative drilling. Demonstrate examples for a given topic.
- Explain how to build on complexity vs intensity in a drill. Demonstrate examples for a given topic.
- Demonstrate how to perform a disarm.
- Demonstrate two different throws.
- Explain how to feint against the sword vs how to feint against the dagger.
- How do you prep a cut?
- How do you prep a thrust?
- How might you coach someone who has issues controlling their calibration?
- Demonstrate how to fight against two opponents at once.
- Explain the progression of crisp, to smooth, to fast.
- How might you ensure you're creating a space that provides students with a sufficient amount of psychological safety?
- For a topic of your choosing, what are a series of drills you could do in order to teach a particular skill?

[105] Boorman, 206.

Rank 5: Everything & Multi-Lesson Coaching

- What are the two primary ways of holding a cloak?
- Demonstrate how to feint using a cut to a thrust.
- Demonstrate how to feint using a thrust to a cut.
- Demonstrate two standing joint locks.
- Demonstrate five throws/takedowns.
- What is the difference between strategy and tactics?
- How might you use this system to fight against a Meyerist?
- How might you use this system to fight against someone who primarily studies Fiore?
- A student approaches you saying they've had difficulty learning in the past due to their own physical limitations. How might you adapt a lesson plan to better fit them? Provide at least three different examples.
- Explain the three kinds of problems a student might have (mechanical, tactical, psychological).
- A student is demonstrating a failure to successfully feint by disengage to provoke a tempo from their opponent and land a strike, you have ascertained that the problem is mechanical. Design a drill to address it.
- The student is demonstrating a failure to successfully feint by disengage to provoke a tempo from their opponent and land a strike, you've ascertained that the problem is tactical. Design a drill to address it. The student is demonstrating a failure to successfully feint by disengage to provoke a tempo from their opponent and land a strike, you've ascertained that the problem is psychological. Design a drill to address it.
- Demonstrate how you could use a rapier to fight against a polearm.
- With a partner, please demonstrate how you might teach someone how to properly fall.
- Explain what it meant to engage in a duel in 16th/ century Northern Italy.
- Demonstrate how to fight against three opponents at once.
- How would you lead a class with students of varying skill levels, ensuring each one of them gets something out of it?
- How might you adapt your teaching for one on one as opposed to group lessons?
- How might you adapt your teaching to fit in a one day workshop as opposed to an ongoing class?
- With a topic of your choosing, please break down how you would approach teaching it across a series of four classes.
- What is the difference between instruction and coaching?
- What can you do to help instill a love for this art?

Glossary

Longsword - A two-handed European sword. In Italian -
spada a dui mani (sword in two hands).

Quillons - The crossguard on a sword.

Pommel - The weighted end on the bottom of the sword.

Inside Line - Extend your dominant hand forward with the thumb up.
All the space on the side of your palm is you inside line.

Outside Line - Extend your dominant hand forward with the thumb up.
All the space on the side of the back of your hand is your outside line.

Mandritto - A forehanded cut.

Roverso - A backhanded cut.

Fendente - A cut that's aimed across from head to toe.

Sgualimbratto - A cut that is aimed across from shoulder to hip.

Tondo A horizontal cut.

Ridoppio - A rising cut.

Falso Dritto - A rising cut with the false edge from your dominant side.

Falso Manco - A rising cut with the false edge from your non dominant side.

Stringere - To constrain someone's blade, controlling the line of their sword.

Imbrocatta - An overhanded thrust

Punta Dritta - A thrust from the dominant side done with the palm of your
dominant hand pointing downward.

Punta Roversa - A thrust from the nondominant side done with the palm of
your dominant hand pointing upward.

Stocatta - A rising thrust.

Punta Ferma - A rising thrust that doesn't require your arm to move forward.

Punta Infalsata - A thrust where your false edge points toward your
opponent's blade.

Falso Impuntanto - A descending strike where the false edge leads.

Stramazonne - A circular wrist cuts performed on your inside line.

Molinetto - A circular elbow cut performed on your outside line.

Mutation - A change in line or plan after the first intention didn't work.

Tutta Volta - Full turn.

Mezza Volta - Half turn.

Volta Stabile - Stable turn.

Gioco Stretto - Constrained play.

Gioco Largo - Unconstrained play.

Measure - The distance between two fencers.

Tempo – Time, or a single beat of time during a fight.

Gorget - Throat protector.

Presa - Press/grapple.

Spada da Gioco - Blunt sword.

Spada da Filo - Sharp sword.

Inside Yield - Yield via *stramazonne.*

Outside Yield - Yield via *molinetto.*

Covered Attack - An attack that ends with your sword between your opponent's sword and you.

Uncovered Attack - An attack that doesn't end with your sword between your opponent's sword and you.

Attack-Direct – An attack where you fire straight into your opponent's opening without having to go around.

Attack by Disengagement – An attack where you have to go around your opponent's blade in order to hit your target.

Feint-Direct – A feint where the initial action is to threaten an opening that doesn't require you to disengage in order to reach.

Feint by Disengagement – A feint where you first have to go around your opponent's blade.

Half-Swording - When you grab your blade with your nondominant hand.

Mezza Spada - When two swords meet toward the middle of their blades.

Find - Putting your sword just a bit over your opponent's in order to establish a bit of control.

Gain - Putting more of your sword over your opponent's, locking in control of their blade.

Counter-Find - A find done in response to one made by your opponent.

Full Cut - A cut in which the point of your sword ends out of presence.

Half Cut - A cut in which the point of your sword ends in presence.

Parry - Stopping your opponent's action by pointing into it with the tip of your blade.

Collection - Gathering your opponent's blade into your hilt.

Deflection - Hitting your opponent's blade out of the way with your own.

Forte - The strong part of the blade, the half that's closer to your hands.

Debole - The weak part of the blade, the half that's further away from your hands.

Tutta Coperta – A position where you're fully covered by your blade pointing down.
Stabile Guard – A guard you can comfortably sit in.
Instabile Guard – A guard you move through, but don't stay in.
Palmo – A handspan.
Double Feint – When you throw two feints in a row in order to strike on the third action.
Compound Feint – Any time you string multiple feints together in a row.
Half Disengage – When your disengage only goes along a quarter of a circle as opposed to the more normal half circle.
Stesso tempo – An action that occurs in a singular tempo

Works Cited

1. Bolognese, Anonimo. 2020. *with Malice & Cunning: Anonymous 16th Century Manuscript on Bolognese Swordsmanship.* Translated by Stephen Fratus.
2. Boorman, Devon. 2017. *Introduction to the Italian Rapier.* Wheaton, Illinois: Freelance Academy Press.
3. Brainard, Lindley L., et al. "Gender Differences in Head Impacts Sustained by Collegiate Ice Hockey Players." *Medicine & Science in Sports & Exercise* 44 (2): 297–304. https://doi.org/10.1249/mss.0b013e31822b0ab4.
4. Chen, Tony Lin-Wei, Duo Wai-Chi Wong, Yan Wang, Sicong Ren, Fei Yan, and Ming Zhang. 2017. "Biomechanics of Fencing Sport: A Scoping Review." Edited by Tiago M Barbosa. *PLOS ONE* 12 (2): e0171578. https://doi.org/10.1371/journal.pone.0171578.
5. Franklin, Sean. 2023. "Block vs Random - When Improvement Isn't Really Improvement." Sword STEM. July 18, 2023. https://swordstem.com/2023/07/18/block-vs-random-when-improvement-isnt-really-improvement/.
6. dall'Agocchie, Giovanni. (1572) 2018. *The Art of Defense, on Fencing, the Joust, and Battle Formation.* Translated by Jherek Swanger.
7. Gaugler, William M. 2004. *The Science of Fencing a Comprehensive Training Manual for Master and Student ; Including Lesson Plans for Foil, Sabre and Épée Instruction.* Bangor, Me. Laureate Press.
8. Hananya, Rabbi Yehoshua ben. n.d. "Eruvin 53b: 22-23." Www.sefaria.org. Accessed April 29, 2024. https://www.sefaria.org/Eruvin.53b.22?lang=bi.
9. Harmenberg, Johan. *Epee 2.6: The New Fencing Paradigm Revised and Explained.* Washington, D.C., InterAlias. 2023.
10. Leoni, Tom. *In the Service of Mars.* Vol. I, Freelance Academy Press, 2010.
11. Manciolino, Antonio. (1531) 2010. *The Complete Renaissance Swordsman : A Guide to the Use of All Manner of Weapons : Antonio Manciolino's Opera Nova (1531).* Translated by Tom Leoni. Wheaton, Illinois: Freelance Academy Press.
12. Marozzo, Achille. (1536) 2019. *The Duel, or the Flower of Arms for Single Combat, Both Offensive and Defensive.* Translated by Jherek Swanger.

13. Wiest, Joshua. 2023. "What Is Viridario, Who Was Achillini?" The Art of Arms. May 31, 2023. https://theartofarms.substack.com/p/what-is-viridario-who-was-achillini.

14. Wilson, Luke. *Tactile : Juggling and Other Touchy Subjects : A Collection of Essays, Blogs and Rants.* London, Gandini Juggling, 2017.

15. Windsor, Guy. *The Swordsman's Companion.* Swordschool Ltd, 8 Oct. 2013.

Further Reading

1. Academia Nazionale di Scherma Editore. *The Swordmanship of Renaissance Italy. Rules and Principles of Historical Fencing.* Accademia Nazionale di Scherma, 2021.

2. Altoni, Francisco. *The Monomachia.* Translated by Stephen Fratus, 2024.

3. Bloom, Benjamin. *Taxonomy of Educational Objectives: The Classification of Educational Goals. Handbook 1, Cognitive Domain.* New York, Longman, 1956.

4. Coblentz, David, and Dori Coblentz. *Fundamentals of Italian Rapier.* Ska Swordplay Books, 2018.

5. Davis, Ian. *The Anonimo Riccardiano.* 2020.

6. dei Liberi, Fiore. *Flowers of Battle : The Complete Martial Works of Fiore Dei Liberi, a Master at Arms at the Turn of the Fifteenth Century.* Wheaton, Il, Freelance Academy Press, Inc, 2017.

7. Dr. Guy Windsor. *The Medieval Longsword.* The School of European Swordsmanship, 20 Aug. 2020.

8. ---. *The Theory and Practice of Historical Martial Arts.* Spada Press, 20 Aug. 2020.

9. Giganti, Nicoletto. *Venetian Rapier.* Translated by Tom Leoni, Freelance Academy Press, 2010.

10. Giovanni Filoteo Achillini. *Viridario de Gioanne Philotheo Achillino Bolognese.* 1513.

11. Katejan Sadowski. *Fear Is the Mind Killer : How to Build a Training Culture That Fosters Strength and Resilience.* Vancouver, British Columbia, Kaja Sadowski, 2019.

12. Manciolino, Antonio. *How to Fight and Defend with Arms of Every Kind.* 1531. Translated by Jherek Swanger, 2021.

13. Melville, Neil. *Two Handed Sword.* Pen & Sword Military, 11 Jan. 2019.

14. Mondschein, Kenneth C. *On Time.* Johns Hopkins University Press, 15 Sept. 2020.

15. Viggiani, Angelo. *Lo Schermo.* Translated by Tom Leoni, 2019, p. Book III.

Acknowledgements

Bunch of folks to thank here. First of all, thank you so much to Terry Tindall and Tim Lyon. The two of them are the fount from which all swordplay knowledge in Chicago comes from. The two of them have done so much work to make it so that a young punk like me could make it to where I am. Without their tutelage I wouldn't be half the fighter or a quarter the scholar I am today.

Next, I want to thank my initial proofreaders. Ernesto Maldonado, Nita Lewis, Dylan McDowell, Patrick Bailey, Luke Kramer, and Tim Lyon (again), you all helped take what I've been teaching for years and translate it into something readable. Without all of you this would likely just have been a collection of teaching notes, but with your help you made it into something anyone can pick up.

I'd also like to thank everyone who helped out with the photoshoot. Sam Halote, thank you so much for not only posing for photos, but also forging the absolutely wonderful swords we used. Feel free to check out his stuff over at https://www. SevenEmbersForge.com/. I tried not to get too far into gear recommendations in this book, but at this point I buy all of my swords from Sam and would highly recommend you do the same. Thank you as well to Xavier Claudio for serving as our photographer. You're a joy to work with, especially when I greatly underestimate how long everything is going to take and you're cool as a cucumber. Big thanks to Laurie Erickson, Dylan McDowell, and Corey Duffey for serving as models. Half the notes I got from my proofreaders were something along the lines of, "I'm sure this will make more sense once there's pictures". It's one thing to write about a physical art, but being able to see what's going on really helps make sure the message gets across. As well I want to thank Jesse Kulla of the Chicago Swordplay Guild for helping me with my initial interpretations of the Anonimo Bolognese's longsword section. I could not ask for a more dependable friend.

Finally, a huge thank you to Guy Windsor. Guy has been a huge help in mentoring me through the process of how to get this whole thing out. I can't think of anyone else who knows the ins and outs of publishing a book on historical fencing better than he does. Go sign up for his courses and buy all of his books at GuyWindsor.net.

About the Author

Arik first stumbled into historical fencing back in March of 2007 and hasn't stopped since. A passionate practitioner of everything Bolognese, as well as the rapier of Nicoletto Giganti, Arik has taught workshops and classes all across the continent including at KWAR (the Known World Academy of Rapier), VISS (the Vancouver International Swordplay Symposium), multiple standalone weekend workshops, and dozens upon dozens of SCA (Society for Creative Anachronism) events. He has won over five dozen fencing tournaments across both the SCA and HEMA worlds and plans to continue doing such. A circus school graduate, Arik spends a lot of his time training and pondering the limits of the human body. He is also the cofounder, along with his friend Tony Francis, of a fencing school that largely operates inside of the SCA, named The Carbonari. Having spent the majority of his life as a member of the SCA, Arik has been recognized for his skill as both a competitor and an instructor and has officially been granted the title of Master of Defense, the highest award a fencer can achieve as a part of the organization. Additionally, Arik is also an avid practitioner of Wing Chun kung fu and has trained in both the Leung Ting and Ip Chun lineages. When not trying to hone his martial skills, Arik spends his time at his home in Chicago, Illinois working as a consultant and working toward his latest juggling trick. You can find out more about his work sword related work at his website, **FoolOfSwords.com.**